More Praise for *MBA In A Day*®

"Steve Stralser is a unique talent. It is unusual to meet people who are both highly professional as well as generous with their knowledge. Not only is Professor Stralser's advice invaluable for business professionals, but those in the arts who are more focused on their creative endeavors would benefit from reading *MBA In A Day*® to help strengthen their business skills."
—Bobi Leonard, CEO, Arcara Enterprises, Inc.

"Steve's book is a valuable asset to anyone needing to avoid the pitfalls of business, be they a small business owner, a physician, a lawyer, or just about anyone who deals with business. Just because you have not had the opportunity to study for a formal MBA, why be at a disadvantage in the business world? In just a few days of quality reading time you will level the playing field. Let your own brainpower do the rest."
—George Reiss, MD, Clinical Instructor, Mayo Clinic;
Eye Physician, Phoenix Coyotes Professional Hockey Club

"Professor Stralser's *MBA In A Day*® contains insights that are incredibly valuable for any entrepreneur obsessed with success. They provide quick access to sound practical thinking on the real-world business issues most likely to confront the busy start-up entrepreneur."
—Michael Hool, Partner, Rogers & Theobald, LLC;
Chairman, Arizona Venture Capital Conference

"Steve has an uncanny ability to distill business concepts to their true fundamentals without confusing or losing the audience. He also provides user-friendly templates that can help readers begin to improve their knowledge and performance immediately."
—Ed Robinson, Capacity Building Solutions Inc.;
TEC Chair, Group 663

"I have personally seen *MBA In A Day*® in action. Our company has organized several live seminars for physicians based on the *MBA In A Day*® content. The information was highly relevant, easily understandable, and highly valued by the participants. Based on this, I believe anyone who reads this book will take away something practical and actionable that will improve their approach to the business side of their professional careers."
—Sidney Auerbach, RPh, President,
Worldwide Healthcare Communications

"If you want the knowledge to build your business, whatever your industry, you must understand business. *MBA In A Day*® is an essential guide to everyday practical decision making."
—Croom Lawrence, MBA, Senior Marketing Manager,
Wyeth Pharmaceuticals

"Professor Stralser has been teaching MBA principles for years in top-tier business schools. His *MBA In A Day*® treatment of these same principles is your 'graduation' into the world of business!"
—R. Glenn Williamson, Partner, Nest Ventures LLC,
providers of early stage financing and equity

"You could read this book in a day, but the nonbusiness professional can go back and refer to it every day!"
—Barry Moltz, Author, *You Need to Be a Little Crazy:*
The Truth about Starting and Growing Your Business

"Easy to read, highly practical, and comprehensive in nature. I highly recommend this book to both experienced and new business owners alike."
—Scott Gabehart, MIM, CBA, Business Valuation Consultant

"Professor Stralser has the ability to impart entrepreneurial attitudes and processes. His teachings give one a solid guide to incorporating business techniques into professional practice. For those who have no business experience, he explains things in understandable terms and for those who understand business, he reinforces what they have been doing all along."
—Martin Blume, DO, MBA, Parkway Medical, PLC

"Dr. Stralser has provided physicians with a focused, structured, and comprehensive resource for the business side of their practices—an area they have typically managed by trial and error. His book is a valuable tool to help them maintain and grow their bottom line."
—Rick Nevins, MD, FAAFP, President,
Nevins & Associates Consulting

"Having recently benefited by being a 'student' in an *MBA In A Day*® seminar, I am looking forward to being able to offer this book to our 2,000+ physician members. *MBA In A Day*® will provide our physician members with a quick reference to deal with the practical, business side of medicine they have not yet experienced."
—Beverly Hurt, Executive Vice President,
Indianapolis Medical Society

"This book is an absolute must-read for anyone who finds that knowledge of business principles and concepts would be helpful, available here in a concise, clear manner that immediately elevates your expertise in this area."
—Gerald Jacobs, Attorney

"This book is a must for any type of entrepreneur who has become successful to a certain point using 'street skills' and deep knowledge of an industry combined with a unique idea. The MBA fundamentals made real by Professor Stralser in his new book will provide a handy tool kit that will enlighten and empower the reader to take his or her organization successfully beyond the start-up phase into sustainable growth."
—Stephen Lindstrom, Co-founder, Behcon, Inc.,
medical practice owners and managers; Adjunct Instructor,
McGuire Entrepreneurship Program, University of Arizona

"*MBA In A Day*® contains insightful and applicable information to anyone interested in running a business, or already doing so. As the president of a young, growing company, I found that the fundamental concepts addressed in the book not only complemented my practical experience, but also provided a helpful, supplementary education in important business principles."
—Alison Chozen, Entrepreneur and President,
Sterling Truffle Bar; Co-founder, Mosaic Event Management

"As an advanced-practice nurse, I highly recommend Dr. Stralser's book as an essential road map on how to navigate today's complex health-care terrain. As more nurses are looking beyond hospitals and exploring entrepreneurship, they will find the fundamentals of business explained here. A must-read."
—Carol E. Heiser, RN, MA, ND (Clinical Nursing Doctorate),
Clinical Education Specialist, Immersion Medical, Inc.

"*MBA In A Day*® has proven to be as essential in my daily practice as my stethoscope. I wish I had had Professor Stralser's book when I started my medical practice."
—Robert S. Knight, MD, FAAFP, Medical Director,
Plumtree Family Health Center, LLC

"Professor Stralser's book is an easy-to-understand guide about business for busy professionals whose intense professional training missed important topics like marketing, accounting, finance, and management."
—Quinn Williams, Chair, Emerging Business and Venture
Capital Group, Greenberg Traurig, LLP

"In advising clients, I often get the sense that they do not have a good grasp of how to manage their businesses or employees. Professor Stralser's book is a straightforward and invaluable primer that will assist readers in the development and management of their businesses."
—Charles S. Mishkind, Miller, Canfield,
Paddock and Stone, PLC

MBA In A Day®

MBA In A Day®

What You Would Learn at Top-Tier Business Schools (If You Only Had the Time!)

Steven Stralser, Ph.D.

WILEY

John Wiley & Sons, Inc.

Published by John Wiley & Sons, Inc., Hoboken, New Jersey.
Published simultaneously in Canada.

For general information on our other products and services please contact our Customer Care Department within the U.S. at (800) 762-2974, outside the United States at (317) 572-3993 or fax (317) 572-4002.

Designations used by companies to distinguish their products are often claimed by trademarks. In all instances where the author or publisher is aware of a claim, the product names appear in Initial Capital letters. Readers, however, should contact the appropriate companies for more complete information regarding trademarks and registration.

Wiley also publishes its books in a variety of electronic formats. Some content that appears in print may not be available in electronic books. For more information about Wiley products, visit our web site at www.Wiley.com.

Library of Congress Cataloging-in-Publication Data:
Stralser, Steven, 1945–
    MBA in a day® : what you would learn at top-tier business schools (if you only had the time!) / Steven Stralser.
      p. cm.
      ISBN 0-471-68054-0 (cloth)
      1. Business education.   2. Industrial management—Study and teaching
      (Graduate)   3. Master of business administration degree.   I. Title.
    HF1111.S77 2004
    658—dc22   2004007668

Printed in the United States of America.

10 9 8 7 6 5 4 3 2

To my father, Harold, a hero in many ways

Contents

Preface

Of course you can't get an MBA degree in a day—ask anyone who has put in the months and years needed to accomplish this challenging and rewarding achievement—but this book is where you will find, in basic, easy-to-understand language, MBA concepts and principles that are presented in the gold standard of business education throughout the world—the master of business administration.

The story behind this book comes from my years teaching in a full-time MBA program where I began to notice something I found very interesting. Every semester, in addition to the traditional MBA students who had taken time off from their corporate life to enroll in the MBA program, I would find one or two students who were clearly "outliers" to these mainstream corporate types—for example, a physician, an attorney, an executive director from a nonprofit organization, or a small business owner or entrepreneur.

It did not take long to realize this trend was an indicator of an underlying interest, and need, for these well-educated professionals— well trained in the education of their profession—to learn about the "business side" of their professional lives.

These non-business-trained professionals wanted to fill a gap and learn business principles and concepts needed in their professional practices but not taught in medical schools or other professional schools such as law, engineering, architecture, veterinary, or other highly specialized training programs.

I also realized that for every physician, attorney, architect, or entrepreneur who can take the time to enroll in an MBA program, there are many more who are pressed for time and focused on the day-to-day challenges of running a successful practice, operating a small business, or launching a new venture but who would benefit from learning the essential principles and concepts found in the coursework of an MBA program. It is for these successful—albeit time-sensitive—professionals that this book is written.

In this book, you will learn the fundamental concepts and principles that full-time MBA students learn and that also have applicability to professional services providers, small business owners, and entrepreneurs as well as corporations and industry. These principles and concepts are not industry or profession specific—they are classic, strategic, and essential in performing in today's complex economic environment.

The book begins with Section I: People, Management, and Policy, which focuses on the human side of business. Chapter 1, "Human Resources," explores how human assets are critical to success and competitive advantage. Chapter 2, "Organizational Behavior," explores the dynamics of how people work together in an organizational setting. Chapter 3, "Leadership and Team Building," explores the differences between managing and leading and presents concepts behind the effective use of teams as a means to achieve organizational goals. Chapter 4, "Ethics," focuses on the complexities and issues that managers face in doing the right thing in an increasingly ambiguous and uncertain organizational environment. Chapter 5, "Negotiation," presents essential processes for navigating through the dynamics of conflict and agreement, providing a useful understanding of how this subject is critical to managers who must negotiate to some degree, on several levels, every day.

Section II: Money: Economics, Finance, and Accounting, focuses on the concepts and principles we associate with the financial side of an organization and its economic context. Chapter 6, "Accounting and Finance," explores the way we keep score in business, providing the essentials of accounting systems and financial statements. Chapter 7, "International, National, and Local Economics," provides a vocabulary of economic fundamentals to understand how nations, corporations, and individuals behave in markets to efficiently apply and allocate scarce resources and make their way through global economic systems.

Section III: Markets and Strategy explores the way organizations read, adapt, and communicate with their customers, competitors, and constituencies. In Chapter 8, "Marketing, Strategy, and Competitive Analysis," we review how organizations analyze their industry and their competition and then develop the way they communicate with their target customers. Chapter 9, "Advertising and Promotion," looks at the specifics of companies' communication with customers and clients. Chapter 10, "Communications and Presentations," presents principles and concepts about an increasingly important part of managing a business today—how to present our ideas and communicate effectively.

Section IV: Systems and Processes explores the key areas for organizations to implement their strategies and maintain competitiveness and sustainability. Chapter 11, "Project Management," explains how managers can tackle specific projects from start to finish and efficiently manage them. In Chapter 12, "Management Information Systems," we explore the increasingly important essentials of today's cyber-environment and how technology can be harnessed to achieve organizational excellence. Chapter 13, "E-Commerce and Uses of the World Wide Web," explores the use of the Web both as a means to communicate with customers, clients, and constituencies and also as a tool for organizational efficiency and productivity. And finally, in a world where quality is the key driver to market success and sustainability, Chapter 14, "Quality Management Systems," explores the concepts and principles of developing a culture and organizational purpose focused on quality.

Acknowledgments

This book would not have been possible without the collaboration and participation by a great team of researchers, writers, and contributors, composed of recent MBA graduates from Thunderbird: The Garvin School of International Management, many of whom I had the privilege of teaching and mentoring at this exceptional school that produces exceptional managers and leaders of global business and enterprise.

Lenora E. Peppers, MBA-IM, the team leader, is managing director of Kick-Start Marketing in Phoenix, Arizona. Arthur Holcombe, MBA, is associate director of the Corporate Executive Board, Washington, D.C. Ronald J. Greene, MBA, is a business analyst living in Phoenix, Arizona. Jaxon Ravens, MBA, is a political consultant in Seattle, Washington. Suchi Patel, MBA, is a strategy consultant in Phoenix, Arizona. Allison Kaiser, MBA, is a marketing strategist for Kick-Start Marketing in the Bay Area, in Northern California. Rachel Neft, MBA-IM, is a marketing strategist in Phoenix, Arizona.

I also want to acknowledge the collective great work of my partners in bringing *MBA In A Day*® to publication. To Rick Frishman at Planned Television Arts special thanks for sharing his knowledge of the publishing business, for mentoring me during the process, and for introducing Jane Dystel and Michael Bourret, who well applied his expertise in advancing *MBA In A Day*® into the market. Matthew Holt, Senior Editor, and Tamara Hummel, Michelle Becker, and Mike Onorato, all at John Wiley & Sons, are a top-notch team of publishing professionals to whom I am grateful for their belief in the book and their collective support and energy in making its publication possible.

Finally, I wish to express my thanks and appreciation to some important women in my life: to my new bride, Rosemary, my love and appreciation for signing up for an adventure and for being a great partner as that adventure in life together has been unfolding; to my mother, Janice, whose memory includes teaching me how words and writing are so important; to Deanne, for her love and support; to my sister Carol for always being there with encouragement and love; and to my daughters Amy and Marcy—you have made me so proud of your own achievements both as moms and wives, and as successful professional women!

About the Author

S teven Stralser received his Ph.D. from the University of Michigan, where he taught marketing and marketing strategy. He holds a BS in marketing from the University of Arizona and an MBA from Arizona State University.

He is currently Clinical Professor and Managing Director of the Global Entrepreneurship Center at Thunderbird: The Garvin School of International Management.

During fall 1999, he was a Fulbright Senior Scholar, teaching marketing management in the MBA program at the Budapest University of Economic Sciences and Entrepreneurship at the University of Miskolc.

His interests outside academe and the professional world include playing left defenseman for his men's adult ice hockey team, driving and just being around vintage sports and touring cars, sharing adventures with his new bride, Rosemary, and enjoying their growing clan of grandchildren.

SECTION 1

PEOPLE, MANAGEMENT, AND POLICY

Chapter 1

Human Resources

The process of recruiting, hiring, and retaining competent employees has always been an important part of any business. In the business world today, this function has become ever more complex and important. The business environment is forever changing, and managers and human resources departments must be flexible enough to adapt to these changes, including the evolving laws, demographics, and business strategies.

HUMAN RESOURCES PLANNING AND STRATEGY

Just like any other aspect of business management, planning and strategy development are the first items on the agenda when tackling a project. Managers, professionals, and entrepreneurs are often faced with the task of developing a plan for how human resources will be needed to meet short- and long-term goals and objectives. For example, a company is interested in expanding its production capacity with a new plant to serve its western U.S. markets. As part of the strategic planning for this new facility, a human resources component of this expansion will be essential.

3

In its simplest form, human resources planning starts by conducting an analysis of staffing needs throughout the organization. This could mean either assessing the current staffing requirements or projecting future requirements if changes are expected. In either situation there are several questions that need to be answered and fully understood prior to the analysis.

1. What is the organization's strategic vision?
2. What are the short-term and long-term goals?
3. Are there any major changes in the market that will impact the organization's future?
4. What changes in staffing requirements, if any, are needed to support the strategic vision of the organization?
5. If changes are needed within the organization, what type of resistance can be expected to the changes?

Once these questions are answered, assessing the staffing requirements can be completed.

Assessing the staffing plans involves evaluating the human capacity needed to meet the goals and objectives of the organization, estimating the number of people needed for each department or role, and making adjustments as needed. This process does take a lot of experience and understanding of the specific business, but experienced managers should be able to make good assessments. If the managers are new to the industry, a good benchmark would be comparing the number of employees needed in similar organizations.

Signs that the current staffing needs are not in line with the condition of the organization:

✔ Regular breakdowns in the process flows, which jeopardize relationships with clients and customers. These include missed deadlines, increased returns, decreased customer loyalty, and regular administration mistakes.

✔ Frequent employee absenteeism and turnover caused by employees being overstressed, having poor morale, or looking for other employment.

✔ Regularly occurring overtime caused by employees being overworked or given too much responsibility. Overworking employees can lead to burnouts and increased costs in the long run.

Once the staffing plan is developed that meets the current and future plans for the organization, job descriptions can be created. This process involves analyzing each job in the organization in order to generate a job description and job specifications, and then these are aggregated at a company-wide level. Job descriptions can be a very important management tool in some organizations. Some thought should be put into them due to the nature of employees using job descriptions to define and defend their actions or inactions. Job descriptions can be either a restraint or an open door for employees or teams.

The job analysis involves collecting sufficient information to form a complete understanding of what is entailed to perform the job. A job description lists the activities that the employee performs, as well as the skills and qualities that are needed to successfully meet the job objectives. Think of this stage of human resources planning as if you were a newly appointed coach of an expansion football franchise. You would identify first the positions you would need to complete the roster, then the qualities you would like for each player, specific to each position.

Once the job analysis and job descriptions are determined, this information can then be aggregated to form a human resource inventory to track what skills and capabilities need to be filled in to complete the human resources requirements.

When completed correctly, job descriptions can be a very important tool and can be used in many different functions, including:

✔ Giving employees a gauge of how they will be evaluated within the organization.

✔ Helping determine the compensation level for individual positions.

✔ Establishing hiring criteria for specific positions, and giving candidates responsibility expectations.

A typical outline of a job description:

Job Title: Specific title that would be included in an organizational chart.

Overall Description: A brief description of the responsibilities an individual holding this position would have.

Reporting To: List of person(s) to whom this position reports, and any subordinate positions.

Duties: A detailed list of regular duties this position would be expected to perform.

Requirements: A list of mandatory or preferred requirements for the position, including number of years of experience, certifications, and licenses.

Criteria: A list of standards that will be used to evaluate the possible candidates, including specific skills, experience, or knowledge.

IMPLEMENTATION OF THE HUMAN RESOURCES PLAN

Once the planning part of the process is complete, the firm will set forth to implement that plan through the next set of human resource concepts and tactics: recruitment, selection, appraisal, rewards, and employee personal and professional development.

Recruitment

Recruitment is the process by which companies attract candidates to fill present and future positions, and the appropriate method varies from company to company. In most cases, the human resources department in the company will work together with managers in departments throughout the company or with others familiar with the personnel needs to determine a recruitment method and approach.

Many recruitment methods are available, including Internet and print advertisements, employee referrals, and outsourced agencies ("headhunter" executive placement firms, job placement agencies, etc.) that perform recruitment services for the company, either on a fixed-fee arrangement, much like a consulting relationship, or on a performance-based basis where the fee is a percentage of the employee's salary. In some cases, the employee will pay the fees associated with such outsourced services, but more often the company will pay these fees. Other recruitment tactics include job fairs and college recruiting and might involve a combination of several methods.

Employee Leasing and Outsourcing. In the past decade, the use of "employee leasing" and temporary, or project-based, outsourcing of human resource needs has become more prevalent. In this scenario, the company contracts with another company that provides the employees for a specific need or project. The contracted worker is an employee of the provider company, with the provider company responsible for payroll, employee taxes, benefits, and other employee-related expenses. The company hiring these contract employees is thus free of the associated bookkeeping and administrative costs of maintaining these employees on its payroll—it makes a single payment to the company from which it is leasing the employees, rather than paying the workers individually.

These leasing or outsourcing arrangements are attractive to new or emerging companies or mature companies that may be experiencing an unusual spike in demand, or some other kind of nonrecurring event, presenting a solution for a company that needs to modify its workforce capacity with some upside or downside flexibility.

Recruitment: Inside versus Outside the Company. One of the first questions the company's human resources department is likely to ask is whether to fill job needs internally or to look outside the company. Hiring internally allows the manager to choose from a known pool of talent and can minimize misperceptions among candidates about the actual requirements of the position. In addition, hiring from within can be cost-effective and provide motivation for existing employees.

Generally, it is advisable to look outside the company when specific skills are required for the position and existing employees may not be reasonably expected to train for or learn these skills. The decision to look outside the company tends to be more appropriate when there is a specific need to fill, such as technical requirements. Hiring from outside also helps to avoid the ripple effect of frequent internal staffing changes and the employee "musical chairs" syndrome that does not give staff time to mature into their respective jobs. (Though sometimes well-planned cross-training for different jobs within a company is a productive long-term strategy.)

Finally, recruiting outside the company can be an effective way to import experience and creativity or new ways of doing things. This infusion of outsider perspectives and approaches can infuse the company with a fresh look at its processes and systems.

Selection

The recruitment process just described will result in a pool from which to select the right employee—and this usually involves a combination of different selection methods in order to make the best employee selection decision.

Interviews and reference checks are the most commonly used, but other methods are available depending on the specific demands of the position. For example, background checks are appropriate when a position requires that the employee have significant customer interaction or if the prospective employee has a fiduciary involvement or responsibility with the company. Other selection methods include:

- ✔ Skill performance tests/work samples—for example, a graphic artist may bring in a portfolio of past projects, or a data entry candidate may be given a simulated work assignment.
- ✔ Personality tests—used especially in customer contact recruitment and selection (e.g., salespersons and customer service candidates).
- ✔ Physical abilities tests—used in many job requirements where physical condition is an essential element in job productivity or success (e.g., a product installation or delivery job).
- ✔ Drug tests—an increasingly used tool to ensure selection of candidates who do not involve themselves in chemical or substance dependency.

Interviewing. Face-to-face interviews can be extremely revealing but must be well prepared. The goal of an interview should be to learn whether the candidate has the competencies and technical skills that are most critical to the job, and questions should be prepared for each area. The interviewer's questions should focus on behaviors, not opinions, and may involve asking applicants to provide examples from their past experiences. Interviews provide an opportunity to read body language and the applicants' ability to "think on their feet," often replicating the realities of life on the job. Additionally, to ensure good fit with the culture of the company, an initial interview is often followed up by several more representing the other employees with whom the potential hire may work, as well as company representatives at different levels and areas within the company. An important step in the interview process is to check on a prospective employee's past performances by making inquiries to former employers and references. Four rules for more effective reference checks:

1. Ask the applicant to inform prior employers that you intend to contact them. Former managers are much more likely to provide useful information if they are aware beforehand that they will be contacted.

2. Open the call by describing the corporate culture of the organization. This provides some context for the previous employer's comments on the previous employee.

3. Reassure the previous employers that the information they provide will not determine the final hiring decision, but that your goal is to learn how best to manage the prospective hire.

4. Save formal questions such as dates of employment and title until the end of the call.

Employee Training and Development

It is one thing to be able to recruit and hire good employees, but to tap into and help them attain their full potential is just as or even more important. Training and development is an essential part of all organizations today. The main benefits of employee development and training:

- ✔ Increases the value and capacity of the human assets of the company.
- ✔ Provides an alternative to recruiting, by having qualified personnel to fill vacant positions.
- ✔ Creates potential future leaders of the company.
- ✔ Helps reduce employee turnover by keeping individuals motivated and interested in their positions with the possibility for advancement.

Orientation. Training should begin on day one of employment, with every employee given an orientation. Getting employees off to the right start is a very easy way to build a company that embraces learning and development. Most small companies do not have formal orientation programs, but rely on individuals finding their way when they first get hired. This seems to work fine in smaller organizations when there is more informal means of communication, but as organizations grow most have found that formal orientation programs are necessary to get employees up to speed and productive in a timely fashion.

Formal orientation programs can range from an hour to several days, and the level of orientation usually depends on the level of the positions. Whereas entry-level or unskilled labor will need very little orientation, experienced professionals will need quite a bit more to get up to speed with the organization. Each organization needs to define its own orientation needs and programs. Assigning mentors is often done in place of an orientation program to give new employees a helping hand during the first few weeks on the job. At a minimum for small or large organizations, orientation programs should include:

- ✔ Detailed company history and overview of the current structure and products.
- ✔ Overview of employment policies and handbook (if applicable).

✔ Basics of compensation, benefits, and all other legal issues that arise.

✔ Health and safety issues.

✔ Information about business systems such as phone, e-mail, voice mail, and office equipment.

✔ Employee rewards and incentives.

Skill Training. Skill training is exactly what it says—training employees on new skill sets. This could take many forms, including training on new software, accounting, customer service techniques, or even team-building exercises. Skill training has two main goals: (1) to maintain employees' current skill level with ever-advancing technology and business practices, and (2) to give employees the necessary skills to advance through the organization.

Every organization is going to have a unique set of skills required of its employees. Of course many skills transfer from organization to organization very easily, but the scope of skills is usually unique for every organization. Prior to implementing training, organizations need to follow a few basic steps:

1. Conduct complete skill assessments, involve all levels of employees, develop core skill competencies for each position, and assess current gaps in the skill set.

2. Choose the training source. Whether you choose outside consultants, assign internal trainers, or devise online training, the source has to be effective for the given skill set.

3. Align training with the broad goals and objectives of the organization. This will help employees see the importance and be more likely to jump on board with the training.

4. Conduct training during work hours; this will help keep a positive attitude toward the training.

5. Conduct training in suitable facilities. Sticking a class in a dirty warehouse is not likely to be very effective.

6. Plan for feedback and assessment of all training programs.

Professional Development and Leadership Training

As organizations grow, adapt, and mature, there comes a time when existing managers and leaders will begin to think about stepping down and looking for replacements either inside the organization or out. When this situation arises, very often managers find themselves not being able to find qualified candidates with the right experience and who will be a good fit with the current organization. Managers typically find that internal candidates are very good at their current jobs but do not have the breadth of experiences it takes to manage multiple departments successfully. External candidates are also very experienced, but the right fit is very hard to find. One way to ensure that suitable replacements for top managers and leaders are available is to have a program or plan to develop leaders internally.

Leadership development programs are very common in today's business world; the risk of not planning for the succession of current leaders is too high for most organizations to bear. One common measurement tool used by organizations is to ask the question "Would the organization be able to survive successfully if the CEO or head manager was the victim of a fatal accident?" If the answer to this question is no, it would be wise for management to address this issue.

Leadership development programs take many forms, but they all have similar goals of providing certain employees with the necessary skills and experience to fill the shoes of top management in the future. The programs can be formal or informal, usually span several years, and should be a recurring program that is well accepted within the organization. Leadership development programs usually involve scheduled job rotations with increased responsibility with every step. High-potential individuals are usually hired into the programs, mentors are assigned, and their progress is measured regularly. Of course, every individual who enters the program is not guaranteed a top management position. All program participants will have to prove themselves and take a proactive approach to develop themselves professionally; and hopefully when the time comes for management succession, there will be qualified candidates to choose from.

The 360-Degree Assessment

The 360-degree assessment is a commonly used tool in organizations as a way of giving and receiving feedback at all levels within the organization. Simply put, a 360-degree assessment is a system used to gather input on individual employees' performance, not only from managers and supervisors, but from coworkers and from direct reports as well. Some companies also involve customers in a 360-degree assessment, especially in the case of customer-contact personnel. More traditional feedback tools, in which only the direct manager provides feedback, can very easily lead to a one-sided and incomplete employee review. The 360-degree assessment is much more likely to provide an accurate review and assessment of an employee's performance.

Almost all large companies today use a form of the 360-degree assessment for their employees; sometimes it takes on a different name, such as full-circle or multisource assessment. Here's how it works.

Typically all employees are given the opportunity to rate and give comments on all employees they work with on a regular basis, including managers, peers, and subordinates. Each assessment includes several different categories for employee assessment—for example, leadership, performance management, communication, teamwork, integrity, quality, problem solving, vision, trust, adaptability, and reliability. Each organization develops the assessment criteria based on what it feels is important.

Once the assessment is complete, employees have the opportunity to view how their coworkers assessed their performance, and managers get to see how they are generally viewed by their subordinates.

Dell, the U.S.-based computer manufacturer, has used 360-degree assessment, and the results have led to substantial management policy changes, including forcing upper management to be more in touch with the daily operations and allowing for routine opportunities for management to interact with subordinates.

Implementing the 360-degree assessment can sometimes be very difficult and can cause more harm than good if management is not careful. Giving feedback has to be done with caution given the sensitive nature of the data and the possible defensiveness of the employees who receive it. Some employees will not be comfortable giving frank feedback to their peers. An organization needs to have a very high level of trust among the employees for this assessment to work effectively. If the level of trust is not established prior to the 360-degree evaluation, human tendencies such as protectiveness, revenge, and development of hierarchies take precedence and will skew the results, creating even more distrust within the ranks. If this trust level cannot be established, the 360-degree evaluation should be postponed to a later date.

Steps for Implementation of 360-Degree Evaluation. If a 360-degree evaluation has not been used previously in the organization, it might be wise to introduce the program as an internal program for personal improvement, not for management decisions. This will take the pressure off employees and allow for a more relaxed environment during the process. It may even be wise for upper management not to have access to the company-wide results the first time in order for employees to feel comfortable with the process. Many large companies have the 360-degree assessment in place for more than a year before they are able to see any benefits from the program and use it to make decisions. Employees need to feel comfortable with the system before they will actually use it as a learning tool.

Start out with a test group. When first implementing the 360-degree evaluation, start out with one department or a small group of employees. The time and resources needed for a company-wide implementation could end up being substantial. Starting with a test group will provide insight on issues and problems that likely will arise and will limit the cost if the 360-degree evaluation does not work within the organization.

Link the 360-degree evaluation's goals with the overall company goals. The 360-degree evaluation needs full cooperation from all employees along with a significant business reason for the implementation. If the program is linked to the overall goals, individual employees will have an easier time accepting and providing value.

Train employees. The 360-degree evaluation may include hiring an outside firm to handle the process, or if it is handled internally, there need to be assigned roles and responsibilities. The employees who are responsible need to be trained on all aspects of the evaluation; they must ensure that complete trust is held throughout the process.

Turn the results into an action plan. Once the evaluation is complete, request ideas for an action plan from all employees. Hold meetings if necessary or provide other means for feedback opportunities. Ongoing goals and objectives need to be set for the future in order for everyone involved to feel that the program is effective and useful.

Questions that should be answered prior to implementing a 360-degree evaluation program include:

- ✔ How ready is the organization for the 360-degree evaluation?
- ✔ Who is going to be involved?
- ✔ Is this a mandatory or voluntary project?
- ✔ What criteria will be evaluated?
- ✔ How will the information be collected, compiled, and distributed?
- ✔ Who is going to be responsible for each activity, including planning, assessing, compiling the information, distributing the results, developing the action plan, and following through?

The 360-degree evaluation, if used correctly can be a valuable organizational tool that will provide a path for personal and organizational development. It can help direct and mold the corporate culture, define and set goals, and create camaraderie among employees.

HUMAN RESOURCES MANAGEMENT AS A COMPETITIVE TOOL

Human resources planning has evolved over time from a basic tool used by companies to identify personnel needs to an integral part of an organization's strategy for making the most of its "human capital."

Increasingly, companies are finding that the strategic management of human resources can actually be a source of competitive advantage. For example, one company that has clearly used its human resources as the key driver of its competitive advantage is Southwest Airlines.

In the airline industry, competitors are using essentially the same kind of equipment, maintenance, and aircraft, and also utilize the same physical locations (i.e., airports), yet Southwest consistently outperforms its competition, using the very same hard assets as its competitors. The main, telltale variable explaining the difference in relative performance between Southwest and its less profitable competitors is its focus on the human side of its business model. Southwest has focused a great deal of its energy in developing a highly productive organizational culture by crafting a human resources strategy that has driven its sustainable competitive advantage.

Additionally, companies like Whole Foods Market, SAS Institute, and Men's Warehouse proactively address personnel issues in order to keep their employees happy with their jobs. It has been proven time and again that when organizations take care of their employees, the employees will take care of the organization.

Men's Warehouse, for example, has a corporate philosophy to uncover untapped human capital in all of its employees. It operates under well-defined values and believes the employees are the organization. They provide training for all levels and, as an added bonus, provide very low-interest loans to employees. As a result, Men's Warehouse has reaped unprecedented growth of more than 30 percent annually in recent years in an industry that is very competitive with very low margins. The company also benefits from low-to-zero employee theft and does not use any devices to try to prevent employee theft.

The Men's Warehouse model can be transferred to any industry. It starts with well-defined goals and values to make human capital a competitive advantage for the organization. In the Men's Warehouse example, the company's goal was to develop every employee to his/her fullest potential. Then once the goals and values are decided on, programs are developed to make them attainable and a reality.

SUMMARY

Human resource planning, recruitment, and selection are the initial steps in effecting the company's strategy by maximizing its investment in human capital. Think of the recruitment and selection like a funnel, with the wide part of the funnel collecting a wide assortment of candidates, and the selection process sorting the candidate pool into a smaller group of qualified candidates, both in terms of the skills needed for the job and from the standpoint of their fit with the organizational culture of the company. Both kinds of suitability are needed to effectively advance the company strategy via its human resources capabilities.

REFERENCES

Conger, Jay A., and Robert M. Fulmer. "Developing Your Leadership Pipeline." *Harvard Business Review*, Reprint R0312F.

Harvard Business Essentials: Hiring and Keeping the Best People. Boston: Harvard Business School Press, 2002.

Messmer, Max. *The Fast Forward MBA in Hiring*. New York: John Wiley & Sons, 1998.

Pfeffer, Jeffery. "Six Dangerous Myths about Pay." *Harvard Business Review*, (May–June 1998).

Chapter

2

Organizational Behavior

A n organization consists of individuals with different tasks attempting to accomplish a common purpose. (For a business, this purpose is the creation and delivery of goods or services for its customers.) Organizational behavior is the study of how individuals and groups perform together within an organization. It focuses on the best way to manage individuals, groups, organizations, and processes. Organizational behavior is an extensive topic and includes management, theories and practices of motivation, and the fundamentals of organizational structure and design.

From the smallest nonprofit to the largest multinational conglomerate, firms and organizations all have to deal with the concept of organizational behavior. Knowledge about organizational behavior can provide managers with a better understanding of how their firm or organization attempts to accomplish its goals. This knowledge may also lead to ways in which a firm or organization can make its processes more effective and efficient, thus allowing the firm or organization to successfully adapt to changing circumstances.

This chapter will help you better understand the theories and structures of organizational behavior. The chapter begins by discussing some of the basic characteristics of managers and management. It then describes some of the popular theories and practical applications related to motivation and helps answer the question "What motivates employees and why does it motivate them?" The chapter then examines some of the fundamentals of organizational structure and describes ways in which organizational structures differ from one another. Finally it discusses a few methods by which organizations can control processes and outcomes.

MANAGEMENT

As discussed in the next chapter, "Leadership and Team Building," management used to be focused on direction and control. Now it is more involved with support and facilitation and the evolving notion of the manager as "coach." In conjunction with this role as a supportive facilitator, managers are now focusing on efficiently and effectively utilizing the intellectual capital of an organization. Intellectual capital consists of the knowledge, expertise, and dedication of an organization's workforce. The management of intellectual capital is necessary in order to get the most out of an organization's material resources and achieve organizational goals.

In practice, managers accomplish organizational goals through the process of defining goals, organizing structures, motivating employees, and monitoring performance and outcomes. In performing these processes a manager often takes on several different roles. These roles were described by Henry Mintzberg and include interpersonal roles, informational roles, and decisional roles. Interpersonal roles are ways in which a manager works and communicates with others. Informational roles are ways in which a manager acquires, processes, and shares information. Decisional roles are how a manager uses information to make decisions, which involves identifying opportunities and problems and acting on them appropriately, allocating resources, handling conflicts, and negotiating.

In order to fill these roles effectively managers use skills that allow them to translate knowledge into action. Robert Katz describes three different sets of skills that managers use, including technical, human, and conceptual skills. Technical skills are used to perform a specialized task. They are learned both from experience and from education, and they can involve using a specific type of technology or process. Human skills are used when working with others and include, among other things, basic communications skills, persuasive ability, and conflict resolution. Conceptual skills are used in analyzing and solving complex interrelated problems. They require having a good understanding of the organization as a whole and understanding how the interrelated parts work together—for example, a good understanding of an organization's behavioral attributes, its weaknesses, and actions needed to achieve its goals and objectives.

Emotional Intelligence and the Manager

Daniel Goleman defined an important aspect of human skills in his work on emotional intelligence. Emotional intelligence is tied closely to management effectiveness and ultimately organizational behavior; it suggests that a manager's performance may be influenced by several factors:

- ✔ Self-awareness—understanding your moods and emotions.
- ✔ Self-regulation—thinking about your actions and controlling destructive ones.
- ✔ Motivation—working hard to accomplish your goals.
- ✔ Empathy—understanding the emotions of others.
- ✔ Social skills—developing good connections and relationships with others.

Understanding emotional intelligence is especially important in light of changes in organizational structures, which have created firms with less hierarchy and closer peer contact.

Motivation

Motivation is an important driver in an organization and is crucial to the management of intellectual capital. Motivation underlies what employees choose to do (quality and/or quantity), how much effort they will put into accomplishing the task, and how long they will work in order to accomplish it. Employees who are motivated will work more effectively and efficiently and shape an organization's behavior. A motivated workforce will have a strong effect on an organization's bottom line. Motivation is strongly tied to job satisfaction. Job satisfaction is how individuals feel about the tasks they are supposed to accomplish and may also be influenced by the physical and social nature of the workplace. The more satisfied employees are with their jobs, the more motivated they will be to do their jobs well.

There are several important studies relating to motivation. These include Abraham Maslow's hierarchy of needs, Frederick Herzberg's study of hygiene and motivational factors, Douglas McGregor's Theory X and Theory Y, Theory Z, Victor Vroom's Expectancy Theory, J. Stacy Adams' Equity Theory, and Reinforcement Theory.

Maslow's Hierarchy of Needs. In 1943 Abraham Maslow developed a theory about human motivation called the hierarchy of needs. This theory has been popular in the United States and describes human needs in five general categories. According to Maslow, once an individual has met his needs in one category, he is motivated to seek needs in the next higher level. Maslow's hierarchy of needs consists of the following general categories:

> *Physiological needs.* These are the first and lowest level of needs. They relate to the most basic needs for survival and include the need for food and shelter.
>
> *Safety needs.* The second level of needs involves an individual's need for security, protection, and safety in the physical and interpersonal events of daily life.
>
> *Social needs.* The third level of needs is associated with social behavior. It is based on an individual's desire to be accepted as part of a group and includes a desire for love and affection.
>
> *Esteem needs.* The fourth level of needs relates to an individual's need for respect, recognition, and prestige and involves a personal sense of competence.
>
> *Self-actualization.* This is the fifth and highest level of needs. Needs of this level are associated with an individual's desire to reach his full potential by growing and using his abilities to the fullest and most creative extent.

As individuals move higher in the corporate hierarchy, they may see higher-order needs as being more important than those of lower orders. Needs may also vary based on career stage, organizational structure, and geographic location. The hierarchy of needs could also lack effective application in different cultural contexts. Certain cultures may value social needs over psychological and safety needs. In addition, the theory necessitates that a manager be able to identify and understand an employee's needs. This is not always easy and can lead to inaccurate assumptions. Taken in the proper context, however, recognizing the importance of needs is a useful method for conceptualizing factors of employee motivation and thus being able to direct an organization's behavior.

Herzberg's Factors. In the 1950s Frederick Herzberg studied the characteristics of a job in order to determine which factors served to increase or decrease workers' satisfaction. His study identified two factors related to job satisfaction: "hygiene" factors and motivational factors.

Hygiene factors are those that must be maintained at adequate levels. They are related more to the environment in which an employee is working rather than the nature of the work itself. Important hygiene factors include organizational policies, quality of supervision, working conditions, relationships with peers and subordinates, status, job security, and salary. Adequate levels of these factors are necessary to prevent dissatisfaction; improving these factors beyond adequate levels, however, does not necessarily lead to an increase in job satisfaction.

A different set of factors, identified as motivational factors, is associated with having a direct effect on increasing job satisfaction. These factors include achievement, recognition, responsibility, growth, the work itself, and the opportunity for advancement.

Like Maslow's hierarchy of needs, Herzberg's factors must be tempered by sensitivity to individual and cultural differences and require that managers identify what employees consider to be "adequate levels." Managers sometimes simplify both of these theories and inappropriately assume that they know what their employees need.

McGregor's Theory X and Theory Y. Douglas McGregor's theories focus less on employee needs and more on the nature of managerial behavior. These theories are based on the assumption that a supervisor's perceptions of her employees will strongly influence the way in which she attempts to motivate her employees. McGregor created two theories based on his studies, called Theory X and Theory Y.

In the case of Theory X, a supervisor assumes that her employees are adverse to work and will do everything they can to avoid it. Acting on this assumption, the supervisor will exert tight control over employees, monitor their work closely, and hesitantly delegate authority.

In this case of Theory Y, a supervisor assumes that, contrary to Theory X, workers are willing to work and would be willing to accept increased responsibilities. In light of these assumptions, the supervisor will provide employees with more freedom and creativity in the workplace and will be more willing to delegate authority.

Managers will seek to motivate their employees based on their perceptions of the employees' interests. This theory brings to light the variation in practice that can exist depending on the assumptions that managers make about their employees.

Theory Z. Theory Z emerged in the 1980s. It attempts to motivate workers by giving them more responsibility and making them feel more appreciated. It was developed, in part, in the light of Japanese management practices, which allowed for more worker participation in decision making and provided for less specialized career paths.

Expectancy Theory. Developed by Victor Vroom, this concept assumes that the quality of employees' efforts is influenced by the outcomes they will receive for their efforts. They will be motivated to the degree that they feel that their efforts will result in an acceptable performance, that that performance will be rewarded, and that the value of the reward will be highly positive. In order for managers to practically apply the theories associated with expectancy theory, they need to define the desired behaviors clearly. Once this is accomplished, the manager should think about rewards that could serve as possible reinforcers and how these rewards will have different values for different individuals. Employees must then be informed about what must be done to receive these rewards, and managers need to provide feedback on employee performance. If a desired behavior is achieved, the reward must be given immediately.

Equity Theory. Equity theory was a result of the work of J. Stacy Adams and states that when individuals determine whether the compensation they receive is fair compared to their coworkers' compensation, any perceived inequity will affect their motivation. This sense of inequity can either be felt as negative inequity, when employees feel they have received less than others who performed the same task, or felt as positive inequity, when workers feel they have received more than others who performed the same task. Either type of inequity can motivate a worker to act in a way that restores the sense of equity. Examples of employee behavior may include not working as hard, asking for a raise, quitting, comparing themselves to a different coworker, rationalizing that the inequity will be only temporary, or getting a coworker to accept more work. To limit a perceived sense of inequity, employees should be compensated to the degree that their efforts contribute to the firm. This theory, however, is difficult to implement given the differences of opinion that might arise between an employee and a supervisor regarding what constitutes equitable pay. To apply this theory successfully it is important to address the employee's perceptions. This can be accomplished first by recognizing and anticipating that inequities can and will exist. It is then important to communicate clear evaluations of any rewards given and an appraisal of the performance on which these rewards are based. There may also be comparison points that are appropriate to share.

Reinforcement Theory. A carrot-and-stick approach to motivational behavior, the reinforcement theory is concerned with positive and negative reinforcement. It applies consequences to certain behaviors. There are four basic reinforcement strategies: positive reinforcement, negative reinforcement, punishment, and extinction. Positive reinforcement motivates workers by providing them with rewards for desirable behavior. To be effective a reward must be delivered only if the desired behavior is displayed. It should also be delivered as quickly as possible after the desired behavior is exhibited. Negative reinforcement, in contrast, involves withdrawing negative consequences if the desired behavior is displayed. This method of reinforcement is sometimes called "avoidance" because its aim is to have the individual avoid the negative consequences by performing the desired behavior. Unlike positive and negative reinforcement, punishment is not designed to inspire positive behavior, but to discourage negative behavior. Extinction is the withdrawal of reinforcing consequences for a desired behavior. Its intent is to eliminate undesirable behavior.

Conclusions from Motivational Theories

In shaping and directing an organization's behavior, the seven theories discussed previously provide some insight into the organization's behavior. Several conclusions can be drawn from these theories.

Needs. Employees have needs. In order to motivate employees, supervisors should attempt to understand the breadth of their employees' needs. This is not always an easy task and requires open and frequent communication between managers and employees. By structuring a job so that it meets these needs a supervisor can increase an employee's motivation.

Compensation. Compensation is an important part of motivation, with a goal to compensate employees according to the contribution each employee makes to the firm. Employees will be dissatisfied if they feel that they are getting less than they deserve. In order to decrease the likelihood of perceived inequities, a manager needs to be proactive and informative regarding reward structures.

Rewards. Employees need to know that the goal they are working toward is achievable and that when they accomplish this goal that they will be rewarded in an appropriate and timely manner.

MOTIVATION: FROM THEORY TO PRACTICE

The insights drawn from the discussion of motivational theory highlight the importance of assessing needs, compensation, and rewards when creating an organizational structure that will increase an employee's job satisfaction and motivation and direct organizational behavior; some of these actions include implementing an adequate compensation program, increasing job security, allowing for flexible work schedules, and establishing employee involvement programs.

Adequate Compensation Program

Before determining how compensation should be set, it is necessary to align the compensation program with several elements of the business.

- ✔ *Business goals.* A compensation plan should be developed in light of a firm's business goals. Employees should be compensated to the degree that their efforts help the business accomplish its goals.

- ✔ *Employee goals.* A compensation plan should be clear in stating individual employee goals. In order to effectively motivate employees, they need to know what goals they will be expected to achieve.

- ✔ *Achievable goals.* The goals that individual employees are expected to accomplish must be realistic and achievable. If employees feel that the goals associated with their positions are unreachable, they will not be motivated to work. If a supervisor can set reasonable goals and make the employee aware that numerous achievable bonuses will be given if these goals are met, the employee will be motivated.

- ✔ *Employee input.* Employees will be more satisfied with their jobs if they are consulted about the compensation plan before it is put into effect.

An adequate compensation program, taking these issues into account, will affect employee motivation; a compensation plan should give the highest relative raises to the individuals who achieve the highest levels of performance. This type of system is referred to as a merit-based pay system and bases pay on performance. It can be effectively implemented in conjunction with an incentive plan that rewards employees for achieving specific performance goals. These plans stand in contrast to a system that provides across-the-board pay raises, which will not motivate workers to put extra effort into achieving set goals.

Job Security

Employees who feel they are in danger of losing their jobs may not show high work productivity. Worker satisfaction can, and productivity may, be increased by providing job security. One way firms can increase job security is by providing cross-training in other functions. This will give employees the versatility to accomplish new tasks if their current positions change or are no longer available.

Flexible Work Schedules

In today's time-pressed world, many employees view time away from work as an important factor shaping their at-work motivation and on-job productivity. There are several methods for allowing flexible work schedules that meet the needs of employees seeking greater home/work flexibility. One of the more common is a compressed workweek. This system lets an employee work the same number of hours over the course of fewer days. Instead of working five eight-hour days, an employee might work four ten-hour days. Other examples of flexible work schedules include job sharing where two or more people share a certain work schedule.

Employee Involvement Programs

Employee involvement programs seek to motivate employees by increasing their responsibilities or getting them more involved in decision-making processes. There are several types of employee involvement programs; the more basic programs include job enlargement, job rotation, and teamwork. More ambitious programs include open-book management and worker empowerment.

Job Enlargement. Job enlargement is a direct way to increase job responsibility. It involves expanding a position and giving an employee a greater variety of tasks.

Job Rotation. A job rotation program periodically reassigns employees to new positions. In addition to increasing employees' involvement in the firm and adjusting their responsibilities, job rotation can also improve employees' skill sets, thereby increasing their job security. In addition, it can also relieve the boredom in the workplace associated with doing the same job over a long period of time.

Teamwork. This program attempts to increase motivation by putting individuals with different positions onto a team and setting them the task of achieving a specific goal. Teamwork serves to increase an employee's responsibilities and involvement in the firm. The best types of teams are self-directed. This provides the team with the authority to make decisions regarding planning, accomplishing, and evaluating the task they are working on. For more on this topic of teamwork, see Chapter 3, "Leadership and Team Building."

Open-Book Management. Open-book management is a challenging, but direct way of increasing employee involvement and responsibility. It involves allowing employees to see how their job performance affects key performance indicators important to the firm. In order to institute this program a firm needs to make key indicators available to employees and educate them on how to interpret key performance measures. Employees also need to be empowered to make decisions related to their positions and training and be given the opportunity to see how these decisions affect the rest of the firm. Open-book management also necessitates an adequate compensation program whereby compensation is tied to performance.

Worker Empowerment. Worker empowerment attempts to increase employee job responsibility as well as employee involvement. It does this by giving employees more authority and involving them in the decision-making process. Employees who are empowered can often make better and more informed decisions than can a manager who is not directly involved in the process. Participative management is similar to worker empowerment. Although it does not provide employees with direct decision-making power, it encourages managers to consult closely with workers before making decisions. Another type of participatory management is management by objective. This approach allows employees to set their own goals and provides them with the freedom to decide how they can best achieve these goals.

Measuring Job Satisfaction

How do managers know that after gaining an understanding of the theories of motivation and applying different approaches to increase job satisfaction that their efforts have been successful? In practice a manager must draw conclusions on a daily basis from social observations and interactions in the workplace. Sometimes, however, it is a good idea to conduct a more formal survey. This can be accomplished through either interviews, surveys, or focus groups that often involve only a specific group of employees. Two useful surveys are the Minnesota Satisfaction Questionnaire and the Job Descriptive Index. Both of these surveys address areas of employee satisfaction in regard to different aspects of an organization and provide managers with useful information. They cover work, working conditions, rewards, opportunities for advancement, and the quality of relationships with managers and coworkers.

ORGANIZATIONAL STRUCTURE

Whether you are in the beginning stages of starting your own business or you are looking for ways to improve an existing business, it is important to think about the firm's organizational structure. Examining organizational structure will help answer questions about the ways in which a firm conducts business. Who is responsible for accomplishing various tasks within the firm? How are these individuals grouped? Who manages these individuals or groups? How do they manage them?

Five Structural Factors

In essence, the primary goal of an organizational structure is to coordinate and allocate a firm's resources so that the firm can carry out its plans and achieve its goals and objectives. The fundamentals of organizational structure revolve around five factors: the division of labor, departmentalization, the nature of the managerial hierarchy, the managerial span of control, and the amount of centralization or decentralization in the organization.

Division of Labor. The division of labor involves two steps: dividing work into separate tasks and assigning these tasks to workers. What are the different tasks carried out by your firm? Who is responsible for accomplishing these tasks?

Departmentalization. Departmentalization is the process of grouping similar types of jobs together so that they can be accomplished more efficiently and effectively. There are five different ways in which to departmentalize business activities. Different types of departmentalization can exist to varying degrees within a business. What types of departmentalization exist within your firm? Could your firm be departmentalized differently?

1. *Function.* An example of functional departmentalization would be a firm that has a marketing and finance department. It involves grouping tasks based on the function that the organizational unit accomplishes within a firm.

2. *Product.* A consumer electronics firm that has separate departments for camera and MP3 players is using product-based departmentalization. In this case departments are based on the goods or services that an organizational unit sells or provides.

3. *Process.* A manufacturing firm that includes separate departments for assembly and shipping is an example of a firm with process-based departmentalization. In this case departmentalization revolves around the production process used by the organizational unit.

4. *Customer.* A bank with separate departments for its business customers and individual customers is using customer-based departmentalization. Its departmentalization is based on the type of customer served.

5. *Geographic.* An example of a firm using geographic departmentalization is an automobile manufacturing company that has different departments for each country in which it sells cars. In this case departmentalization is based on the geographic segmentation of organizational units.

Managerial Hierarchy. Managerial hierarchy relates to the way in which management is layered. It usually includes three levels—upper or top management, middle management, and supervisory roles. The higher levels of management generally have fewer employees, but more power.

Span of Control. Span of control is closely related to managerial hierarchy. At each level of management within a firm an individual is responsible for a different number of employees. Span of control relates to the number of employees that a manager directly supervises. Span of control is determined by a number of factors, including the type of activity, the location of the workers, a manager's ability to delegate tasks, the amount and nature of communication between the manager and the individuals being supervised, and the skill level and motivation of the individuals being supervised.

Centralization versus Decentralization. Centralization is the degree to which formal authority is centralized within a unit or level of an organization. Decentralization is the process of actively shifting authority lower in a firm's hierarchical structure. This effectively gives more decision-making power and responsibility to those in supervisory roles. Centralization and decentralization have their benefits and costs. While centralization provides top-level managers with a better overview of operations and allows for tighter fiscal control, it can result in slower decision making and limit innovation and motivation. Decentralization, by contrast, can speed up decision making and increase motivation and innovation, but this is done at the expense of a top manager's view of the firm and financial control.

Mechanistic and Organic Organizational Structures

The five structural factors just discussed give rise to numerous organizational possibilities. Mechanistic and organic structures are two possibilities at opposite ends of the organizational spectrum. They give shape to the concept of the factors of organizational structure. A mechanistic organization is characterized by the following structural factors:

- ✔ Degree of work specialization is high.
- ✔ Departmentalization is rigid.
- ✔ Managerial hierarchy has many layers.
- ✔ Span of control is narrow.
- ✔ Decision making is centralized.

✔ Chain of command is long.

✔ Organizational structure is very tall.

An organic organization is characterized by the following factors:

✔ Degree of work specialization is low.

✔ Departmentalization is loose.

✔ Managerial hierarchy has few layers.

✔ Span of control is wide.

✔ Decision making is decentralized.

✔ Chain of command is short.

✔ Organizational structure is flat.

Informal Organizations

A formal organizational structure, represented by an organizational chart or written job descriptions, is not the only structure that exists within an organization. Between different departments and levels of hierarchy, various informal organizations exist within an organizational structure. An informal organization consists of a network of channels of communication based on informal relationships between individuals within a firm. These networks are often based on friendships and social contacts. In addition to providing information and a sense of control over the work environment, they can also be a source of recognition and status. Informal organizations can be examined more closely through social network analysis. This process maps the social relationships between individuals within an organization. Once they are recognized and understood, informal organizations can be utilized within an existing organizational structure in order to increase communication and overall effectiveness and efficiency.

Line and Staff Organizations

The factors related to organizational structures also help describe different positions for individuals within a firm. Two examples of this are line positions and staff positions. Organizational structures often involve the interrelation between these two types of positions.

Line positions are directly related to the production of goods and services. They are common in firms that involve production, manufacturing, or providing financial services.

Staff positions are supportive in nature, helping those in line positions and top management more effectively achieve the firm's goals and objectives. Staff positions provide, for example, legal, public relations, human resources, and technology support services.

Reengineering

Reengineering involves the complete redesign of a firm's structures and processes. It is done in the hope of increasing a firm's operational efficiency and effectiveness by controlling costs, improving quality, improving customer service, and increasing the speed at which business is conducted. Once a firm has examined itself in light of the five factors of organizational structure, it can better understand where it can make changes to align its structure with the firm's goals and objectives.

High-Performance Organizations

The goal of the high-performance organization is to effectively and efficiently utilize intellectual capital. High-performance organizations focus on employee involvement, teamwork, organizational learning, total quality management (TQM), and integrated production techniques. Employee involvement is accomplished through worker empowerment or participative management. Teamwork is accomplished though self-directed groups. Organizational learning involves gathering, communicating, and storing organizational information in order to anticipate changes and challenges and make more informed decisions about the future. TQM focuses on high quality, continuous improvement, and customer satisfaction. Integrated production techniques implement flexibility in manufacturing and services and involve job design and information systems to more effectively and efficiently utilize the resources, knowledge, and techniques that a business uses to create goods or services. It stresses the use of just-in-time production and service systems and relies heavily on computers to assist, control, and integrate different organizational functions. Implementing integrated production techniques requires speeding up communication and decision making within the organizational structure.

The process of transforming an organization into a high-performance organization begins by actively seeking to understand an organization's work site problems and opportunities and its purpose, mission, strategy, and vision. These elements must be tied together into a new mission statement and vision for the firm that is aligned with the organization's core values. In order to be successful, this process requires the active involvement of individuals from various levels and groups within the organization. The broad level of participation will also ensure a greater level of acceptance in the organization. Once these initial steps have been taken, the factors of employee involvement, teamwork, organizational learning, total quality management, and integrated production techniques can result in organizational, individual, and community benefits. The organization will be more effective in achieving its goals, job satisfaction and employee motivation will increase, and the organization will be better able to contribute to the community as a whole.

Although there are numerous benefits associated with high-performance organizations, establishing and maintaining them is a difficult task. One of the most daunting elements is successfully integrating employee involvement, teamwork, organizational learning, total quality management, and integrated production techniques. These are not separate functions; teamwork must contain elements of employee involvement, organizational learning, and total quality management. This can be especially challenging for managers who, in addition to their regular functions, are asked to implement these changes. Managers can experience many kinds of resistance. Employees may feel that the changes could put them out of a job. They may be resistant to participating in group decision making or in team-based activities. Managers may also experience obstacles related to cultural differences regarding hierarchy and participation. In light of these challenges, some firms succeed in implementing only some of the elements associated with high-performance organizations.

Successfully creating a high-performance organization requires a high degree of cooperation and a strong level of commitment and acceptance from all employees. It is a challenging and difficult process, but it offers significant rewards throughout the organization.

METHODS OF CONTROL

Managers achieve organizational goals by managing intellectual capital in order to get the most out of organizational resources. An important part of this process is monitoring performance and outcomes. This can be done in several ways. Two of the more common ways that directly affect organizational behavior are output controls and process controls. Controls relate to setting standards, obtaining measurements of results related to these standards, and taking corrective actions when these standards are not met. Managers must be judicious in their use of controls so as not to overburden the organization.

Output Controls

Output controls are about setting desired outcomes and allowing managers to decide how these outcomes can best be achieved. Output controls promote management creativity and flexibility. This type of control serves to separate methods from outcomes and subsequently decentralizes power by shifting it down the hierarchical structure.

Process Controls

Once effective methods have been determined for solving organizational problems, managers sometimes institutionalize them in order to prevent the problem from recurring. These types of controls are called process controls and are a way of regulating how specific tasks are conducted. Three types of process controls are (1) policies, procedures, and rules; (2) formalization and standardization; and (3) total quality management controls.

Policies, Procedures, and Rules. These are often used in the absence of direct management control. Policies are general recommendations for conducting activities, while procedures are a more focused set of guidelines. Rules are the strictest set of limits and establish things that should and should not be done.

Formalization and Standardization. Formalization involves creating a written set of policies, procedures, and rules that simplifies procedures in order to guide decision making and behavior. Standardization is the degree to which the actions necessary to accomplish a task are limited. It attempts to make sure that when certain tasks are carried out they are carried out in a similar fashion.

Total Quality Management Controls. The previous methods of process control are based on organizational experience. TQM management controls differ in that they are based on an ongoing statistical analysis of a firm's operations. TQM involves all levels of management and has proved to be the most effective when it is instituted in an organization that has clearly defined outcomes and is done in conjunction with employee empowerment or participatory management programs.

CURRENT TRENDS IN ORGANIZATIONAL BEHAVIOR AND DESIGN

Modern organizational structures are currently undergoing changes in response to new trends in the global business environment.

One of the more prevalent trends is the increase in the network organization. A network organization is one that consists of a group of independent firms communicating via the latest advances in information technology. It can include suppliers, customers, and even competitors. These firms operate as an alliance in order to share skills, costs, and access to each other's markets in order to work together quickly and take advantage of business opportunities. These types of firms are characterized by technology, opportunism, trust, and a lack of borders. They assemble and disperse in response to business opportunities.

Another trend affecting organizational structures is the increase in large global mergers. By their very nature these types of mergers necessitate that a firm reexamine its existing structure in light of its new position within the larger structure. In addition, management decisions designed to increase employee motivation must take into account the culture context in which they are made. Global mergers can also increase the use of virtual groups and the diversity of membership characteristics.

SUMMARY

Organizational behavior is the study of how individuals and groups perform together within an organization. It focuses on the best way to manage individuals, groups, organizations, and processes. This chapter has covered the basics of organizational behavior by defining the nature of managerial behavior, addressing the fundamental theories and practices of motivation, explaining the basics of organizational structure, and discussing some methods of control.

REFERENCES

Goleman, Daniel. *Emotional Intelligence.* New York: Bantam, 1995.

Kahn, Jeremy. "What Makes a Company Great?" *Fortune* (October 26, 1998): 218.

Katz, Robert L. "Skills of an Effective Administrator." *Harvard Business Review* 52 (September/October 1974).

Mintzberg, Henry. *Mintzberg on Management.* New York: Free Press, 1989.

Schermerhorn, John, Jr., James Hunt, and Richard Osborn. *Core Concepts of Organizational Behavior.* New York: John Wiley & Sons, 2004.

Chapter 3

Leadership and Team Building

What are the qualities of good leaders? What makes them successful? Think of some of the greatest leaders of all time. What made them stand out from others? We may think of adjectives such as "heroic," "charismatic," and "strategic." These are all leadership qualities, but what really makes for a strong and successful leader?

Successful leaders are able to influence others. They use their innate qualities to inspire a workforce, a team, or a nation to achieve goals. Leaders can see beyond themselves and beyond the task at hand to look at achieving long-term goals by utilizing their strengths combined with the strengths of others. Effective leaders are able to manage relationships with others and create positive outcomes.

Winston Churchill often comes to mind as one of the greatest leaders in history. He was a talented orator and politician, but what made Churchill a phenomenal leader was his ability to mobilize and strengthen the will of his people through his words and policies. Although his strategic actions were often criticized at the time for being impulsive, Churchill allowed his belief in democracy and his intolerance for fascism to dictate his wartime policies. It was not only his passion for the policies but his ability to carry out his plans that made him a successful leader.

38

Leadership, such as that demonstrated by Churchill, is about inspiring others and doing the right thing. Leaders make change happen, but their values remain steady and unchanging. Most leaders not only have a long-term perspective on goals, but they also have innovative ways of achieving their goals.

World leaders and business leaders alike can create triumph from disasters. Leaders learn from failure and have a steadfastness of purpose that keeps them focused on a goal or objective in spite of near-term setbacks or adverse conditions. Leaders are flexible in their execution and will make midcourse corrections and iterative improvements—leaders "bend but don't break." They inspire those around them to stretch and do their best to fulfill the organizational mission. Leaders are able to energize those around them in order to create desired results without compromising their ethical standards.

LEADERSHIP VERSUS MANAGEMENT

Management is doing things right; leadership is doing the right things.

—Peter F. Drucker

Although sometimes used synonymously, leadership and management can be quite different. Leaders may be managers, but not all managers are leaders. So just what are the differences?

While managers tend to have their eyes on the bottom line, leaders are more often looking toward the horizon, trying to find new opportunities for growth and development. A manager is usually satisfied with the status quo, whereas the leader is often challenging it.

Leadership often involves reinventing the job; strong leaders create their role in an organization or in the world system. Managers are often responsible for executing the task at hand, not thinking of future goals. Managers are responsible for maintaining, but leaders look to innovate. Managers may involve employees in their activities, but often on a "need to know" basis. Leaders, in contrast, work to inspire those around them by trying to help others gain personal growth and development from their activities and by turning weaknesses into strengths.

Companies that have "leader-managers" throughout the corporate hierarchy are the most successful.

ROLES OF MANAGERS

Management is often expressed as the process of achieving an organization's objectives through guiding development, maintenance, and allocating resources. The primary roles of managers are planning, organizing, leading, and controlling.

Planning

> The very essence of leadership is that you have to have vision.
> You can't blow an uncertain trumpet.
> —Theodore M. Hesburgh

Planning is the process of determining a course of action for future conditions and events with the goal of achieving the company's objectives. Effective planning is necessary for any business or organization that wants to avoid costly mistakes. There are four different types of planning that are associated with management: strategic, tactical, operational, and contingency planning.

Strategic planning involves creating long-range goals and determining the resources required for achieving these goals. Strategic planning is the most far-reaching level of planning and involves plans with time frames from one to five years. Essential to the notion of strategic planning is that it involves an assessment and consideration of the organization's external environment, and that the organization is adaptive to these outside, noncontrollable variables, adjusting and possibly redirecting its strategy to account for this changing environment.

Tactical planning denotes the implementation of the activities defined by the strategic plans. Generally, tactical planning involves shorter-range plans with time frames of less than one year.

Operational planning involves the creation of specific methods, standards, and procedures for different functional areas of an organization. In addition, the organization chooses specific work targets and assigns employees to teams to carry out plans.

Contingency planning involves the creation of alternative courses of action for unusual or crisis situations. In today's society, companies are placing greater importance on contingency planning in order to respond to crisis situations. For example, realizing the impact of terrorism on businesses in the wake of September 11, 2001, many companies have developed contingency plans to respond to potential terrorism events.

Organizing

This management role involves blending human and capital resources in a formal structure. The manager will divide and classify work by determining which specific tasks need to be carried out in order to accomplish a set of objectives.

Leading

Managers also have the role of leading or directing employees and plans. Some managers may be more successful at leadership than others. The goal of leading is to guide and motivate employees in order to accomplish organizational objectives. This role involves explaining procedures, issuing directives, and ensuring that any mistakes are corrected.

Controlling

Controlling allows a manager to measure how closely an organization is adhering to its set goals. It is also a process that provides feedback for future planning.

1. *Setting performance standards*. A company needs to set the standards by which performance will be measured. In a sales organization it may be sales growth or quarterly sales figures. Perhaps the manager will set the dollar amount for sales that are to be made that quarter.
2. *Measuring performance*. Using the previous example, measuring performance for sales will require tallying up the number of sales made during the quarter.

3. *Comparing actual performance to the set performance standards.* Now the difference between the set performance sales and the dollar amount of actual sales made during the quarter must be determined.

4. *Taking the necessary corrective action steps.* If the sales were much below the set level, it is important to analyze what went wrong and try to correct it.

5. *Using information from the process to set future performance standards.*

LEADERSHIP STYLES

Leadership is the art of getting someone else to do something you want done because he wants to do it.
— Dwight D. Eisenhower

Individual managers have their own styles of managing, and within organizations there is often a predominant style of leadership. The predominant leadership styles—autocratic, democratic, and laissez-faire—have many variations. We can compare and contrast the effectiveness of each of these styles as it affects employee performance.

Autocratic Leadership

This style of leadership is both directive and controlling. The leader will make all decisions without consulting employees and will also dictate employee roles. Micromanaging is a form of autocratic leadership in which upper management controls even the smallest tasks undertaken by subordinates. The autocratic style of leadership limits employee freedom of expression and participation in the decision-making process. It may result in alienating employees from leadership and will not serve to create trust between managers and subordinates. Further, creative minds cannot flourish under autocratic leadership.

Autocratic leadership may best be used when companies are managing less experienced employees. U.S. companies operating in less developed countries often use autocratic leadership. It allows the parent corporation more control over its overseas investment. In countries where the government controls the economy, U.S. corporations often use autocratic leadership because the employees are used to making decisions to satisfy the goals of the government, not the parent corporation.

Managers should not use the autocratic leadership style in operations where employees expect to voice their opinions. It also should not be used if employees begin expecting managers to make all the decisions for them, or if employees become fearful or resentful.

Democratic Leadership

This style of management is centered on employee participation and involves decision making by consensus and consultation. The leader will involve employees in the decision-making process and they will be encouraged to give input and delegate assignments. Democratic leadership often leads to empowerment of employees because it gives them a sense of responsibility for the decisions made by management. This can also be a very effective form of management when employees offer a different perspective than the manager, due to their daily involvement with work. A successful leader will know when to be a teacher and when to be a student.

Democratic leadership may best be used when working with highly skilled and experienced employees. It is most useful for implementing organizational changes, for resolving group problems, and when the leader is uncertain about which direction to take and therefore requires input from knowledgeable employees. One of the downsides of democratic leadership is that it may lead to endless meetings and therefore create frustration among employees if used for every decision made by a company. Democratic leadership is not a good idea in situations when the business cannot afford to make mistakes—for instance, when a company is facing a crisis situation such as bankruptcy.

Laissez-Faire Leadership

> *Delegating work works, provided the one delegating works, too.*
> —Robert Half

This free-rein form of leadership, if it is to be successful, requires extensive communication by management with employees. It is the style of leadership that makes employees responsible for most of the decisions that are made, and in which they are minimally supervised. Employees are responsible for motivating and managing themselves on a daily basis under this leadership style.

Laissez-faire leadership may best be used when employees are educated, knowledgeable, and self-motivated. Employees must have the drive and ambition to achieve goals on their own for this style to be most effective. Laissez-faire leadership is not a good idea in situations where employees feel insecure about the manager's lack of availability or the manager is using the employees to cover for his or her inability to carry out his or her own work. This type of situation can create resentment and result in an unhealthy work environment.

As with many categories that describe business concepts, an organization and its leadership may apply any or all of these leadership styles. For instance, the managing partners of an architectural firm may utilize autocratic leadership style with the lower levels in its clerical and administrative functions but employ a democratic or laissez-faire leadership style with its professional staff of architect-associates and partners.

Transformational and Transactional Leadership

Two additional styles of leadership worth exploring are transformational and transactional. Both have strong ethical components and philosophical underpinnings.

Transformational Leadership. Leaders who have a clear vision and are able to articulate it effectively to others often characterize this style of leadership. Transformational leaders look beyond themselves in order to work for the greater good of everyone. This type of leader will bring others into the decision-making process and will allow those around them opportunity to learn and grow as individuals. They seek out different perspectives when trying to solve a problem and are able to instill pride into those who work under them. Transformational leaders spend time coaching their employees and learning from them as well.

Transactional Leadership. This leadership style is characterized by centralized control over employees. The transactional leader will control outcomes and strive for behavioral compliance. Employees under a transactional leader are motivated by the transactional leader's praise, reward, and promise. They may also be corrected by the leader's negative feedback, threats, or disciplinary action.

The most effective leadership style is using a combination of styles. Leaders should know when it is best to be autocratic and when to be democratic. They can also be transformational and transactional at the same time; these are not mutually exclusive styles and in fact can complement one another extremely well.

LEADERSHIP AND MOTIVATION

An important role for a leader is motivating employees to do the best job possible. There are many ways a leader can motivate employees, and many of them do not require additional monetary compensation.

Sometimes motivation is brought about through creative means. The Container Store, a Dallas-based retailer, offers its employees free yoga classes, a personalized online nutrition diary, and a free monthly chair massage. These techniques help relieve employee stress and make workers feel appreciated. The company has ranked near the top of *Fortune*'s 100 Best Companies to Work For since 2000.

Open communication is also a key to motivating employees. When employees feel that they will be listened to and managers openly discuss matters with employees, a trusting relationship is created. At Harley-Davidson's headquarters executives don't have doors on their offices, creating an open, trusting environment.

Another method to motivate is to ensure that employees are matched up with the right job. It is the leader's job to learn what employees' abilities and preferences are and match them accordingly to tasks that utilize their skills and when possible match with their preferences.

If a leader is a good role model, showing enthusiasm for his or her work and pride in the company, this will positively affect employee motivation.

At W. L. Gore, a salesperson's motivation will come from the approval of his or her peers. Compensation is based on rankings by the sales team members. Further, the company bases monetary rewards or bonuses on long-term growth and customer retention, unlike most companies that base bonuses on the bottom line. Gore also presents a Proud Octopus award trophy to employees who have performed "special achievements" during the quarter.

CORPORATE CULTURE

A corporate culture is the system of beliefs, goals, and values that an organization possesses. Many aspects of an organization influence the corporate culture including workplace environments, communications networks, and managerial philosophies.

Strong cultures cause employees to march to the same beat and create high levels of employee motivation and loyalty. Corporate culture also provides control and structure to the company.

Having a strong corporate culture is not always the key to an organization's success. If the corporate culture is an obstacle to change, it can hinder a company's performance and ultimately its success. A misdirected culture can lead employees to strive for the wrong goals.

Leadership and Culture

Leadership style is extremely important in an organization, as it often affects the organization's culture. Which style of management is right? It depends greatly on the type of organization and on the top management within the organization.

If managers are strong leaders, their style of leadership often predominates throughout the different levels of management within the organization. The leadership style is then responsible for creating the culture of the organization. There are good and bad hallmarks for leadership within an organization. If the corporate leadership style is deceptive, then often the management culture within the organization will be deceptive. The same would hold true if the leadership was ethical.

It takes a strong leader to create a lasting culture within an organization. For ordinary leaders it can take years to shape the attitudes and environment; only an extraordinary leader is capable of making revolutionary change.

Characteristics of Successful Corporate Culture

Here are some examples of characteristics of successful corporate cultures. By no means is this list exhaustive.

Caring. This involves employees taking responsibility for their actions, caring about both the customer and the good of the company. It creates high-quality customer service and a positive atmosphere in which to work.

Challenge. If the CEO of a company states that employees should "think outside the box," but then squashes ideas because of their perceived chance of failure, a contradictory environment is created. In this type of situation, a challenge to conventional thinking and performing causes employees to fear losing their jobs; creative employees will leave and a culture of yes-men will be created.

Risk. A successful company will be able to manage risk and even turn it into a strategic and profitable advantage. It involves paying attention to reputation and earnings. Employees must anticipate the consequences of their decisions and actions. This type of risk management can add significant shareholder value.

Ethics. Often ethics can be the glue that holds the culture of an organization together. An effective leader should create a written ethical code for the organization. This code of ethics should not only be enforced but continuously reinforced. The employee's ethics should serve as a standard by which performance is evaluated.

Focus. There is a saying, "If you don't know where you are going, then any road will take you there." A leader has done his or her job well if the managers have a sense of continuity, if they know where the company or organization is heading. If managers feel that the direction of the organization is decided on by which way the wind is blowing that day, goals will not be met. It is important for employees to know where they are going and what they should be achieving, and it is the job of the leader to define this for them. The leader should always know where he or she is going at all times.

However, this does not mean that a leader should not be willing to change. In fact, a leader should be an agent for change, because stagnation does not often lead to success. It is important that while being accepting to change a leader is able to align employees with goals.

Trust. Mutual trust is an important hallmark of effective leadership. Management should trust the leader and the leader should trust management. It is important to note that micromanaging can kill the trusting culture. When employees come to trust one another, it creates a team environment, where everyone is working for the common goals of the organization.

Merit. Organizations often meet their goals by rewarding employee performance based on merit. Merit systems create fairness and help to further foster a team environment.

LEADERSHIP TRENDS

In today's competitive environment, leaders are continually searching for new ideas and approaches to improving their understanding of leadership. Here are thumbnail descriptions of current leadership trends.

Coaching

A new trend in effective leadership, coaching, has become extremely popular throughout different organizations. This style of leadership involves guiding employees in their decision-making process. When coaching, management provides employees with ideas, feedback, and consultation, but decisions will ultimately be left in the hands of the employees. Coaching prepares employees for the challenges they will face. The lower an employee's skill and experience level, the more coaching the worker will require. The interactions that an employee has with the manager are the best opportunities they have for enhancing their respective skills. Coaching enables the employees to excel at their tasks. Instilling confidence in employees is extremely important. If management conveys the belief that employees will exceed expectations, it helps them do so.

A good coach will draw out the strengths of each employee and focus on how those strengths can be directed most effectively to achieve the organization's purpose and objectives. A good coach will also facilitate personal development and an improvement process through which the employee will be able to play a more effective role in achieving the organization's purpose and objectives. An effective coach also realizes that each employee is unique, with different strengths and weaknesses, and that a coaching strategy must reflect this individualistic approach.

Employee Empowerment

As organizations and companies become increasingly borderless, employee empowerment becomes ever more important. This trend in leadership has allowed employees to participate in the decision-making processes. Employee empowerment is also a method for building employee self-esteem and can also improve customer satisfaction. It also ties them more closely to the company goals and will serve to increase their pride in their work and loyalty to the organization.

Global Leadership

As corporations become increasingly international in scope, there is a growing demand for global leaders. Although many of the qualities that make a successful domestic leader will make a successful global leader, the differences lie in the abilities of the leader to take on a global perspective. Global leaders are often entrepreneurial; they will have the ambition to take their ideas and strategies across borders. They will also have to develop cultural understanding; global leaders must be sensitive to the cultures of those working under them, no matter where they are based. Global leaders must also be adaptable; this is part of accepting the cultural norms of different countries in which they are operating. They must know when to adapt the operational structure of the organization or adjust their leadership styles in order to relate to those around them. However, as adaptable as they must be, the global leader should not adapt his or her ethics or values to suit local tastes. Global leaders must also serve as role models, fighting corruption, not giving in to it.

Equitable Treatment

An important trend in leadership is the equitable treatment of employees. This does not mean that each employee will be treated the same; it means that every employee will be given the amount of individual attention they require, and it will involve leadership knowing his or her employees. A good leader will get to know employees well enough to give them what they need in order to best perform. For some employees that may mean more structure; for others it may mean more freedom. Some employees may need to be monitored more carefully, while others may work better independently. Leaders must know how to bring out the best in employees and how to build solid relationships with them; the most effective way of doing this is by getting to know them individually.

Feedback

Employees thrive on feedback, and by providing feedback and communicating effectively, managers can give employees the tools they need to improve their performance.

Providing feedback will not dampen employee morale in most cases, but will allow opportunities for employees to learn from their mistakes and move on to performing their tasks better. Positive reinforcement should be used to encourage employees' positive behavior, but when criticism is necessary, make sure it is constructive. Managers can do this best by telling employees exactly what was observed and how they interpreted it; this also will allow employees to better understand what the manager saw in their performance and to explain if there has been a misunderstanding. The 360-degree assessment tool discussed in Chapter 1 provides an effective means of feedback. This type of open dialogue between management and employees creates a more trusting atmosphere and is more likely to generate positive performance results.

PURSUING A LEADERSHIP ROLE

When pursuing a leadership role in an organization, it is important to gain insight into effective leadership.

Firsthand Experience

Draw upon your firsthand experience in leadership roles; think of the lessons you have learned from leading clubs, teams, or other groups.

Leader Memoirs

It is also important to read about other leaders. Most world leaders read books about leaders whom they admire. The books provide important insights into what it takes to be a leader and how to make decisions.

Find a Mentor

Learning from an accomplished leader is a great way to improve your own leadership abilities; find someone in your organization or community whose leadership you admire and ask this person to serve as your mentor; they will probably be flattered and happy to help.

Research

It is important to research management and leadership trends and to learn skills and techniques that are relevant to the particular field in which you are working so that you can then implement them.

TEAM BUILDING

"Teamwork" is defined as a group of people working together to achieve a common goal. Team members are mutually responsible for reaching the goal toward which they are working. Team building is a process meant to improve the performance of the team and involves activities designed to foster communication and encourage cooperation.

Additionally, the objective is to avoid potential disputes and problems and to keep the morale of team members high.

Many different industries and organizations use teams to accomplish goals, because people working together can often achieve more than they could individually. How do you know if you need a team to complete a project? Ask yourself the following questions: Can I achieve this goal by myself? Do I have the resources and time to undertake this project? Can other people or a team of other people be more effective than I would be in achieving this goal? If your answers favor the involvement of others, it's time to consider forming a team.

In an increasingly complex environment, organizations are using a team approach to bring a diverse set of skills and perspectives into play. An effective use of teams often draws upon a creative approach of bringing together specialists who combine their efforts and develop intrateam synergies to meet the challenges of their often complex organizational environment.

An example of an industry that often uses teamwork is the construction industry. A successful construction project cannot take place without the formation of teams. A design team will be formed at the beginning of the project and is made up of architects, engineers, and project consultants. The design team alone, however, will not be able to complete the project. They will also need to form a team with the owner of the project and the contractor.

TYPES OF TEAMS

Throughout different organizations there are different types of teams that are used to accomplish goals. Two of the most common team varieties are problem-solving and cross-functional teams.

Problem-Solving Teams

These teams are formed for a temporary period until a problem is solved, and then they disband. Team members often consist of one level of management. Let's say XYZ Corporation has lost 10 percent of its North American market share to MNO Widgets. XYZ wants to get this back by increasing sales across North America. All of XYZ's regional salespeople will be called in to form a team to regain that market share. Although their regional focus will remain, they will have to work together to solve the problem of regaining that market share, and when they achieve that goal, they will individually work on maintaining their hold in their market.

Cross-Functional Teams

This type of team is made up of members from different areas of the business and often from a common managerial level.

If a shampoo company wants to bring a new conditioner to market, a team will be formed and its members will consist of managers from different departments such as brand management, product development, market research, and finance. It is also likely that there will be involvement by marketing, communications, and design when the product comes closer to being launched.

STAGES OF TEAM DEVELOPMENT

Team development has been broken into four stages: form, storm, norm, and perform.

Forming the Team

The first stage involves assembling the team and defining the goals, which should provide focus and be attainable. It is important that the team leadership understands the strengths of each of the team members in order to assemble a cohesive team. Often in the forming stage, team members will be extremely polite to one another; they will be feeling each other out.

An example of a goal that the team may set would be the project schedule. For a construction team, for example, there are many stages of the project that should be completed in a certain time frame to ensure that the project is completed on time for the owner. The design team designates the appropriate amount of time for the construction phase in which the builder will make a profit. It is important to agree upon and set this schedule from the beginning.

Storming Stage of Team Development

The second phase involves coordinating efforts and solving problems. If the teamwork starts to slip because of a difficult problem, it is necessary for the team members to get the project back on track. Team members should be conscious of the team's health and whether the team is taking steps in the right direction to reach the goals. It may be necessary to think creatively about approaches to solving a problem.

Communication is extremely important to effective team performance in the storming stage. Effective teams communicate clearly and openly about problems. Ineffective communication can cause unnecessary tension and stress to team members. It is important that communication be relevant and responsive. Relevant communication is task-oriented and focused. Responsive communication involves the willingness of team members to gather information, to actively listen, and to build on the ideas and views of other team members.

Establishing Team Norms

The project norms are an informal standard of conduct that guides the behavior of team members. This stage involves defining team roles, rights, and responsibilities. It is important to establish these norms at the beginning of the team-building process in order to avoid problems along the way. In addition to allocating responsibilities, it may also be necessary to allocate the risk that is to be undertaken by each team member. Each member of the team should have a sense of ownership of the project.

Allocating responsibility also means establishing a team leader. Team leadership should not be a top-down effort, but should be more of a coaching role. The team leader must act as a cheerleader, encouraging the team members to work together, providing ideas, and serving as a role model.

There is often a period after the team has been formed when a conflict of personalities or ideas will arise. Team members begin to show their own styles; they are no longer worried about being polite. At this stage, there will be pessimism on the part of team members in relation to the project and there may also be confusion.

Team Performance Stage

By this stage, the team is working together effectively, problems have been smoothed out, and achievements begin to become evident. A great deal of work will be accomplished at this stage. The team will be able to tackle new tasks easily and confidently. They will be comfortable using creative means. It is essential at this point to evaluate and report on progress that has been made.

Project Completion and Team Disbanding Stage

The last phase of the project is completion. Often at this time the team will evaluate the results, debrief, and take time to learn and improve its processes for use in future team-based projects.

SUMMARY

Leadership can greatly affect an organization, both by determining its success in the market and by defining the corporate culture. Strong, ethical leadership is extremely important in today's business climate. Although there are several different leadership styles, some of the most effective leaders are able to tailor their management practices to suit employee needs. Leadership is not only about being a great speaker or politician; it is about having a vision and being able to make that vision a reality.

Team building is another important aspect of business today. Many companies use teams to complete projects, and building an effective team is necessary to complete a project. Teams are most successful when they have a "coach" who is able to help see them through some of the more difficult stages of the team-building process.

REFERENCES

Bass, Bernard M., and Paul Steidlmeier. *Ethics and Authentic Transformational Leadership.* Binghamton, NY: Center for Leadership Studies, School of Management, 1998.

Bender, William J., and Darlene M. Septelka. "Teambuilding in the Construction Industry." *AACE International Transactions* (2002).

Blundell, R. C., Jeffrey Gandz, George A. Peapples, Ian D. Clark, J. E. Newall, Donald H. Thain, David Morton, Jennifer R. McQueen, Geoffrey Relph, and John M. Thompson. "Best Practices in Management." *Business Quarterly* (September 22, 1990).

Feiner, Michael. "*FT* Report: Mastering Management." *Financial Times* (November 15, 2002).

Furash, Edward E. "Leadership = Culture (Management Strategies)." *RHA Journal* 86, no. 4 (December 1, 2003).

Kotter, John, and James Deskett. "The Caring Company." *Economist* 323, no. 7762 (June 6, 1992): 75.

Pentilla, Chris. "Missed Mission." *Entrepreneur* (May 2002).

Peters, John. "On Structures." *Management Decision* 31, no. 6 (1993).

Tkaczyk, Christopher. "Container Store." *Fortune* 149, no. 1 (January 12, 2004).

Weinreb, Michael. "Power to the People." *Sales and Marketing Management* 155, no. 4 (April 2003).

Chapter 4

Ethics

$\mathbf{A}$lthough ethics in business has been an issue for centuries, today there are numerous examples of corporations and individuals who have run into legal and financial trouble due to their questionable ethics. Martha Stewart is an example of an individual whose ethics have been called into question. The accusation that she lied when asked if she participated in insider trading, a violation of Securities and Exchange Commission (SEC) regulations, brought her to court and made her the center of a negatively charged media frenzy. While she is accused of committing the violation with her personal investments, the question of character has already cast a shadow on her business. She stepped down from her role as CEO of her company, Martha Stewart Living Omnimedia, Inc., and Kmart, which carried her brand-name products, is bringing a lawsuit against her. This is a clear situation where ethical standards, whether it is the individual representing the company or the company itself, are tied to the company's bottom line.

ENRON

An example of a company that committed serious ethical violations was Enron, the energy trading company. In 15 years Enron grew to be one of the largest companies in the United States, with more than 20,000 employees in over 40 countries. But by December of 2001 it became clear that Enron was involved in a huge accounting scandal, the ramifications of which were the largest Chapter 11 bankruptcy filings in U.S. history and subsequent government hearings were conducted to evaluate just how severe the wrongdoing was.

As a result of Enron's deceptive accounting practices, thousands of Enron employees lost their retirement savings, while several Enron executives received multimillion-dollar bonuses.

WORLDCOM

The largest financial fraud in U.S. history began to unravel WorldCom in 2002. WorldCom had overstated its income by more than $9 billion by means of its misleading accounting practices, and the CEO at the time was granted $400 million in loans with the approval of the company's board of directors. By July 2002, WorldCom was forced into bankruptcy and laid off thousands of workers.

WorldCom changed its name to MCI and hired a chief ethics officer in 2003. The company now requires that all 55,000 remaining employees take an online ethics course, and more than 2,000 MCI employees have participated in a full-day ethics training seminar. MCI is being closely watched by the government and by competitors for any future ethical errors, and the company is not willing to take any chances.

ETHICS—A DEFINITION

Ethics are the moral standards used to judge right from wrong. In the business setting, ethics are the standards of moral values and conduct that govern decisions made and actions carried out in the work environment.

Unethical decisions are often made for the benefit of the decision maker as opposed to the organization's stakeholders. Some examples of unethical behavior in business practice are:

- ✔ Saying things that you know not to be true.
- ✔ Taking something that doesn't belong to you.
- ✔ Buying influence.
- ✔ Hiding or divulging information.

CORPORATE GOVERNANCE

Often thought of as the system by which organizations are directed and controlled, corporate governance has come to take on more of an ethical slant over the past decade. According to World Bank president James Wolfenson, "Corporate governance is about promoting corporate fairness, transparency, and accountability."

CREATING AN ETHICAL STANDARD

Deciding what is right and what is wrong is not always clear-cut. The subjective nature of ethics creates the need for organizations to define their ethical standards. Company leaders often set the example for ethical standards. As discussed in Chapter 3, the job of the leader is to serve as a role model for employees. This is part of the reason why Martha Stewart's personal financial dealings are a concern to the company bearing her name.

Creating an ethical standard is an important way for a leader to spread his or her ethical beliefs throughout an organization. Often the ethical standards will cover a wide range of business areas.

Interorganizational Relations

An organization's ethics policies cover the areas of internal policies, which explain the company's responsibility to employees. These policies often include equal opportunities, sexual harassment, diversity, and employee safety.

Equal opportunity employment is protected by the Civil Rights Act of 1964, which prohibits employers from discriminating against prospective employees due to their race, religion, gender, or national origin. Today, employers include sexual preference as being protected by this act as well. Many companies have enacted policies of affirmative action to increase the employment opportunities for minorities and women within their organization. The Equal Employment Opportunity Commission (EEOC) enforces equal opportunity employment. Employees who feel their civil rights have been violated can file an official complaint with this organization.

Sexual harassment lawsuits have been much publicized over the past 20 years, and for that reason many companies have enacted stringent policies and comprehensive employee training. These measures have been taken in order to increase employee awareness of what behaviors are not acceptable, as well as to make employees aware of their rights for dealing with sexual harassment by fellow employees.

Diversity in the workplace refers to the numbers of women and minorities employed by an organization. Many organizations hold diversity seminars in order to break down barriers and to increase cultural awareness and understanding among employees.

External Organizational Relations

Many firms also create an ethical standard that covers issues concerning the organization's effect on the outside world, including its responsibility to shareholders, customers, and the community.

One of the firm's responsibilities to shareholders is to make decisions with the best interest of the shareholders in mind. Many organizations encourage shareholder activism, which gives the shareholders the opportunity to influence management practices. As ethical concerns have been embraced by shareholders, activism has also included influencing practices such as employee relations, social awareness, environmental practices, and other socially oriented concerns.

An organization has an obligation to its customers with regard to its production practices. Customers expect that a company will not produce a product or provide a service that has inherent defects or safety issues. Companies also will establish a standard for sales practices that discourages deceptive or aggressive sales methods, ensuring that employees understand what is acceptable and not acceptable behavior.

The social obligation that a company has can include environmentally sound practices. Environmental obligations include preventing air, water, and land pollution. A growing movement suggests that a company's social obligation also includes producing products that somehow benefit society or are not harmful.

Importance of Written Standards for Ethical Policies

Many organizations opt for a written document that not only outlines the company's ethical policies, but also follows government regulations. This document is then distributed throughout the organization so that there can be no question of what the company policies are. This standard will often include guidelines for internal company behavior as well as for product quality and customer relations.

ETHICS TRAINING

As noted in the case of MCI, with increasing frequency companies are conducting ethics training sessions with employees. These training sessions involve the discussion and analysis of ethical dilemmas. Ethics training seminars are helpful in providing employees with the tools to make the right decisions in situations where their ethics are being tested.

CONSEQUENCES OF POOR ETHICAL DECISIONS

Enron illustrates how large-scale ethics violations can cause the downfall of a company and legal entanglements for executives. Enron filed for Chapter 11 bankruptcy and sold off many of its holdings. Several executives face trial. The ethics violations did not stop with Enron, but spread to its accounting firm, Arthur Andersen, whose reputation was also irreparably tarnished for covering up Enron's accounting wrongdoings.

Despite the attention that has been given to ethics abuse by large corporations, smaller businesses suffer most from fraudulent activities. Small organizations reported losses of up to 25 percent more than those of larger organizations due to fraud.

MONITORING COMPLAINTS AND ENCOURAGING FEEDBACK

Companies can deal with ethical violations by monitoring complaints and encouraging feedback. Companies monitor complaints against the company made by customers, shareholders, and employees. Many companies also encourage feedback by having toll-free telephone lines for customers to call or by providing suggestion boxes for employees. This system of feedback makes customers, employees, and shareholders feel as though the executives are hearing their voices. Organizations that have hotlines set up were able to cut their losses from fraud by 50 percent, according to a 2002 survey by the Association of Certified Fraud Examiners.

GOVERNMENT REGULATIONS

As is the case when a social harm is identified, the federal government will step in and design regulations that will prevent further damage by unethical companies. Currently the government protects consumers from unethical companies in several ways.

The Federal Trade Commission (FTC) monitors advertising to ensure that companies are not misleading the public with false advertising. The goal is to stamp out deceptive practices. Another government agency, the Food and Drug Administration (FDA), protects consumers by monitoring the safety and quality of many products. Additionally, the government has many policies in place to encourage competition in the market in order to ensure that consumers will not be charged unfair prices for goods and services. To this end, the government's antitrust statutes prevent monopolies from forming. The government has also protected consumers from unfair pricing by deregulating industries, such as the telecom industry, in order to allow more competition to enter the market.

WHISTLE-BLOWING

A common method for detection of occupational fraud is employee tips. While many employees choose to handle fraud accusations internally by reporting wrongdoings to executives, whistle-blowing is the employee's disclosure to the media or government of a company's unethical activities. Before employees step forward with information, there are several factors that they must consider.

✔ Can the ethical problems that a company is having be better handled internally?

✔ Is it worth staying with a company that does not value ethics?

✔ Does the unethical damage that has been done outweigh the risk of retaliation by the company?

✔ Can the whistle-blower risk the possibility of being harassed, disciplined, or fired, in spite of regulatory protection?

There are some state and federal regulations that have been put in place to protect whistle-blowers once they have decided to step forward. According to the Sarbanes-Oxley Act of 2002:

> (e) Whoever knowingly, with the intent to retaliate, takes any action harmful to any person, including interference with the lawful employment or livelihood of any person, for providing to a law enforcement officer any truthful information relating to the commission or possible commission of any Federal offense, shall be fined under this title or imprisoned not more than 10 years, or both.
>
> (www.sarbanes-oxley.com)

ETHICS TODAY

Enron and WorldCom have caused many citizens to take a skeptical view of large corporations. The managerial negligence that has been brought to light in recent years has caused global distrust of the U.S. financial markets. The economic impact of these scandals, combined with distrust, has taken a financial toll on many U.S. investors.

As evident in the Sarbanes-Oxley Act, the U.S. government is doing more these days to protect citizens against unethical corporations. Attempts have been made by creating new regulations, requiring more stringent accounting practices, encouraging an increase in transparency, and protecting those who step forward with information regarding corporate wrongdoings.

The cynical view of business ethics in the United States has caused organizations to go above and beyond what was done in the past to ensure that ethics are being enforced. As seen with MCI, corporations are now creating positions for chief ethics officers. Tyco is another company whose past questionable ethics led it to create this position in the organization.

But will these moves toward stringent ethical policies be enough to convince the world that U.S. companies are ethical? A new term has been created: "Enron ethics," meaning an ironic difference between a company's outwardly ethical appearance and its internal ethical failure. From the outside, Enron appeared to be a model company, with its corporate social responsibility practices and thick book of ethical guidelines that was handed out to employees, while on the inside, the company was falling apart due to its faulty accounting practices. But Enron managed to pull the wool over the public's eyes for years. It's difficult for people to trust that other companies are not doing the same.

BEST PRACTICES

Some businesses stand out from others as far as their attempts at good corporate governance and business ethics are concerned.

General Mills

In 2003 *Business Ethics* magazine ranked the 100 Best Corporate Citizens. General Mills, the Minnesota-based producer of cereals and other food products, ranked number one on the list. So what is this company doing that sets it apart from other companies?

At General Mills, the corporate culture is based on business ethics and corporate social responsibility. Employees are successful at being ethical because they follow their own standards and adhere to their core values. Employees are supplied with the company's written code of ethics and are expected to uphold the values of the corporation:

- We strive for the highest quality in our products, services, and relationships.
- We set and maintain the highest standards for all aspects of our work.
- We advance and grow our businesses honestly and ethically, taking no shortcuts that might compromise our high standards.
- We comply with local laws in every nation where we operate. We recognize and respect the cultures, customs, and practices of our consumers and customers in nations around the world.
- We steer clear of conflicts of interest and work to avoid even the perception of conflict.
- We set very high expectations for ourselves—and for the integrity of our company. We will not compromise those standards.
- We deliver on our promises.
- We are ever mindful of the trust our consumers, customers, partners, and employees place in General Mills. We will never knowingly or willfully undermine that trust.

(www.generalmills.com/corporate/about/ethics/)

Hewlett-Packard

Another company that has been recognized internationally for its outstanding corporate governance and ethics is Hewlett-Packard (HP), the computer and accessory manufacturer. HP has set high ethical standards to which employees are expected to adhere. Its core ethical values are:

- **Honesty** in communicating within the company and with our business partners, suppliers, and customers, while at the same time protecting the company's confidential information and trade secrets.

- **Excellence** in our products and services, by striving to provide high-quality products and services to our customers.
- **Responsibility** for our words and actions.
- **Compassion** in our relationships with our employees and the communities affected by our business.
- **Citizenship** in our observance of all the laws of any country in which we do business, respect for environmental concerns and our service to the community by improving and enriching community life.
- **Fairness** to our fellow employees, stakeholders, business partners, customers, and suppliers through adherence to all applicable laws, regulations, and policies, and a high standard of behavior.
- **Respect** for our fellow employees, stakeholders, business partners, customers, and suppliers while showing willingness to solicit their opinions and value their feedback.
  (www.hp.com/hpinfo/globalcitizenship/ethics/index.html)

CORPORATE SOCIAL RESPONSIBILITY AND CITIZENSHIP

Corporate social responsibility (CSR) can be defined as the concern of a business for society as a whole that goes beyond contractual or legal obligations. Many firms today are taking on CSR initiatives because, although they may not appear to help the company's bottom line in the short term, they often coincide with long-term sustainability and profitability.

Areas for Corporate Social Responsibility

CSR covers a wide range of issues, including, but not limited to the following areas:

Unfair Business Practices. Firms will adhere to fair selling tactics, produce quality products, and price their products fairly. They will obey laws regarding business practices.

Workplace and Employee Issues. This includes upholding the rights of employees' individual freedoms, equal opportunity employment, and protecting employees from sexual harassment. It also involves paying employees fair wages, adhering to legal employment statutes, and ensuring employee safety. Firms may also try to promote a balance of family life and work for employees by offering family leave, flexible hours, or day care services.

Organizational Governance. As outlined earlier, it is necessary that the firm be governed ethically. Leadership must be ethical and spread the message of ethics from the top down.

Environmental Impact. Firms must ensure that their impact on the environment is at a minimum. This includes using environmentally sound manufacturing processes and producing products that do not damage the environment. Many companies have found that they can be successful financially while also being ecologically sound.

Marketplace and Consumer Issues. This involves ensuring consumer safety with the products that are produced and may involve monitoring and responding to consumer complaints. It may also involve ensuring fairness in the marketplace, giving consumers a choice, and pricing products fairly.

Social Development. Companies can aid the social development of communities by creating jobs and contributing resources.

Community Involvement

Corporate social responsibility also involves becoming active in the communities where the company operates. Activities may include funding local charitable organizations, sponsoring cultural events, or having volunteer days for employees to go into the community and participate in community service projects. An organization may also choose to create its own philanthropic arm, such as the Gap Corporation's Gap Foundation, which matches employee giving to philanthropic organizations.

Another term used frequently is *corporate citizenship*, the concept of companies holding to high ethical standards, demonstrating environmental responsibility, providing safe and reliable products, and working to improve conditions in the community. Corporate citizenship encompasses business ethics, but also has an element that goes above and beyond the legal and contractual obligations, similar to CSR.

A theory that has been cropping up recently is called the "triple bottom line." The basis of this theory is that companies should be working just as hard at increasing their social and environmental worth as they do with their financial results. The three bottom lines are society, economy, and environment, and the lines are interdependent. But how can working hard at social and environmental worth benefit a company's bottom line financially?

Benefits of Corporate Citizenship

According to the World Economic Forum white paper *The Business Case for Corporate Citizenship*, there are eight areas where corporations can benefit from good governance and corporate citizenship:

1. *Reputation management.* Companies can avoid a damaged reputation by adhering to ethical practices.

2. *Risk profile and risk management.* Companies that adhere to more stringent policies (environmental, for example) are less likely to pose as much risk for investors because they are not taking chances with their reputations.

3. *Employee recruitment, motivation, and retention.* Companies that are better corporate citizens are more attractive to potential employees; companies whose reputations are tarnished may have much difficulty recruiting new employees.

4. *Investor relations and access to capital.* Recent studies have shown that companies with sound environmental policies and environmentally safe products have been able to increase their earnings per share and are more likely to win contracts.

5. *Learning and innovation.* Adopting corporate citizenship principles can lead to creativity and employee innovation because

it requires finding solutions to problems while enhancing the company's bottom line.

6. *Competitiveness and market positioning.* Today, consumers are very concerned about trusting companies and their products. Being a good corporate citizen will make a company more competitive and will help its position in the market.

7. *Operational efficiency.* Becoming more environmentally efficient often means reducing material use and waste, which enhances a company's bottom line.

8. *License to operate.* Companies that are good citizens are more likely to be given a second chance in case of a slipup than companies that have a negative image in the minds of citizens.

SUMMARY

Ethics and corporate social responsibility are very important topics in today's business environment. With the recent ethical downfall of Enron and the ethical violations of telecom giant WorldCom, citizens are wary of investing in U.S. markets. Companies must do their best today to adhere to ethical standards. These ethical standards are a top-down effort from leadership. Ethics and good corporate governance can lead to success in business. Organizations have also found that being a good corporate citizen can benefit the company's bottom line, while protecting it from a damaged reputation if minor ethical infractions do occur. Companies are realizing that in order to achieve sustainability, they must become more socially aware and ethically conscious in the post-Enron business climate.

REFERENCES

Gunther, Mark. "Tree Huggers, Soy Lovers and Profits." *Fortune* (June 23, 2003).

Joyner, Brenda E., and Dinah Payne. "Evolution and Implementation: A Study of Values, Business Ethics and Corporate Social Responsibility." *Journal of Business Ethics* (December 2002).

Leonard, Dennis, and Rodney McAdam. "Corporate Social Responsibility." *Quality Progress* (October 2003).

Mehta, Stephanie M. "MCI: Is Being Good Good Enough?" *Fortune* (October 27, 2003).

Mellema, Greg. "Responsibility, Taint and Ethical Distance in Business Ethics." *Journal of Business Ethics* (October 2003).

Petrick, Joseph A., and Robert F. Scherer. "The Enron Scandal and the Neglect of Management Integrity Capacity." *Mid-American Journal of Business* (Spring 2003).

Roberts, Sara, Justin Keeble, David Brown, and Arthur D. Little. The Business Case for Corporate Citizenship. White paper prepared for World Economic Forum, Geneva, Switzerland.

Sims, Robert R., and Johannes Brinkmann. "Enron Ethics (or Culture Matters More Than Codes)." *Journal of Business Ethics* (July 2003).

Verschoor, Curtis C. "New Evidence of Effective Ethics Systems." *Strategic Finance* (May 2003).

Negotiation

Business owners' ability to negotiate skillfully is important because typically, whether they realize it or not, they spend hours every week negotiating with subordinates, suppliers, lenders, significant others, children, parents, in-laws, car dealers, and others. Deciding how much to pay a new office manager or where to go to lunch with a client involves negotiation. The office manager may choose to accept less money if 100 percent of health benefits are paid, while a client may agree to go for Mexican food if Chinese food will be the choice on the next occasion. Even though all business owners are experienced negotiators, they may not be *skilled* negotiators. Being a skillful negotiator requires patience, attentiveness, flexibility, and awareness of personal negotiation style, issues and details of the case, as well as the goals and objectives of the other party.

Negotiation can be described as nonviolent communication between two or more parties who may have conflicting and common interests in an attempt to reach an agreement that meets the goals of one or both parties. In simple terms, negotiation is a process for getting something you want. Gary Karrass, author of *Negotiate to Close*, once said, "We don't get what we want in this life, we get what we negotiate."

COMMON MISCONCEPTIONS ABOUT NEGOTIATION

Many people are afraid to negotiate because of all the stereotypes associated with negotiation. Although business owners spend up to half their time at work negotiating, many still feel uncomfortable with the process. Some fear that they may come across to the other party as impolite, pushy, unfair, or even cheap.

One common misconception about negotiation is that good negotiators use tactics similar to the stereotypical deceitful, conniving used car salesman. Being a good negotiator does not mean you have to resort to being a slick, smooth talker.

Contrary to popular belief, negotiating should not be compared to a game or a war in which both parties enter the process with the goal of winning and crushing the other party's spirit. The end result of war or a game is that one party comes out as the clear winner and the other as the absolute loser. Upon completion of a successful negotiation, in contrast, both parties should feel that they have won something.

Another reason business owners feel uncomfortable negotiating is because they feel they have to make trade-offs between getting along with the other side and getting what they want. It is not uncommon for business owners to feel that they have to either give in to the other side's demands or play hardball in order to avoid conflict, damaging their future relationship, or being taken advantage of by the other party.

Many people feel more relaxed when they find out that they will be negotiating with a woman because they assume that women are not as aggressive as their male counterparts and, therefore, cannot be as effective as negotiators. This is another common misconception. While women tend to be more concerned with preserving relationships and men with arriving at an agreement as quickly as possible, this is not always the case. Some men are patient and are more interested in achieving a deal that meets the needs of all parties while some women prefer to enter the negotiation with a competitive drive to win. Whether you are negotiating with women or men, you should always do your homework. Learn as much as you can about the members of the other team, develop a relationship with them and, if necessary, alter your negotiation style so that it resonates with the other team's personality.

PRIMARY GOAL OF NEGOTIATION

Negotiation is like neither a game nor a war. It is about cooperation and signing an agreement that makes both parties feel that they have been successful. The primary goal of effective negotiation should be to achieve a deal that both parties can live with and that accomplishes your goals without making the other party walk away from the deal or harming a valuable relationship. Basically, the whole point of negotiating with someone is to get something better than what you would get without negotiating.

NEGOTIATION STYLES

There are two main types of negotiation styles, hard and soft. Hard bargaining is also referred to as positional, aggressive, contending, or competitive bargaining; and soft bargaining is synonymous with relational or cooperative bargaining.

Hard Bargainers

In a nutshell, hard bargainers want to be victorious and are willing to jeopardize relationships to accomplish their goal of winning. While this negotiation style eliminates the need to make concessions, it also increases the likelihood that the other party will walk away, resulting in no agreement, and that the relationship will be severed or severely damaged.

Hard bargainers consider satisfying the other party's needs only if it helps to accomplish their goals and objectives. They tend to withhold important information, purposely provide incorrect bottom-line figures, and embellish facts. As a result of their sometimes deceptive behavior, they tend to distrust the other party. Other traits displayed by hard bargainers are their inflated demands and threats, impatience, pressure tactics, and insistence on their own positions.

Because this approach involves little to no preparation, it is used by many negotiators. However, this negotiation style usually does not yield the best results because it alienates the opposing party and leaves them dissatisfied with the outcome. Before deciding to use this approach, serious consideration should be given to the following questions:

- ✔ How important is it that the other party does not walk away from the negotiation?
- ✔ How much do you value your relationship with the other party?
- ✔ How complicated are the issues?

If you value the relationship you have with the other side, it is important to you that the other party not walk away from the negotiation, or if the matter involves complex issues, hard bargaining will most probably not yield the desired results.

Soft Bargainers

In contrast to hard bargainers, the primary concern of soft bargainers is to maintain or improve relationships by finding a solution that appeases all parties. However, to avoid conflict with the other side, soft bargainers will quickly concede, make concessions, and agree to conditions that are clearly unfavorable for them. The major disadvantages of this approach are that often soft bargainers feel that they are taken advantage of or become bitter and resentful following a negotiation. Soft bargainers tend to be more patient, indirect, accommodating, and trusting than their hard-bargaining counterparts.

So, which negotiation style should you adopt—hard or soft bargaining? According to Roger Fisher, director of the Harvard Negotiation Project, and William Ury, director of the Negotiation Network, the answer is neither. Fisher and Ury suggest a third negotiation style called principled or win-win negotiation. The main idea behind principled negotiation is that both sides explore the interests of both parties and discover a creative solution that makes both sides feel like winners. Fisher and Ury base principled negotiation on the following four points:

1. Focus on the *interests* of all parties, not their positions.
2. Separate the people from the issue.

3. Make a list of creative options that meet the interests of both parties.
4. Base the end result on an objective standard.

PRENEGOTIATION HOMEWORK

To be a successful negotiator, it is imperative that you do your homework. Fisher and Ury suggest that you spend about half the time you spend negotiating on preparing for the negotiation.

Ideal Meeting Location

Once you have established a relationship with someone or have negotiated with that party before, you may feel comfortable negotiating over the telephone. Otherwise, conducting the meeting in person would be better than over the phone because it will give you the opportunity to observe the other person's body language and maintain eye contact.

If you decide to meet in person, offer to meet at your office if possible. Not only will you feel more comfortable in your office, but you also will be able to get quicker approval from senior people (if necessary); and it gives you the home advantage. The main advantage of meeting at the other side's offices is that you can withhold information until you return to your office. Of course, if neither party is willing to agree to meet at either office, you can always meet at a neutral location.

Evaluate Your Negotiation Style

Before you can improve your negotiation style, you should think about evaluating your current style and your personality. Thinking about the last few negotiations you participated in, what tactics do you think were successful? In what areas do you think you could improve? Would you say you used hard or soft bargaining techniques? Did you tend to be direct or indirect in your negotiation dealings? What would you say are your hot buttons? If you think about how you react in different situations and what your turn-ons and turnoffs are, you will be better prepared to handle yourself professionally while maintaining your composure during your next negotiation. And this can be an advantage when dealing with people whose tempers get the best of them.

Establish Your Goals and Objectives

You need to determine your primary goal and objectives—that is, what you want to get out of the negotiation. Your primary goal should be realistic and accessible. Let's say your main goal is to hire a new office manager. It is unrealistic to assume that you will be able to hire an office manager at $0 per year and no benefits. You should expand your main goal to include other objectives. For example, you would like to hire a new office manager and pay $4,000 per month and 75 percent of health and dental insurance, offer 10 days of vacation and 5 days of sick time for the first year, and match up to 3 percent of salary in the company's 401(k) plan.

Research the Other Team's Members and Personalities

Once you have established your goals and objectives and those of the other party, the next step in preparing for negotiation is gathering as much information as you can about the opposing party's personalities. If you do not have a relationship with them already, begin to establish one by setting up a meeting or two prior to the negotiation. Perhaps you can meet informally over lunch one afternoon. If you are unable to meet with your counterparts prior to the negotiation, consider calling their assistants to find out more information regarding how to make them comfortable during the negotiation. Ask their assistants what they like to eat and drink so that you can have things prepared at the time of the negotiation.

Also think about how you will get their attention at the start of the negotiation meeting. What do you have in common with them? Perhaps you both like to hike and you can discuss trails you have hiked recently. What do they like to do for fun? If they like to play tennis, you can ask about the last game they played or how well they played. Or you could bring up the latest professional tennis tournament that you recently saw on television. This is a great way to get their attention before you begin negotiating.

Do you think the other side uses a hard or soft bargaining strategy? Can you trust them? How long do they anticipate the process will take? Do you know anyone acquainted with a member of the opposite team who can give you some information about them? What makes them tick? Are they impatient? Demanding? How long do they anticipate this process to take?

The more you know about the people on the other side, the more prepared you will be for the negotiation. And the more prepared you are, the more confident you will be because you will know what to expect.

Make a List of Assumptions

Skilled negotiators realize that people sometimes have mistaken assumptions that they believe to be facts. When negotiating with another party for the first time, we have to make certain assumptions as to what some of their body language, expressions, or phrases mean. Ask for clarification! Don't assume anything. Make a list of assumptions to bring to the negotiation and clarify any points that are unclear or uncertain.

Gather Facts and Conduct Research

The next step involves gathering as much information as you can about the subject of the negotiation. Let's say that you own a pizza restaurant and you are negotiating prices with the landlord who owns the building in which you operate your restaurant. To persuade the other side that you are asking for something that is reasonable, you need to provide supporting data.

For example, if you would like to renew your lease at the same price you paid the previous year, you would need to prove why it would be unfair of your landlord to increase your rent. Research regarding real estate prices in similar buildings located in the surrounding area of your restaurant, restaurant occupancy rates in your city, the number of new restaurant openings in the past year in your city, and the average increase in rent in your city would be some topics worth researching prior to the negotiation. You can find this type of information on the Internet, by asking for assistance at your local community library, by speaking to a local real estate leasing agent, or by meeting with other building owners in your area. You may also want to find out about what the current issues are in the real estate industry. Another way to get the latest news and information regarding the real estate industry is to read trade publications or visit the web sites of real estate trade associations for current articles.

Focus on the Other Side's Interests Rather Than Stated Positions

It is almost always in your best interest to find a win-win solution for both parties, to complete a negotiation knowing that both sides are satisfied with the results. If the other party is dissatisfied, it can have negative consequences for you. For example, if a customer feels he was cheated, you will lose her as a customer and perhaps future customers because of her negative comments. If a new hire feels cheated out of a better salary, he may quit his job in a few months when he finds something else that pays more after you just invested time and money in training him. Leaving the other side feeling disgruntled, cheated, or deceived destroys relationships, which could be risky for your business.

The next step in preparing for negotiation is to imagine that you have to negotiate for the other side and develop a list of questions you should ask them. Put yourself in their shoes and do their homework. What questions will they ask your team? Be prepared to answer them.

Although it seems like the most important question to ask the other side is what they want, Roger Fisher states that there is another even more crucial question that looks at the underlying interests of the other party. *Why* do they want what they want? Walk a mile in their shoes and determine what you think motivates their stated positions.

You may already be familiar with this story, but imagine that one of your coworkers, Lisa, finds a bag of 30 oranges on sale at a local grocery store. She needs only 10 of them so she brings the remaining 20 oranges to the office to share with anyone who wants them. Both Karen and Anna decide they want them. After negotiating for a few minutes, they decide to each take home 10 oranges.

However, if they had focused on their interests (one wants just the peels and the other wants only the juice) instead of their stated positions (wanting the oranges), they would have been able to share the 20 oranges and achieve their goals. Karen wanted the oranges so she could squeeze fresh orange juice in her juicer. Anna wanted the oranges so she could grate the orange peels for an orange muffin recipe. Since neither side asked the opposing side why she wanted the oranges, both Karen and Anna had to make a trip to the supermarket. Anna's recipe called for the rinds of 20 oranges and Karen needed enough juice for her family of five for breakfast, which also required the juice from 20 oranges. If they had focused on interests, they would not each have had to make a trip to the grocery store, and the peels of Karen's oranges and the orange juice from Anna's oranges would not have been wasted.

Don't assume that every party's interests and motivations revolve around money. Let's assume that you own a small marketing research firm and are looking for a new project manager. You have completed the interviews and are in the process of negotiating an offer with a prospective candidate. When you offer him a salary of $50,000 a year, he states that he thinks you should offer him $55,000. When you ask him why he thinks he deserves $5,000 more than you offered him, you realize that money is not what is motivating him. He feels he should get an extra $5,000 in return for settling for the title of project manager. He has 10 years of project management experience and thinks he should have the title of project director instead of project manager. He is considering applying to an executive MBA evening program at the local university and feels that the title of project director would be viewed more favorably by the university. Once he has shared his true interests with you, you agree to give him the title of project director and agree to pay your new project director a salary of $50,000 a year.

Consider this example:

Boss: Based on our conversations over the past few days, I would like to extend an offer to you for $44,000 a year plus 10 days of vacation time and 5 sick days.
Employee: Well, I'm going to be honest and say that I am a bit surprised. I was expecting the offer to be closer to the $50,000 salary range.
Boss: Why were you expecting an offer of approximately $50,000?

Employee: Well, since I have been freelancing for the past few years, I have grown accustomed to having more time to go on vacations. I work hard for most of the year but I am also able to take a few weeks at a time to travel abroad. I will be unable to do much traveling if I have only two weeks of vacation time a year. So if I won't be able to travel as much, I should at least make more money.

Boss: I see. How about this? I'll throw in an extra week of vacation for the next three years so you'll have 15 days of vacation time. In addition to those 15 days of vacation time, you will have 5 days of sick time. If you do not get sick during the year, you can use them as vacation days during the last quarter of the year. So, you could have up to 20 vacation days your first three years! And, if you work with me for three years, I'll increase that to 20 vacation days plus 5 sick days. And, once a quarter, you can work 10 hours either Monday through Thursday or Tuesday through Friday and take a long weekend off. I think that sounds fair. What do you think?

Employee: I think I'll accept the offer—$44,000 sounds good as long as I have enough vacation time to travel.

Boss: Great, welcome aboard then!

At first glance it may appear that both parties want completely different things and have no interests in common. However, once you start to think about what motivates the other team and what their goals are, you will notice that sometimes both teams have more shared interests than opposing ones. Let's go back to the example about the small marketing research firm owner and the newly hired project director. You, as the business owner, and your new employee have a few interests in common. First, you both want the company to perform well. You both rely on your company's sales to support your families. Second, you both want stability. You, the owner, want your company to grow and would like to keep your valuable employees; you do not want to lose them to the competition, so you offer them competitive salaries, vacation time, and benefits. Your new project director is also looking for job security. He doesn't want to have to switch jobs and move his family every few years to get a competitive salary and benefits. Third, you are both interested in maintaining a good relationship with each other. You want your employee to be happy with his job so that he stays around, and your project director wants to be able to use you as a reference or for networking possibilities in the future.

Use Objective Standards

In order to convince the other party that what you are asking for is fair and reasonable, try to use objective standards whenever possible. If you are in the negotiation process with a prospective candidate, you will want to pay her as little as possible and she will want to earn as much as possible. Rather than feeling that the other party is trying to rip you off and haggling back and forth, the easiest solution is to use an independent objective standard. Independent objective standards may include market value, replacement cost, depreciated book value, competitive prices, precedents for similar cases, scientific judgment, professional standards, moral or ethical standards, or government standards. You can also speak to experts in the field to learn what is considered fair market value for whatever goods or services the negotiation is about. Using objective standards can reduce the amount of time it takes to conclude a negotiation because they are more likely to be accepted by the other party as a fair and reasonable offer.

If the other party offers to pay or accept a specific amount, always ask how they arrived at that specific number. Did they use an objective standard? If so, which one? If not, suggest one be used in order to eliminate bias and be fair, and to create a win-win situation for both parties. If they are unable to provide you with details for how they arrived at that amount and refuse to budge, you should seriously consider to agree to disagree and not negotiate. If, however, the price seems fair and is based on a trustworthy objective standard, be willing to be open-minded when confronted with a reasonable offer. Think about the following example:

> *Doctor:* I am pleased to tell you that I met with everyone you interviewed with and would like to extend you an offer of $45,000 per year as your salary.
> *Employee:* How did you arrive at that amount exactly?

Doctor: Well, we think it is a very fair salary. According to our human resources department, the average salary paid to pediatric nurses with your level of experience in this city is $43,789. Not only do we pay slightly more than average, but we also offer additional benefits. While most doctors offer their nurses two weeks of vacation, we would give you three. You would also be able to begin contributing to your 401(k) plan immediately rather than waiting for six months as in many other offices. Additionally, the vast majority of our nurses have been with us for more than 10 years. The average tenure at our office for nurses is 14.5 years. And every year for the past five years, we have been working with a market research firm to conduct an employee satisfaction survey. According to last year's results, 92 percent of our employees are either satisfied or very satisfied with their jobs, 94 percent with the benefits, and 90 percent with their bosses. We really value our employees here and I think they recognize that.

Employee: Sounds like once nurses are hired at your office, they don't want to work anywhere else.

Doctor: Exactly. We have one of the highest retention rates in the city for nurses.

Employee: Well, now that you explained how happy your employees are, I think I would like to work here as well.

Doctor: I'm glad to hear it. I'll notify the human resources department and have them send your paperwork by the end of the day. You should receive it by the end of the week.

Generate Options That Meet Interests of Both Parties

Once you have figured out what the opposing party really wants, you can start to develop a list of creative options that meets the interests of both parties. Remember, if you meet only your own interests, you risk alienating the other party and the possibility that they will lose their patience and walk away.

You may want to consider Fisher and Ury's suggestion of holding a brainstorming session with five to seven colleagues off-site with a facilitator to generate a comprehensive list of ideas. Have the facilitator display the ideas on an easel or whiteboard and record all ideas mentioned, realistic or not. Remind all participants that all ideas should provide a win-win solution for both sides. The unrealistic ideas can be tossed out when the group meets again before the negotiation to select the best ideas that will be discussed during the negotiation.

Make sure that all the ideas selected meet the following basic human needs that motivate the positions people choose so that you can reach mutual agreement more quickly:

- ✔ *Risk reduction and security*—job security.
- ✔ *Sense of belonging*—fitting in at home and at work with specific roles and responsibilities.
- ✔ *Economic security*—being able to afford basic necessities (food, shelter, etc.).
- ✔ *Recognition and approval*—feeling valued for accomplishing challenging work.
- ✔ *Control over one's life*—managing, organizing, and running one's life in the desired way.

Consider this next example:

Employee: Thank you for agreeing to meet with me to discuss my raise for next year.

Boss: I want you to know that I think you are an asset to my company and I appreciate everything you do around here. I think your review went well this year, and I have decided to give you an 8 percent raise for all your hard work.

Employee: I appreciate the 8 percent but I have to say that I was hoping for 15 percent.

Boss: Please tell me why you were hoping for 15 percent.

Employee: Well, I really like my job but it's expensive to keep my kids in day care from 3:30 to 5:30 every day. I was hoping for a 15 percent raise so that I can keep up with the rising costs of day care.

Boss: I'll tell you what I can do. What about letting you work flexible hours? Maybe you could work from 6:30 A.M. to 3:00 P.M. each weekday with a 30-minute lunch. This way you can still work 40 hours a week and be home in time to take care of your kids when they come home from school. Not only would you get to spend more quality time with your kids, but you also wouldn't have to send them to day care.

Employee: Wow, that's a great idea. The 8 percent raise sounds fine. Thank you.

The boss was able to meet his own needs of wanting to give his employee a raise of 8 percent and those of his employee by solving his day-care cost increase problems, leaving both parties feeling that they had won.

Determine Your BATNA

In order to negotiate better, you must determine what your BATNA is prior to negotiating. BATNA, first coined by Fisher and Ury, stands for "best alternative to a negotiated agreement." If you are unable to reach an agreement with the other party, what is your next best option? Knowing your BATNA helps you to decide at what point the deal the other side is offering you is no longer beneficial to you. Remember, the whole point of negotiating with someone is to get something better than what you would get without negotiating. So, you should consider sealing a deal only if you are able to come out ahead.

For example, let's say you own a small advertising agency and are looking for a seasoned account executive for one of your largest accounts. You are in the process of negotiating an offer with the leading candidate. Generate a list of as many alternatives as you can think of for not hiring this candidate and then pick the one option that seems to be the best. Bear in mind that you have a stronger position if your BATNA is to hire a freelancer who used to be an employee of your company until a permanent employee is hired. This person would require little or no training since she is familiar with how your company does things and would be able to produce work immediately. If, however, you have no other prospects in mind, have to advertise the position to generate resumes, and the official start date of the project is next week, you have a weaker BATNA.

Once you have determined your BATNA, you should consider the BATNA of the other party, keeping in mind that the party with the stronger BATNA tends to be the more powerful party in the negotiation process. If the prospective candidate you are interested in hiring has another job, she has a more powerful BATNA than if her second best alternative is to remain unemployed for an indefinite amount of time until another suitable job is offered. If both parties have strong BATNAs, the best solution may be to not negotiate with each other and instead negotiate with other parties or not at all.

THE NEGOTIATION PROCESS

Put the Other Side at Ease

Once the negotiation process has started, the first thing you should do after you introduce yourself to the other party is make the other side feel at ease. If the meeting takes place in your office, make sure they are comfortable with the temperature of the room, and offer them coffee or water and something to eat. Give them a tour of the facilities so they know where the restrooms, phones, and computer access (if available) are in case they need to use them. Once everyone is comfortable, initiate small talk based on the research you did earlier. Talk about any interests you may have in common, ask about their children, or discuss hobbies or any other interests they may have.

Be a Good Listener

Active listening skills are crucial if you want to be a skilled negotiator. Being a good listener is challenging because you may feel stressed during the negotiation. Additionally, listening requires concentration and patience. Although you may want to interrupt with your comments, try to be patient and concentrate on what is being said. Many people find it difficult to concentrate because they are too busy preparing what they will say next in reaction to what was said. If you do your research, plan, and rehearse everything you intend to say prior to the negotiation, you will be able to listen and concentrate much more effectively during the negotiation.

If you prove to the other side that you are paying attention to what they are saying, they will be more likely to listen to what you say. To avoid having the other party feeling like everything they are saying is "going in one ear and out the other," try to appear genuinely interested and use physical gestures to prove that you are paying attention such as tilting your head and nodding. Saying "Go on" or "I see" are other effective ways to show the other side that you are interested in what they are saying. Another way to let the other party know you are paying attention is by reiterating what has just been said in a succinct manner. Although actively listening to someone does not automatically mean you agree with his point of view, make sure you acknowledge that you understand where he is coming from and how the person feels. Acknowledging the other person's emotions helps him feel more comfortable so that you can both move on to the problem-solving phase.

Listening to what someone is saying is a good start, but also pay attention to body language. Is she looking you in the eye when she answers your questions or is she fidgeting and looking at the ground? Does she seem trustworthy? Does she say she agrees with you and then roll her eyes? Lee Miller, managing director of the Advanced Human Resources Groups, states that body language that suggests doubts include touching the nose, rubbing the ears, running fingers through the hair, or turning away.

If something that was said remains unclear or ambiguous to you, be sure to ask for clarification. And, once you think you have understood something, repeat it back in a succinct manner to make sure there are no misunderstandings.

Alter Your Negotiation Style If Necessary

You may find that you need to adjust your negotiation style to match the other team's personality. For example, if your style is to be more indirect but the other side gets right down to business once the meeting begins, perhaps you should be more direct. If the other team seems to be more analytical, focus on your presentation and be sure to include lots of numbers, charts, and graphs that validate and explain your point of view.

Separate People from the Issue

Fisher and Ury state that people become too emotionally involved with the issues of the negotiation and their side's position. When the other side attacks their position or issues, they feel as if they are being attacked personally. It is important that you separate the people on the other side from the issues that you are trying to resolve. Instead of attacking the other party by saying "Your company ripped me off!" explain how the situation made you feel: "I felt let down."

Actively listening to the other side when they are speaking, acknowledging their emotions, and making a sincere effort to understand their point of view are ways to ensure that you have separated the people from the issues at hand. When people become emotional during a negotiation, it is important that you recognize their emotions even if they seem outrageous or unreasonable. Simple phrases such as "I understand your frustration" would suffice. Failure to notice their emotions may lead them to feel alienated or to an even stronger reaction.

Be Confident and Firm but Not Demanding

One way to exude confidence during a negotiation is to practice, practice, practice. For example, you can work on your listening skills next time you get your car fixed at the car shop or negotiate with your spouse about where you want to go on your next vacation. You negotiate every day with your family, friends, and strangers, so you should find ample opportunities to practice.

Another way to show your audience that you are in control is by exhibiting positive body language. Lee suggests that you look your audience members in the eye, stand or sit straight, smile, moderate and project your tone and pitch, and speak slowly. Avoid phrases such as "I should have done more research in this area but . . ." or "I'm not as experienced as the rest of you but . . ." that may give the impression that you are unsure of what you are saying.

Be Patient

It is important to remain calm and patient at all times, particularly when the other side is screaming, personally attacking you or your company, or behaving in an emotional manner. Although it may be difficult to maintain your composure under tense circumstances, try to calm the other person down by acknowledging his emotional state and trying to understand his point of view, followed by a brief 15-minute break. The person probably needs recognition, reassurance, security, or esteem, or perhaps he is just having a bad day. Maybe his spouse lost her job today. The idea is to "kill them with kindness" and avoid bringing up this episode in the future to save face and embarrassment.

Ask Questions

Even though you may have prepared as much as you could for the negotiation, there is no way you could have found answers to everything. Ask the other side questions to make sure you understand what their interests are and to clarify anything they may have mentioned earlier that you find to be unclear.

When you ask questions to find out what the other party is thinking, be sure to ask open-ended questions, questions that must be answered with more than just a simple yes or no. You will get more information from the other side by asking "What did you like and dislike about your last job?" instead of "Did you like your last job?" Or, "How would you describe your management style?" in place of "Do you lead by consensus?" Open-ended questions tend to begin with "who . . . ," "what . . . ," "when . . . ," "why . . . ," "where . . . ," "how . . . ," "describe a time when . . . ," "please explain . . . ," "please tell me . . . ," and so on.

When the person has finished answering your question, refrain from immediately asking another question or making a statement. A few seconds of awkward silence is usually enough to make people uncomfortable, which influences them to continue speaking and you may be able to extract some more information from them.

Don't Be Afraid to Walk Away

Sometimes even though you do your homework, understand the other side's point of view and interests, and come up with a list of creative solutions keeping the interests of both parties in mind, you find yourself unable to reach a satisfactory agreement with the other party. Although it is sometimes tempting to just sign a deal and get it done as quickly as possible so that you can move on to other pressing tasks, be patient. If the offer you are thinking about signing is worse than your

BATNA, do not be afraid to walk away. Sometimes after you declare to the other party that you are walking away, the other side will reconsider the agreement—but not always. Remember that what you are offering to the other side is valuable. Why else would the other party spend time trying to negotiate with you if you were not valuable to them? You should be able to find another party to strike a more reasonable deal with, one that is better than your BATNA.

DIRTY NEGOTIATING TRICKS

While principled negotiation is the ideal negotiation strategy, sometimes you may be faced with a situation in which the other party claims to use principled negotiation but during the negotiation will begin using tricky negotiation tactics, which range from using false data to lying. If you find yourself in this situation, call the other party on the dirty trick they are using, make a counteroffer, keep their interests in mind, and insist on using an objective standard. Although it may seem easier said than done, keep your emotions under control when confronted with dirty tactics. Although it is human nature to respond sharply, you may say something in your state of anger you will regret later, which is precisely what the other party is expecting to happen. Instead, smile, try to relax, and don't be intimidated.

After you confront the other party about their tricky behavior, continue with the negotiation process. Focus on the people, mutual interests, creative options, and objective standards. If you are unable to reach a fair agreement, evaluate your BATNA and consider walking away.

Nibbling

Let's say you own a florist shop and negotiated a contract with a vendor for vases just three days ago. You are meeting today to sign the printed contract. When the meeting begins, the other party says, "I know we agreed to all parts of this contract but when I took it to my boss for approval, he told me that the company now requires payment in 30 days instead of 45." When one party wants just a little bit more toward the end of the negotiation, this is called nibbling. Until you confront them and acknowledge the nibbling, they will continue to do so.

The key when dealing with dirty tricks is to separate the people from the problem. Instead of saying, "You tricked me! I'm not going to negotiate a deal with you liars," try "Well, as long as we're still in the negotiation process, there's one small thing we're not that happy about, either. How about us paying you within 30 days of receiving a vase shipment if you will guarantee these prices through the end of June?" You could also try, "Look, this agreement has already been approved by a lot of people from your side and my side. We have both already agreed that it is a fair contract, and I would prefer that we keep it the way it is."

Good Guy/Bad Guy

The good guy/bad guy routine, often seen on television shows and in movies about detectives and cops, involves two individuals. The bad guy is demanding, abrasive, and tough while the good guy acts friendly, seems more anxious to make a deal, and appears to be almost embarrassed by the partner's harsh behavior. The good guy tries to befriend you while the bad guy tries to intimidate you. Although the two are working together to deceive you, the good guy will try to work out a deal with you so that you can avoid having to negotiate with the bad guy. The best way to handle this situation is to recognize the tactic and call it to their attention. "There seems to be some disagreement between you. Perhaps the two of you need a few minutes to sort out your objectives here today. Why don't we break for 15 minutes while you work it out?"

Ultimatums

This "take it or leave it" technique is usually designed to intimidate you and get you to sign the agreement quickly. The best way to handle this technique is to ignore it and continue with the negotiation process as you normally would.

Limited Authority

If you are in the process of negotiating and the other party says that they do not have the authority to agree or sign off on an issue, you are the victim of the limited authority tactic. Whether this technique is preplanned or legitimate, you should say, "I understand. Let's set up a meeting with the person who does have authority to negotiate on all the issues."

Lateness/Long Interruptions

When you are waiting for someone to show up for a meeting and that other person arrives either very late or not at all, you feel flustered. You have been wondering, "Am I on time? Were we supposed to meet earlier today and I wrote it down incorrectly in my calendar? Or maybe we were supposed to meet tomorrow?"

On other occasions the other party arrives on time but is interrupted during the meeting and does not appear to have any interest in resuming the meeting. Consider someone who accepts a cell phone call in the middle of a negotiation and remains on the phone for more than 30 minutes while everyone else in the room waits. These tactics are designed to make the other party feel intimidated and irritated. If you find yourself as the victim in this situation, you should say, "You're obviously very distracted today, and I wouldn't want to take advantage of your inattention. Let's reschedule." This lets them know that you will not tolerate this behavior and attacks the problem, not the people.

Statistical Data

The other party should be able to justify what they are asking for if they have done their homework. However, pay attention to the source of their information. Just because the source is legitimate, it does not mean it is relevant. For example, imagine you own an advertising agency in Boise, Idaho, and you are interviewing a recent college graduate for a position as junior copywriter. When you ask him what type of salary range he is looking for, he says he expects $35,000 to $40,000. When you ask him why he thinks he should get paid $35,000 to $40,000, he pulls out a document he printed from the Internet. Upon reviewing the document, you realize that the source he is using bases its results on a national study. Therefore, the results have little bearing on getting a job in Boise since it includes national data instead of local data.

CONCLUSION

Being a successful negotiator and using principled negotiation involves a lot of hard work and preparation. However, it can also be rewarding when you walk out after a deal knowing that both sides got what they wanted. During the negotiation process, remember to try to uncover the other side's motivating interests, never lose sight of your goals and objectives, and try to convince the other party to use an objective standard. And, if the other party uses dirty tactics, let them know that you are aware of what they are doing; attack the problem—not the people; maintain your composure; and continue with the negotiation.

Negotiation "Do's"

✔ Use good posture.

✔ Speak slowly.

✔ Smile.

✔ Psych yourself up.

✔ Ask why they want what they want.

✔ Look the other party in the eye.

✔ Be succinct.

✔ Ask open-ended questions that must be answered with more than a yes or no.

✔ Be a good listener—clarify, encourage, appreciate others' efforts, recognize feelings, and summarize.

✔ Think of creative solutions.

✔ Ask for what you want.

✔ Realize that you have something valuable.

✔ Be willing to walk away.

✔ Try to achieve a win-win negotiation.

✔ Know what the other party wants.

✔ Walk a mile in the other side's shoes.

✔ Know your BATNA.

✔ Determine the other side's hidden interests.

✔ Ask for justifications and clarifications.

✔ Ask questions.

✔ Separate the people from the problem.

✔ Use objective criteria.

✔ Be flexible and open-minded.

✔ Be credible—use facts and other supporting evidence.

✔ Exude confidence.

✔ Pay attention to your tone.

✔ Make trade-offs.

✔ Take notes.

✔ Build relationships.

Negotiation "Don'ts"

✔ Make threats.

✔ Interrupt when someone is speaking.

✔ Shout.

✔ Be sarcastic.

✔ Criticize in front of others.

✔ Attack people.

✔ Insult or belittle.

✔ Make the other feel guilty.

✔ Pout.

✔ Cry.

✔ Fidget.

✔ Call anyone names.

✔ Be easily discouraged.

✔ Beg.

✔ Whine.

✔ Take it personally.

✔ Negotiate when you are feeling irritated, stressed, tired, or angry.

✔ Use technical jargon.

✔ Hog the floor.

✔ Give ultimatums.

REFERENCES

Fisher, Roger, and William Ury. *Getting to Yes*. New York: Penguin Books, 1981.

McRae, Brad. *Negotiating and Influencing Skills*. Thousand Oaks, CA: Sage Publications, 1998.

Miller, Lee E., and Jessica Miller. *A Woman's Guide to Successful Negotiating*. New York: McGraw-Hill, 2002.

Nierenberg, Gerard I. *The Complete Negotiator*. New York: Berkley Books, 1986.

Nierenberg, Juliet, and Irene S. Ross. *Women and the Art of Negotiating*. New York: Fairfield Graphics, 1985.

Ury, William. *Getting Past No: Negotiating with Difficult People*. New York: Bantam Books, 1991.

Woolf, Bob. *Friendly Persuasion*. New York: G. P. Putnam's Sons, 1990.

SECTION 11

MONEY: ECONOMICS, FINANCE, AND ACCOUNTING

Chapter 6

Accounting and Finance

A
ccounting is the process of recording, classifying, reporting, and analyzing money. Accountants capture and record all the transactions, operations, and activities that have financial consequences for a business. Accountants are also involved in other activities in finance that impact a business, such as weighing the costs of new ventures, participating in strategies for mergers and acquisitions, quality management, tracking financial performance, as well as tax strategy.

While the accounting requirements of businesses vary, all organizations need a way to keep track of the flow of money within them. The responsibilities of the finance and accounting functional area within an organization or of its chief financial officer (CFO) include:

✔ *Facilitating operations*—payroll, purchasing, cash collections, cash disbursements.

✔ *Management control*—measuring actual performance against goals and expectations.

✔ *Management decision making*—analyzing cash position to make decisions.

✔ *External financial reports*—financial statements prepared according to generally accepted accounting principles (GAAP) and available for audit.

✔ *Tax returns*—federal and state income taxes; property, sales, and payroll taxes.

Accounting and finance are not intuitive. Many small businesses hire accountants to set up and manage their books. Other companies use accounting software such as QuickBooks. Accounting involves periodic reporting of financial data and includes:

✔ *Business transactions.* Businesses keep a daily record of transactions in sales journals, cash-receipt journals, or cash-disbursement journals.

✔ *Debits and credits to a general ledger.* An up-to-date general ledger shows current information about accounts payable, accounts receivable, owners' equity, and other accounts.

✔ *Making adjustments to the general ledger.* General-ledger adjustments let businesses account for items that don't get recorded in daily journals, such as bad debts and accrued interest or taxes. By adjusting entries, businesses can match revenues with expenses within each accounting period.

✔ *Closing the books.* After all revenues and expenses are accounted for, any net profit gets posted in the owners' equity account. Revenue and expense accounts are always brought to a zero balance before a new accounting cycle begins.

✔ *Preparing financial statements.* At the end of a period, businesses prepare financial reports—income statements, statements of capital, balance sheets, cash-flow statements, and other reports—that summarize all the financial activity for that period.

CASH VERSUS ACCRUAL ACCOUNTING

The two principal methods of keeping track of the money that flows in and out of a business are cash and accrual accounting. Most small businesses use the cash method, in which income is reported in the year it is received, and expenses are deducted in the year they are paid. Under the accrual method, income is reported when it is earned and expenses deducted when incurred, regardless of whether money has changed hands yet.

Accrual Accounting

In an organization using the accrual method, an accountant records income and expenses when they happen, not when they are actually received or paid. In practical terms, this difference in timing is relevant if your company keeps inventory on hand or handles transactions on credit. For example, a consultant completes a project in January but isn't paid for it at the time. The business that has been serviced recognizes all expenses in relation to that contract when they were incurred, even though the consultant has not been paid. Both the income and expenses are recorded for the current tax year, even if payment is received and bills are paid the following February.

Cash Accounting

If an accountant uses the cash method, he/she counts income when it is received and expenses when they are paid. Many small businesses, especially retail businesses, use the cash basis method of accounting, which is based on real-time cash flow. On the day a check is received, it becomes a cash receipt.

DOUBLE-ENTRY BOOKKEEPING

Without a system to record and track the flow of money within a firm, a business cannot accurately conduct its operating functions or make clear operating decisions. In order to effectively operate, a business must ensure that the cash inflow from operating, financing, and investing activities is in balance with the cash outflows that are associated with expenditures. To do this, accountants use a system of double-entry accounting to debit (remove) or credit (add) money as it flows into and out of their business. Double entry requires two entries per transaction, which provides cross-checks and decreases errors. In the record of every financial transaction the following equation remains in balance at all times:

$$\text{Assets} = \text{Liabilities} + \text{Owners' Equity (Capital)}$$

Assets are what a company owns, such as equipment, buildings, and inventory. Claims on assets include liabilities and owners' (stockholders) equity. Liabilities are what a company owes, such as notes payable, trade accounts payable, and bonds. Owners' equity represents the claims of owners against the business.

The double-entry system provides checks and balances that ensure that the books are always kept in balance. Each transaction is recorded as a debit or a credit, with total assets equaling the sum total of liabilities and owners' equity.

ACCOUNTING TERMS AND CONCEPTS

There are a few accounting terms and concepts that a business manager must be familiar with in order to make setting up an accounting system easier.

Debits and Credits

An understanding of debits and credits is essential in the effective usage of any accounting system. Every accounting entry in the general ledger contains both a debit and a credit. Further, all debits must equal all credits. If they don't, the double-entry system is out of balance. Therefore, the accounting system must have a mechanism to ensure that all entries balance. Indeed, most automated accounting systems won't let you enter an out-of-balance entry; they will just beep at you until you fix your error. Depending on the type of accounting system, a debit or credit will either increase or decrease the account balance. For every increase in one account, there is an opposite (and equal) decrease in another. That's what keeps the entry in balance.

Assets and Liabilities

Balance sheet accounts are the assets and liabilities for a firm, which, as discussed, must balance.

Identifying Assets. An asset is any item of value owned by a business. A firm's assets are listed on its balance sheet, where they are set off against its liabilities. Assets may include factories, land, inventories, vehicles, and other items. Some assets (short-term assets), like cash, are easy to value and liquidate, while others (long-term assets), such as buildings and farmland, are difficult to value and take longer to liquidate. These kinds of assets are collectively known as tangible assets. Intangible assets, like a valued brand name such as BMW, don't show up on a balance sheet, but do contribute to the value of the firm. There are many other intangible assets owned by a company. Patents, the exclusive right to use a trademark, and goodwill from the acquisition of another company are such intangible assets. Generally, the value of intangible assets is whatever both parties agree to when the assets are created. In the case of a patent, the value is often linked to its development costs. Goodwill is often the difference between the purchase price of a company and the value of the assets acquired (net of accumulated depreciation). Even something that is not physically in hand, such as accounts receivable, is an asset because a company has claim to money due from a customer.

Identifying Liabilities. Liabilities are the opposite of assets. These are the obligations of one company to another. Accounts payable are liabilities and represent a company's future duty to pay a vendor. So is the loan you took from a bank. A business organizes liabilities into short-term and long-term categories on the balance sheet. Long-term debt (claims due in more than one year) and short-term debt (claims due within a year) are liabilities because they are claims against the business. If you were a bank, a customer's deposits would be a liability for accounting purposes, because they represent future claims against the bank.

Owners' Equity

Owners' equity is the difference between assets and liabilities; it increases and decreases just like they do. Owners' equity includes factors like partners' capital accounts, stock, and retained earnings. Stockholders' equity is also what would belong to the company's owners—the holders of its common stock—after selling the assets and paying off the creditors. Literally, it is paid-in capital plus retained earnings.

Retained earnings are the accumulated profits after dividends to common shareholders have been paid. At the end of one accounting year, all the income and expense accounts are compared to one another, and the difference (profit or loss for the year) is moved into the retained earnings account.

Income and Expenses

Further down in the chart of accounts (usually after the owners' equity section) come the income and expense accounts. Most companies want to keep track of just where they get income and where it goes, and these accounts provide that information.

Income Accounts. A business may want to establish an income account for different income-generating departments of a business. In that way, it can identify exactly where the income is coming from, and the income of the various departments can be added together. Different income accounts would be:

- ✔ Sales revenue.
- ✔ Interest income.
- ✔ Income from sale of assets.

Expense Accounts. Most companies have a separate account for each type of expense they incur. A company probably incurs much the same expenses month after month; thus, once they are established, the expense accounts won't vary much from month to month. Typical expense accounts include:

- ✔ Salaries and wages.
- ✔ Telephones.

✔ Utilities.

✔ Repairs.

✔ Maintenance.

✔ Depreciation.

✔ Amortization.

✔ Interest.

✔ Rent.

GENERAL LEDGER

The core of a company's financial records is maintained as a "general ledger." These records constitute the central "books" of all financial transactions since day one in the life of the company.

In setting up the general ledger, one must be cognizant of two points: (1) linkage to the company's financial reports and (2) establishment of opening balances.

The two primary financial documents of any company are the balance sheet and the profit and loss statement (income statement), both of which are drawn directly from the company's general ledger. The general ledger accrues the balances that make up the line items on these reports, and the changes are reflected in the profit and loss statement.

Every account that is on a chart of accounts will be included in a general ledger, which should be set up in the same order as the chart of accounts. While the general ledger does not include every single accounting entry in a given period, it does reflect a summary of all transactions made.

If a business is small and cash-based, a business can set up much of a general ledger out of a checkbook. The checkbook includes several pieces of information vital to the general ledger—cumulative cash balance, date of the entry, amount of the entry, and purpose of the entry. Even for a cash-based business, a checkbook cannot be a sole source for establishing a balance sheet.

An important component of any general ledger is source documents. Two examples of source documents are copies of invoices to customers and from suppliers. Source documents are critical in that they provide an audit trail in case you or someone else has to go back and study financial transactions made in a business. For instance, a customer might claim that he never received an invoice from you. A source document will prove otherwise. And source documents are a required component for an accountant at tax time. Other examples of source documents include canceled checks, utility bills, payroll tax records, and loan statements.

All general ledger entries are double entries. This makes sense because for every financial transaction in a business, the money (or commitment to pay) goes from one place to another. For instance, when a payroll check is written, the money flows out of a payroll account (cash) into the hands of an employee (an expense). When goods are sold on account, a record of the sale (income) is generated; but there must also be a journal entry to make sure that the funds are collected from that account later (an account receivable). As discussed earlier, the system used in recording entries on a general ledger is called a system of debits and credits.

As explained in a previous section, for every debit there should be an equal and offsetting credit. It is when the debits and credits are not equal or do not offset one another that the books don't balance. A key advantage of any automated bookkeeping system is that it polices debit and credit entries as they are made, making it far more difficult for the accounts not to balance.

COMPONENTS OF THE ACCOUNTING SYSTEM

Think of the accounting system as a wheel, and the hub as the general ledger. Feeding the hub information are the spokes of the wheel. These include:

- ✔ Payroll.
- ✔ Accounts payable.
- ✔ Fixed assets.
- ✔ Inventory control.
- ✔ Accounts receivable.

✔ Order entry.

✔ Cost accounting.

The following is an exploration of some of the important elements of the accounting system.

Payroll

Payroll accounting can be quite a challenge for the new business owner. There are many federal and state laws that regulate what must be tracked related to payroll. A business may face fines for maintaining incomplete or nonconforming records. Many small business owners outsource their payroll services and by so doing guarantee their compliance with all applicable laws.

If payroll is maintained in-house, it is advised that a business use an automated payroll system. Even if the books are done manually, an automated payroll system will save valuable time and help considerably with compliance.

Accounts Payable

Accounts payable represent bills from suppliers for goods or services purchased on credit. Generally this debt must be paid within 12 months. It is important to track accounts payable in a timely manner in order to know how much each supplier is owed and when payment is due. If a business has a timely system in place to manage accounts payable, it may often be able to take advantage of discounts that are provided for timely payments. A poorly managed supplier system can damage a relationship with a supplier and earn a business a poor credit rating.

Fixed Assets

Fixed assets are commonly recognized as long-lived property owned by a firm that is used in the production of its income. Fixed assets include real estate, facilities, and equipment. Other types of assets include intangible fixed assets, such as patents, trademarks, and customer recognition. Fixed assets are items that are for long-term use, generally five years or more. They are not bought and sold in the normal course of business operation.

In an accrual system of accounting, fixed assets are not recorded when they are purchased, but rather they are expensed over a period of time that coincides with the useful life of the item (the amount of time the asset is expected to last). This process is known as depreciation. Most businesses that own fixed assets keep subledgers for each asset category as well as for each depreciation schedule.

In most cases, depreciation is easy to compute. The cost of the asset is divided by its useful life. For instance, a $50,000 piece of equipment with a five-year useful life would be depreciated at a rate of $10,000 per year. This is known as straight-line depreciation.

There are other more complicated methods of fixed-asset depreciation that allow for accelerated depreciation on the front end, which is advantageous from a tax standpoint. You should seek the advice of a certified public accountant (CPA) before setting up depreciation schedules for fixed-asset purchases.

Inventory Control

A good inventory-control feature is an essential part of a bookkeeping system. If you are going to be manufacturing products, you will have to track raw materials, work in process, and finished goods, and separate subledgers should be established for each of these inventory categories. Even if you are a wholesaler or retailer, you will be selling many different types of inventory and will need an effective system to track each inventory item offered for sale.

Another key reason to track inventory very closely is the direct relationship to cost of goods sold. Because nearly all businesses that stock inventory are required to use the accrual method for accounting, good inventory records are a must for accurately tracking the material cost associated with each item sold. From a management standpoint, tracking inventory is also important. An effective and up-to-date inventory-control system will provide you with the following critical information:

✔ Which items sell well, and which items are slow moving.

✔ When to order more raw materials or more items.

✔ Where in the warehouse the inventory is stored when it comes time to ship it.

✔ Number of days in the production process for each item.

✔ Typical order of key customers.

✔ Minimum inventory level needed to meet daily orders.

Accounts Receivable

If you plan to sell goods or services on account in a business, you will need a method of tracking who owes you how much and when it is due, the purpose of the accounts receivable subledger. If you will be selling to a number of different customers, an automated system is a must.

A good bookkeeping software system will allow you to set up subledgers for each customer. Thus, when a sale is made on account, you can track it specifically to the customer. This is essential to ensure that billing and collection are done in a timely manner.

ORGANIZING THE ACCOUNTING AND FINANCE DEPARTMENT

Organize a small-business accounting system by function. Often there is just one person in the office to do all the transaction entries. From an internal control standpoint, this isn't desirable because it opens the door for fraud and embezzlement. Companies with more people assigned to accounting functions don't pose as much of a threat for fraud perpetrated by a single person.

Having the same person draft the checks and reconcile the checking account is not a good example of how to assign accounting duties. Small businesses often can't afford the number of people needed for an adequate separation of duties; however, setting up a smart internal control structure within a new accounting system helps mitigate that risk.

Assignment of Duties

Figure out who is going to do what in a new accounting system. A business needs to cover the following accounting responsibilities:

- ✔ Payroll. (Even if the business uses an outside payroll service, someone must be in control and be responsible.)
- ✔ Accounts payable.
- ✔ Fixed assets.
- ✔ Inventory control.
- ✔ Accounts receivable.
- ✔ Order entry.
- ✔ Cost accounting.
- ✔ Monthly reporting.
- ✔ Internal accounting control.
- ✔ Overall responsibility for the accounting system.
- ✔ Management of the computer system (if you're using one).

In many cases the same person will do many of these things. The person assigned to be in overall charge of the system should be the one who is most familiar with accounting. If you are just starting a company, you will want to think about the background of the new employees. At least one of them should have the capacity and integrity to run the accounting system. To determine someone's expertise in a field, one of the following steps would be appropriate:

- ✔ Have the applicant be interviewed by an expert. Your own CPA will probably be glad to interview a few for you.
- ✔ Carefully check references from past jobs. Ask detailed questions on exactly what the candidate did in the accounting function. Compare the reference source's answers with what the candidate said.
- ✔ Ask some accounting questions. This will allow you to assess the applicant's comfort with the language of accounting.

PRACTICAL ACCOUNTING

Though accounting serves a rather perfunctory purpose of control and assessment of the firm's financial performance, there are other, practical financial activities to consider.

Credit Checking Potential Customers

When a business extends credit, it is in effect loaning customers money, and any company wants to be reasonably sure that the money will be paid back. The best assurance of being able to collect is to check each customer's credit history before extending credit. That can be as simple as a phone call to a bank.

However a business chooses to check a customer, it will want to build a credit relationship slowly and carefully. Remember, not every customer deserves the same credit terms; thus, it's best to approach credit on a case-by-case basis. One thing to note is how long the company has been in business. Companies that have been around for at least five years are more likely to pay their bills on time—or they wouldn't be around anymore. The key ways to check a customer's credit include credit reports, credit references, financial statements, personal credit reports on the owner or CEO, and letters of credit.

Credit Reports. It's always a good idea to obtain a potential customer's credit report before you extend credit. Credit reports range in price from $15 for a one-page report to more than $1,000 for a detailed filing. The reports show historical payment data; bankruptcy records; any lawsuits, liens, or court judgments against a company; and a risk rating that predicts how likely customers are to pay their bills. Even if a prospective customer has little or no credit history, running a credit report is still worthwhile because it will reveal relevant data, including bankruptcy filings, corporate records, fictitious business name filings, court judgments, and tax liens.

Credit reporting agencies can send a credit report via mail, fax, or via the World Wide Web. Some agencies also provide reports online. If you request a considerable number of reports, you might be able to sign a contract that will reduce a per-report price.

Credit References. In addition to credit reports, or for companies not covered by commercial credit reporting agencies, you may want to check a customer's credit references yourself. These references can be informative, but they aren't foolproof. After all, a customer picks his or her own references. To gain a more realistic picture, ask a customer for a comprehensive list of suppliers. Call several and ask if a potential customer owes them money. If so, find out if payments are being made in a timely manner. Ask these suppliers for names of other suppliers and other customers and contact them as references.

You might want to call the customer's banker as well. While specific information may be inappropriate or illegal for a banker to provide, you may seek some general information. Ask how long the bank has had a relationship with the company. Has the bank given it any credit? If a loan was given, did the company meet its obligations?

Personal Credit Report of the Owner or CEO. When contemplating doing business with a new, closely held private company, it may not be possible to obtain a credit report, references, or financial statements. However, you can run a personal credit check on the owner or CEO of the business. If that person has a strong credit history, it's likely he or she will see to it that the company pays its bills on time. If the owner or CEO has a history of debt dodging or late bill payment, the company could follow suit. If a review raises concerns, schedule a meeting with management to address the issues. You may want to discuss credit issues with any investors in the firm as well.

Red Flags. In addition to the standard inquiries into a company's credit situation, you should keep your eyes open for other things that could indicate a credit problem:

Does the business engage in unusual price-cutting or discounting strategies? Such practices may hinder the company's ability to pay what it owes in a timely fashion. Does the company already have trade credit relationships with other companies? You don't want to work with a customer that is already overextended. Are any company assets already pledged as collateral? Does the company operate in a cyclical industry or in a business sector that is prone to seasonal turns? What is the general economic climate? When business is good you may be more willing to extend credit. When things are slow, however, you may want to be more tightfisted in extending credit to higher-risk customers.

Finally, pay attention to the results of research. Sometimes "no" is the right answer when it comes to extending credit, no matter how much you want the business.

Reading a Credit Report. A credit report is a snapshot of a company's or an individual's financial activities. Credit reports typically include historical payment data, bankruptcy records, Uniform Commercial Code (UCC) filings, bank loan information, leases, payment trends, and comparative industry data.

A typical credit report on a company contains its corporate name, address, and telephone number. It also includes the name of the chief executive officer, the company's Standard Industrial Classification (SIC) code, a description of its line of business, and the date when the company began operations. Also included are the number of employees, sales, and a net worth figure. In many cases, a report includes a numerical credit rating.

Financial information can run the gamut from basic sales and payment data to detailed transactional analysis. The information should include a summary of any lawsuits, liens, or court judgments that are outstanding, plus any relevant bankruptcy filings. If available, there will also be information on changes in ownership, relocations, company acquisitions, and publicly reported news events, including fires or natural disasters. The amount of information depends on the stature of the company and whether it is publicly owned.

Most credit report services focus on publicly held companies. Credit rating resources for privately held and newer companies are less formalized. To check payment practices for smaller companies, try talking to their customers, suppliers, and bankers.

Remember, too, that while credit reports can be important tools, they're not ends in themselves. Before making decisions based on credit reports, you'll want to back up the information with data gleaned from other kinds of company research, as well as from customers, employees, and personal contacts.

Preventing Overdue Accounts

The best way to prevent overdue accounts is to avoid doing business with customers who have bad credit histories. However, if you limited yourself to doing business with companies with spotless credit records, a pool of potential customers would be quite small. And unfortunately, with a growing business you often have no choice but to do business with anyone who wants to do business with you. Even then, you don't always have complete control of the terms of sales agreements. The reality is that the biggest and best clients want to be billed quarterly and then have 60 days to pay you. And you certainly don't want to cut off those clients.

While you don't want to destroy any potential or established business relationships by laying down harsh payment terms, you must take some control of accounts receivable to avoid wreaking havoc with a cash flow. You're not a bank, after all. The following five steps can help cash flow without endangering it.

1. Watch for new customers with bad credit history. You can't expect that a company or a person with a history of bouncing checks or paying their bills late will change their ways when dealing with you. If you must do business with the chronically late, lay down credit rules early and firmly and start the relationship off slowly. Keep the amount of product or services you offer a company with an iffy credit record to a minimum until they've proven themselves worthy. And no matter how much you need the business, never start doing business with another person or company until you have a signed contract clearly stating and agreeing to payment terms.

2. Once you begin doing business with someone, make sure you stamp invoices with the date that payment is due. Don't rely on the customer to look at the invoice date and add 30

days—or whatever the payment terms are—to determine the pay date.

3. Offer discounts for early payment and add interest to late payments. A typical discount is 2 to 3 percent off the total if the bill is paid within 10 days of the invoice date. The maximum amount of interest that can be charged varies by state.

4. Phone customers and start trying to collect the day after a payment is due. Never wait—let them know that you keep close track of accounts receivable.

5. Until customers pay their bills, don't do any more business with them. Do not bend on this rule—you'll only cause yourself more problems and scuttle any chance of collecting what you are owed. If you really want to keep doing business with a customer who owes you, insist that any new products or services they receive from you are COD—cash on delivery.

Collection Agencies

It's easy to extend too much credit when trying to entice companies into doing more business. Extending too much credit can lead to unpaid accounts, which can quickly and severely limit the cash you have to grow a business. If you don't stay on top of overdue accounts, the chance of collecting the money decreases over time.

One way to recover more from delinquent accounts is to hire a collection agency. A collection agency locates debtors and collects the money you are owed. If brought on board early, a collection agency can often recover a substantial portion of unpaid accounts.

In addition to increasing chances of actually getting paid, using an agency saves you time and money—two of your most valuable resources. With their custom-designed phone systems, computers, and software, collection agencies can be more effective in recovering delinquent accounts than you can. Although collection agencies charge between 15 and 50 percent of what they recover, you still end up with more than you probably could have collected on your own.

When selecting an agency, you should think about these considerations.

Find out if the collection agency is a member of the American Collection Agency or the Commercial Law League of America, which require that their members adhere to a code of ethics and are familiar with the Fair Debt Collection Practices Act.

Make sure the agency has insurance that will protect a business if the agency errs during the collections process.

Ask the agency to disclose its typical recovery rate and provide you with a list of references. Contact some of the companies on the list and find out how long it took the agency to collect on late accounts, if it collected the whole debt or a portion of what was owed, and if the companies were satisfied with the agency's collection efforts.

GAAP Accounting Rules

Generally accepted accounting principles (GAAP) is a set of nationally (United States) recognized accounting standards. Using GAAP accounting standards, costs and benefits are accounted for in a recognized way to assure consistency with other firms' accounting principles and for comparing various projects and investments with one another.

Chart of Accounts

The first step in setting up an accounting system is deciding what you want to track. A chart of accounts is simply a list and is kept by every business to record and follow specific entries. Whether you decide to use a manual system or a software program, you can customize the chart of accounts to a particular business.

Account numbers are used as an easy account identification system. The chart of accounts is the fuel for an accounting system. After the chart of accounts, you establish a general ledger system, which is the engine that actually runs an accounting system on a daily basis.

The chart of accounts is the foundation on which you will build an accounting system. Take care to set up a chart of accounts correctly the first time. Keep account descriptions as concise as possible, and leave plenty of room in a numbering system to add accounts in the future.

MANAGERIAL ACCOUNTING
AND FINANCIAL MANAGEMENT

There are several concepts found in accounting systems that serve as decision-making tools for the business owner, manager, or professional.

Fixed, Variable, and Other Types of Costs

Fixed, variable, incremental, opportunity, and sunk costs describe different types of costs to the business.

Fixed costs include all costs that do not vary with activity for an accounting period. Fixed costs are the inevitable costs that must be paid at any time regardless of the level of output and of the amount of resources used. A fixed cost does not, in theory, vary with activity or sales. Such costs often include offices, factories, depreciation, and insurance or professional indemnity.

Variable costs are costs that are some function of activity. Variable costs include the obvious things such as sales commissions, raw materials, components, distribution, and deal financing.

Incremental costs are those costs (or revenues) that change due to an incremental change in activity, as compared to those that are unaffected. They are costs that would occur if a particular course of action were taken.

Opportunity costs refer to alternatives or opportunities that are sacrificed in favor of the chosen solution. Because resources are limited, any decision in favor of one project (service, goods, upgrade, etc.) means doing without something else.

Sunk costs include prior costs that cannot be recovered.

Activity-Based Costing

A financial analysis costing methodology associates specific efforts and personnel with specific tasks, allowing the tasks to be analyzed and the current costs dedicated to specific tasks to be well understood. A simple activity-based costing analysis can be an analysis of work performed by a specific employee or work unit in a year and the cost associated with each time the work is done to arrive at an annual cost for that activity. For example, a company considering outsourcing its payroll function may analyze how many people in the human resources and accounting departments are involved in processing payroll each pay period, assess the associated salaries and overhead, multiply by the number of pay periods per year, and arrive at an activity-based cost of payroll processing. This assessment may then be compared to the quote from an outsource payroll preparation company to determine the relative cost/benefit of outsourcing versus internally processing the payroll function.

TAXES

Small Business Tax Basics

Next to profits, taxes may be the most important issue facing every small business. You'll want to be sure that you are meeting all your responsibilities to the tax collector—and also seizing every opportunity to reduce taxes. Use these tax tips to make sure you're not giving Uncle Sam more than his due.

Writing It Off: Deductions

You can deduct all "ordinary and necessary" business expenses from revenues to reduce taxable income (see "Tax Deductions" subsection later in the chapter). Some deductions are obvious—expenditures in such areas as business travel, equipment, salaries, or rent. But the rules governing write-offs aren't always simple. Don't overlook the following potential deductions:

> ✔ *Business losses.* Business losses can be deducted against personal income to reduce taxes. If losses exceed personal income this year, you can use some of this year's business loss to reduce a taxable income in future years.

✔ *Employee taxes.* If you hire employees, you'll have to pay—or withhold from their salaries—a variety of taxes:

> *Withholding.* Social Security (FICA), Medicare, and federal and state income taxes must be withheld from employees' pay.
>
> *Employer matching.* You must match the FICA and Medicare taxes and pay them along with employees.
>
> *Unemployment tax.* Federal and state unemployment taxes.

Quarterly Estimated Taxes

This area of the tax code trips up many an entrepreneur and is especially vexing for home-based businesses. Failure to keep up with an estimated tax bill can create cash flow problems as well as the potential for punishing Internal Revenue Service (IRS) penalties. The antidote is simple—know your responsibilities:

✔ Who should pay? You probably must pay quarterly estimated taxes if you expect a total tax bill in a given year to exceed $500.

✔ How much should you pay? By the end of the year, you must pay either 90 percent of the tax you owe for the year or 100 percent of last year's tax amount (the figure is 110 percent if your income exceeds $150,000). An accountant can help you calculate payments. Otherwise, you can subtract expenses from your income each quarter and apply an income tax rate (and any self-employment tax rate) to the resulting figure (your quarterly profit).

Sales Taxes

Many services are under the taxable radar screen, but most products are taxable (typical exceptions are food and prescription drugs). States keep adding to the list of taxable services, however, so check with a state's department of taxation to find out if you should charge sales tax on services. If you do sell a product or service that is subject to sales tax, you must register with the state's tax department. Then you must track taxable and nontaxable sales and include that information on a sales tax return.

Deadlines

As a salaried worker, you have to remember just one or two tax-related dates: April 15 and perhaps December 31. But other dates may matter just as much or more when you are involved in your own business:

- ✔ *Annual returns.* Most annual returns are due April 15 for unincorporated companies and S corporations. A C corporation, though, must file an annual corporate return within two and a half months after the close of its fiscal year.
- ✔ **Estimated taxes.** Estimated taxes are due four times a year: April 15, June 15, September 15, and January 15.
- ✔ *Sales taxes.* Sales taxes are due quarterly or monthly, depending on the rules in a state.
- ✔ *Employee taxes.* Depending on the size of a payroll, employee taxes are due weekly, monthly, or quarterly.

Taxes and Incorporation

For federal tax purposes, it's often best for a start-up company to be an S corporation rather than a regular corporation. This is so even though recent changes in tax rates have made the decision a bit more complex. Still, to make sure an S corporation is best for you, speak to a knowledgeable accountant or tax adviser. Also keep in mind that a limited liability company (LLC) may be an even better choice.

Starting as an S corporation rather than a regular corporation may be wise for two reasons:

1. Income from an S corporation is taxed at only one level rather than two—a total tax bill will likely be less.
2. If a business operates at a loss the first year, you can pass that loss through to a personal income tax return, using it to offset

income that you (and a spouse, if you're married) may have from other sources.

Your decision to be an S corporation isn't permanent. If you later find there are tax advantages to being a regular corporation, you can easily change an S corporation status.

Employee Taxes

A business is responsible for collecting and filing some taxes on behalf of employees. The following is an overview of what you have to do to withhold and match taxes on an employee's paychecks:

✔ *Get an employer identification number (EIN).* A business must report employment taxes or give tax statements to employees; you need an EIN to do this. Get Form SS-4 (Application for Employer Identification Number) from the Web, or by calling 1-800-Tax-Form (1-800-829-3676).

✔ *Deposit employee withholdings on time.* Instead of paying the federal government directly, you deposit with an authorized financial institution such as a commercial bank (1) the income tax you have withheld and (2) both the employer portion and the employee portion of Social Security and Medicare taxes.

✔ *Issue Form 1099-Misc to independent contractors.* Doctors, lawyers, veterinarians, contractors, direct sellers, qualified real estate agents, and others who pursue an independent trade in which they offer their services to the public are usually not employees but independent contractors. A worker is defined as an independent contractor if he controls what he does and how the work is performed. What matters is that you have the right to control the details of how the services are performed.

✔ *Avoid payment penalties.* For an employer, paying and reporting employment taxes is a "fiduciary responsibility," and that responsibility is taken very seriously by Congress, the IRS, and the judicial branch of the government. The IRS can impose deposit penalties ranging from 2 percent of the amount due (for payments that are one to five days late) to 15 percent (for amounts not paid within 10 days after receiving the first IRS notice).

Preparing for a Tax Audit

A tax audit is an experience every businessperson hopes to avoid. If the IRS does pay a business a visit, however, understanding what an auditor might look for can make the difference between a minor inconvenience and a major hardship. During a full-fledged audit, an IRS agent may look at several specific items in a tax return and business records, including:

- ✔ *Income.* The IRS will compare bank statements and deposits to the income you reported. They will also review invoices, sales records, and receipts, along with a general ledger and other formal bookkeeping records. If you received gifts of money or an inheritance, keep records to document how much you received. Without proof, the IRS may classify these as income and tax them as such. They will also classify any exchange of goods or services in lieu of cash (such as barter transactions) as taxable income.

- ✔ *Expenses and deductions.* An auditor may compare canceled checks, bills marked "paid," bank statements, credit card statements, receipts for payment or charitable gifts, and other business records to the expenses and deductions you reported on a return. They may pay special attention to reported debts or business losses; charitable gifts; and travel, meal, and entertainment expenses. Keep a log to substantiate travel, meal, and entertainment expenses and be sure to deduct only legitimate business expenses.

- ✔ *Loans and interest.* An auditor may review loan paperwork, deposits, bank statements, credit card statements, receipts, and canceled checks to verify that you used borrowed money only to cover business expenses. This is important, because you are allowed to deduct interest on business-related loans.

✔ *Employee classifications.* The IRS will review employee classifications on a return and check this data against time cards, job descriptions, benefit plans, invoices, canceled checks, contracts, and other business records. Auditors will pay particular attention to independent contractor classifications, because many firms improperly classify regular employees as contractors.

✔ *Payroll.* Auditors will examine canceled checks, tax returns, deposits, business records, and other forms to check for completeness, accuracy, and timely filing. They will also review records documenting state, federal, and Social Security (FICA) withholding, Medicare taxes, advance earned income credit, unemployment compensation, and workers' compensation premiums. The IRS will also examine salaries and bonuses paid to owners and officers of a business to be sure they are legitimate and within industry standards.

✔ *Other records.* An auditor can also inspect records from a tax preparer or accountant, bank or other financial institution, suppliers, and customers. In addition to inspecting a business, an auditor may inspect personal finances. The IRS may compare a current lifestyle with the income presented on a tax return to determine if they are compatible. An auditor may also talk with others who are knowledgeable about you and your financial situation.

Tax Deductions

Taxes are an inevitable—and painful—part of every business owner's life. But there are ways to reduce, if not eliminate, a company's tax burden, if you know how to use business-expense tax deductions to an advantage.

Most business owners know they owe business taxes only on their net business profit—that is, their total profits after they subtract their deductions. As a result, knowing how to take full advantage of a deductible business expense can dramatically lower taxable profits. You can legally deduct a number of expenses commonly associated with a trade or business. Common deductions include:

- ✔ Employee wages and most employee benefits.
- ✔ Rent or lease payments.
- ✔ Interest on business loans.
- ✔ Real estate taxes on business property.
- ✔ State, local, and foreign income taxes assessed to a business.
- ✔ Business insurance.
- ✔ Advertising and promotion costs.
- ✔ Employee education and training.
- ✔ Education to maintain or improve required business skills.
- ✔ Legal and professional fees.
- ✔ Utilities.
- ✔ Telephone costs.
- ✔ Office repairs.

If you have a home-based business or a home office, you can also deduct a portion of residential real estate taxes, utilities, and telephone expenses as long as you can prove the legitimacy of the home-based business.

Finally, always maintain complete and accurate business records to document deposits, income, expenses, and deductions. If the Internal Revenue Service audits a business, it may require you to demonstrate that each entry on a tax return is correct.

Tax laws change annually, and they can be very complex. Always consult an accountant or tax attorney for assistance, strategies, and recommendations for an individual situation.

REFERENCES

Adelman, Philip. *Entrepreneurial Finance: Finance for Small Business.* Upper Saddle River, NJ: Prentice Hall, 2000.

Gill, James. *Financial Basics for Small Business Success.* Menlo Park, CA: Crisp, 1996.

Livingstone, John, and Theodore Grossman. *The Portable MBA in Finance and Accounting.* New York: John Wiley & Sons, 1997.

www.allbusiness.com/finance&accounting.

www.business.com/accounting.

www.entrepreneur.com/money.

Chapter 7

International, National, and Local Economics

E conomics is a social science that analyzes the choices made by people and governments in allocating scarce resources. While this definition sounds rather scientific, most people have a fairly intuitive understanding of the laws of supply and demand. When making purchasing decisions, we all decide what products or activities fit into our schedules, budgets, and needs; and through these economic choices, we vote for what we want to be available in our market and at what price. The economic system is the social institution through which goods and services are produced, distributed, and consumed. As you can surmise, the economic decisions that we make affect economic systems that are often global in scope. There is a combination of domestic and international policies that allocate resources, commodities, labor, tariffs, and so on that go into the price composition of the goods and services that we purchase and consume. These factors, however, emerge on a couple of different levels that economists study: microeconomics and macroeconomics.

MICROECONOMICS AND MACROECONOMICS

Microeconomics is the study of small economic units such as individual consumers, families, and businesses. It is the study of the individual parts of the economy and how prices are determined and how prices in turn determine the production, distribution, and use of goods and services. Macroeconomics refers to the study of a country's overall economic issues. Although these two disciplines are often addressed separately, they are interrelated, as macroeconomic issues help shape the decisions that affect individuals, families, and businesses.

Another area of economics focuses on the global impact of emerging markets. The financial markets of developing economies in Asia such as China, India, Indonesia, Malaysia, South Korea, Taiwan, and Thailand are among the most important. In Latin America, Argentina, Brazil, Chile, Colombia, Mexico, Peru, and Venezuela are also demonstrating large amounts of economic/financial activity. Africa has five countries considered emerging markets in the international arena: Ghana, Ivory Coast, Kenya, Nigeria, and South Africa. In Europe, the Czech Republic, Greece, Hungary, Poland, Portugal, Russia, and Turkey are all markets that are striving toward the financial stability of the European Union (EU).

SUPPLY AND DEMAND

The basic relationships in the study of economic systems are the factors that drive the forces of these economies: supply and demand. Supply refers to the willingness and ability of sellers to provide goods and services for sale at different prices. Demand refers to the willingness and ability of buyers to purchase goods and services at different prices.

Factors Driving Demand

The study of economics focuses on the "wants" of the players in a market and the limited financial resources that they have to spend on their wants. The dynamics between supply and demand can be best understood when looking at a demand curve. Demand is defined as the relationship between the price of the good and the amount or quantity the consumer is willing and able to purchase in a specified time period, given constant levels of the other determinants—tastes, income, prices of related goods, expectations, and number of buyers. The graph of the demand curve demonstrates the amount of product that buyers will purchase at different prices. Typically demand rises as the price of a product falls and demand decreases as prices rise. The sensitivity of the changes in price and demand is called price elasticity.

Products and services have different degrees of price elasticity. For example, if gasoline increases in price, overall demand may not be proportionately reduced (i.e., a low degree of price elasticity), as people still need gas to fuel their vehicles (assuming there are no substitutes or alternatives—for example, a move toward using public transportation). If, however, the price of airline travel increases greatly, it may be likely that demand for air travel will have a greater than proportionate decline. This means that there is a relatively high degree of price elasticity.

Businesses need to carefully monitor the factors that may affect demand. If they aren't keeping a careful eye on these different demand elements as related to their business, assuredly their competitors will find a competitive advantage that can affect an organization's long-term survival.

Factors Driving Supply

The supply aspect of an economic system refers to the relationship between different prices and the quantities that sellers will offer: Generally, the higher the price, the more of a product or service that will be offered.

The law of supply and demand states that prices are set by the intersection of the supply and the demand. The point where supply and demand meet identifies the equilibrium price, or the prevailing market price at which you can expect to purchase a product. All of these factors of supply and demand, then, come down to setting a price for the product or service that the market will bear.

ECONOMIC SYSTEMS

In the twentieth century, there were primarily two competing economic systems that provided answers to the questions of what to produce and for whom, given limited resources: "command economies" directed by a centralized government and "market economies" based on private enterprise. History has proven that, worldwide, the central command-economy model has not sustained economic growth and has not provided long-term economic security for its citizens.

Private Enterprise

In fact, many government-controlled economies are turning to privatization to improve incentives and efficiency. Privatization is the selling of government-owned businesses to private investors. This trend has provided an opportunity for U.S. firms to own businesses in foreign countries that previously prohibited U.S. investment. Why is this trend appearing? We will take a look at the four different types of market structures that are currently identified in the private enterprise system.

The private enterprise system, or market economy, is centered on the economic theory/belief/philosophy of capitalism and competition. Capitalism is an economic system in which businesses are rewarded for meeting the needs and demands of consumers. It allows for private ownership of all businesses. Entrepreneurs, desiring to earn a profit, create businesses that they believe will serve the needs of the consumers. Capitalist countries offer foreign firms opportunities to compete without excessive trade barriers.

As a result of the ineffectiveness of command economies, governments tend to favor the hands-off attitude toward controlling business ownership, profits, and resource allocations that go along with capitalism and market economies with competition regulating economic life and creating opportunities and challenges that businesses must handle to succeed.

A Taxonomy of Competition. There are four different types of competition in a private enterprise system: pure competition, monopolistic competition, oligopolies, and monopolies.

Pure competition is a market or industry in which there are many competitors. It is easy to enter the market, as there are few barriers to entry and many people/organizations are able to offer products that are similar to each other. In a market where there is pure competition, a lower price becomes the key factor and leads buyers to prefer one seller over another, and there is likely to be little differentiation between products. Additionally, the amount that each individual seller can offer constitutes such a small proportion that when acting alone it is powerless to affect the price. Therefore, individual firms in these commodity-like markets have very little control over the price.

Monopolistic competition means that there are fewer competitors, but there is still competition. In this market environment, it is somewhat difficult to enter the market. The barriers to entry could be due to location, access to commodities, technology, or capital investment levels. The result is that there are usually differences in products offered by competing firms; perhaps they serve the same function, but there are differentiations that rely on consumer preferences to make a choice. Due to the differentiation factor, individual firms are able to have some sort of control over the prices. They can choose to charge a premium or a discount to set their product apart and affect the demand.

Oligopoly is a market situation with few competitors. The few competitors exist due to high barriers to entry, and a few large sellers vie for, and collectively account for, a relatively large market share. The products or services in this market may be similar (telephone companies) or they may be different (supermarkets). In the oligopolistic market situation, the individual firms do have some control over prices (Whole Foods Market can charge more for produce/products than Albertsons) and can create differentiation or vie for more of the market share by having price be part of their consumer acquisition strategy.

Unlike the board game, a monopoly exists in the private enterprise system when there is absolutely no other competition. That means that there is only one provider that exists to provide a good or service. In this case, it is often the government that regulates who can enter the market, so there are no specific barriers to entry. But the government regulations ensure that there are no competing products or services in the market. The lack of competition yields considerable power over prices in a pure, or unregulated, monopoly, but there is little control over prices in a regulated monopoly. An example of a pure monopoly is the issuance of a patent for a drug, in the case of a pharmaceutical company. Some pharmaceutical drugs have no current substitute, in which case the patent holder pharmaceutical company has a monopoly in the production/distribution of that drug. In this case the government guarantees that no other company can produce the drug, and that provides a sufficient market entry barrier. Monopolies of this sort, however, arise rarely because pharmaceutical drugs may have substitutes and the regulatory barriers to entry are typically temporary (for a period of a few years).

Planned Economies

In addition to the private enterprise system, planned economies are another market structure in the world economy. In a planned economy, government controls determine business ownership, profits, and resource allocation. Countries that existed with planned economies, however, have not been highly successful.

The most common theory of a planned economy is communism, which purports that all property is shared equally by the people in a community under the direction of a strong central government. It is an economic system that involves public ownership of businesses. Rather than entrepreneurs, the government decides what products consumers will be offered and in what quantities. As the central planner, the government establishes trade policies that historically have been very restrictive in allowing foreign companies the opportunity to compete. Communism was proposed by Karl Marx and developed and implemented by V. I. Lenin. In Marxist theory, "communism" denotes the final stage of human historical development in which the people rule both politically and economically.

The communist philosophy is based on each individual contributing to the nation's overall economic success and the country's resources are distributed according to each person's needs. The central government owns the means of production and everyone works for state-owned enterprises. Further, the government determines what people can buy because it dictates what is produced.

Looking specifically at China and Russia, we can see what led to the failure of communism. First of all, their constitutions had little or no meaning, so although the government created laws, they bore no power. Second, the government owned the means of production and made all of the economic decisions. Therefore, market forces were not allowed to work, and the laws of supply and demand were not followed. Third, the citizens of these countries had limited rights and all the citizens were subject to Communist Party control. Individuals existed to serve the state and had virtually no freedom for themselves. All of these factors contributed to the downfall of communism and as a result, China and Russia are currently privatizing and borrowing other capitalistic methods in an attempt to improve their economic situations and convert to a more market-based economy. They are desperately trying to get the market to find an equilibrium for their goods and services that we all too often take for granted.

Socialism

Another economic system is socialism, which is characterized by government ownership and operation of major industries. For example, when telecommunications, gasoline, or some other major industry is owned by the government, this is considered a socialistic economy. Socialism is an economic system that contains some features of both capitalism and communism. Socialist governments allow people to own businesses and property and to select their own jobs. However, these governments are involved in providing a variety of public services, such as generous unemployment benefits, comprehensive health care for all citizens, and public transit. These public services are paid for by high tax rates on income. Entrepreneurs, not surprisingly, have less incentive to establish businesses if the tax rates are excessively high.

Socialism is based on the belief that major industries are too important to a society to be left in private hands; however, private ownership is allowed in industries considered to be less crucial to social welfare.

As socialism is retreating, there are new theories of regulation emerging. The new theories aren't aiming to regulate economic relations between individuals, as socialism did, but rather they seek to regulate social relations in general. For example, there is a desire to increase the "social capital" in communities. If "social capital" is defined as norms and networks that encourage cooperation and trust between individuals, then the existence of social capital can be beneficial. It reduces transaction costs, assists the diffusion of knowledge, and can enhance the sense of community well-being. The questions arising now, however, are whether the government *can* create social capital and, even more fundamental, if the government *should* create social capital. Although the traditional form of socialism is no longer touted as a successful market structure, remnants of it can still be seen in today's economy.

The majority of market economies that we see today, however, are mixed market economies. These are economic systems that display characteristics of both planned and market economies. In the mixed market economy, government-owned firms frequently operate alongside private enterprises. Good examples of this can be found in Europe where the respective governments have traditionally controlled certain key industries such as railroads, banking, and telecommunications. What is seen today, however, is a trend toward privatizing many of these state-owned industries. In 1986 the United Kingdom privatized the gas industry, in 1987 it privatized the steel industry, and in 1989 water was privatized. Today, Austria is following suit and is proceeding with the privatization of steel, oil, and chemicals.

FOUR STAGES OF THE BUSINESS CYCLE

The business cycle, also called the economic cycle, refers to the recurring series of events of expansion, boom, bust, and recession. The length of business cycles over time are rarely alike. The business cycle experiences periodic cyclical expansions and contractions in overall economic activity. For example, the United States has experienced 11 complete business cycles since the end of World War II. Business cycles are relevant because business decisions and consumer buying patterns differ at each stage of the business cycle, and it is important to know where you are in a business cycle when developing your organizational strategy.

Prosperity, or the "boom" part of the business cycle, occurs when unemployment is low, strong consumer confidence leads to record purchases and as a result, businesses expand to take advantage of the opportunities created by the market. A good example of the market experiencing prosperity took place in Silicon Valley from 1998 to 2001. Suddenly the market identified technology as the next big business opportunity, so companies were adopting online technologies at a record pace; brick and mortar businesses were creating electronic marketplaces for the first time. As common sense tells us, no economy can sustain a boom forever and as we saw in Silicon Valley, a recession, and sometimes a spot-depression (a short-term slow-down), can follow the prosperity stage.

A recession is a cyclical economic contraction that lasts for at least six months. Economists agree that a recession results in a downturn lasting for at least two consecutive quarters. During a recession consumers frequently postpone major purchases, such as homes and vehicles, and businesses slow production, postpone expansion plans, reduce inventories, and cut workers. As a result, unemployment rises and consumer demand decreases.

A depression is classified as a recession, or economic slowdown, that continues in a downward spiral over an extended period of time. It is also characterized by continued high unemployment and low consumer spending. Many economists suggest that sufficient government tools are available to prevent even a severe recession from turning into a depression. For example, federal, state, and local governments can make investments to improve the country's infrastructure as a means of bringing the market out of a depression. They can invest in transportation systems and public facilities such as schools and universities, or perhaps they can loan money to small businesses to help the economy grow. Governments can also influence the economy through regulations in fiscal and monetary policy, which will be discussed in more detail later in this chapter.

Eventually these tools contribute to the next stage in the business cycle: recovery. The recovery period is when economic activity begins to pick up. Consumer confidence improves, which leads to increased spending on big items such as homes and vehicles. Unemployment also begins to fall, and people are working and contributing to the economy again.

THE STABILITY OF A NATION'S ECONOMY

As already discussed, economies are the result of an interrelated mixture of numerous forces.

Productivity

The gross domestic product (GDP) is the value of all goods and services produced within a nation's borders each year. It is a very popular economic indicator and provides a benchmark for the nation's overall economic activity.

Productivity is the relationship between the goods and services produced and the inputs needed to produce them. During expansionary periods, productivity tends to rise as fewer resources are needed to produce greater levels of output. During recessions, then, productivity might stagnate or decrease overall.

Inflation and Deflation

Price-level changes are related to the value of the economy's currency. Inflation is a period of rising prices caused by a combination of excess demand and increases in the costs of the factors of production. "Inflation" is defined as a rise in the general level of prices of goods and services over a specified period of time. In the United States, the rate of inflation is usually measured as the percentage change in the consumer price index (CPI), which includes the prices of a wide variety of consumer goods and services in categories such as food, clothing, medical services, housing, and transportation.

Demand-pull inflation occurs when there is an excess of demand relative to supply. In these conditions, a relative shortage of products or services gives producers the leverage to increase prices. Cost-push inflation occurs when there are rises in the costs of the factors of production. The costs of either the labor, commodities, or manufacturing rise and push prices up to cover the increased costs.

Hyperinflation is a period characterized by rapidly rising prices. We remember the images of people from Communist Russia standing in long lines to purchase bread because of hyperinflationary costs.

Inflation impacts the economy because more money is needed to sustain a given standard of living. If people receive a fixed income and suddenly the cost of bread increases dramatically, it is easy to see the negative impact caused by this increased price.

Inflation can be good news, though, to those who are experiencing a rising income or those with debts at fixed interest rates. Businesses, however, find it difficult to make long-range plans in high inflationary conditions, because budgeting and forecasting depend largely on the prices of products and services needed to conduct business. Low inflation, in contrast, makes it easier for businesses to make long-term plans—it becomes easier to predict prices and costs. Low inflation is also associated with low interest rates, encouraging major purchases by consumers and fueling business expansion.

Deflation is the price-level change referred to during a period of falling prices. While deflation sounds good, it can have disastrous consequences; the Great Depression was a general period of deflation. Prices fell, but so did employment and wages for those lucky enough to be employed, as well as availability of most goods and services.

Relative price levels are measured by two common indicators. The consumer price index measures the monthly average change in the prices of a basket of goods and specific services. The producer price index (PPI) looks at prices from the seller's perspective (finished goods, intermediate goods, and crude goods).

Employment Levels

Employment levels have a major impact on a nation's economy. In fact, the unemployment rate is one of the most popular economic indicators that most people intuitively use to understand the state of the economy. The unemployment rate is usually expressed as the percentage of total workers who are actively seeking work but are currently unemployed. These indicators tend to increase during recessions and decrease during expansions.

Because the unemployment rate is so important, we're going to discuss some different categories that have been created to characterize an economy's state of unemployment.

Frictional unemployment is when someone is temporarily not working. A good example is a recent graduate who is looking for work but has yet to find a job. *Seasonal* unemployment occurs when people are not working during some months, but they are not looking for a job during that period. People involved in the tourism industry or seasonal farmworkers are good examples of this. *Structural* unemployment results when people are not working because there is no demand for their particular skill set. An example might be someone who graduates with a Ph.D. in medieval economics. There is a relatively low demand for people with this skill set, so structural unemployment results for many in that field. People who fall into this category, however, may be training for a new job and developing new skills while they look for work. *Cyclical* unemployment results when there is an economic slowdown and people are looking for work but there aren't enough jobs. This was the case for many MBAs who graduated in 2001 and 2002. The economic recession resulted in fewer jobs, and even highly skilled graduates with advanced degrees had difficulty finding work.

The unemployment rate does not include the so-called discouraged workers, out-of-work people who are no longer looking for jobs.

International Diversification

As a company, one way to mitigate some of these economic uncertainties is to diversify the effects by maintaining markets in two or more countries. Diversifying into two separate market economies/environments reduces risks by hedging economic bets across multiple economic systems.

Another area in which diversification makes sense for the international business is in the political risk dimension. Political risk represents the risk that another country's political actions may adversely affect a business. Carried to an extreme, a foreign government may take over a U.S. firm's foreign subsidiary without compensating the U.S. firm. A more common risk is the threat of higher tax rates or restrictions on the repatriation of profits to the U.S. parent firm. In general, large-scale political events—such as military coups, social unrest, and currency crises—are referred to as macropolitical risks. Conversely, small-scale events—such as expropriation, discriminatory regulation, and terrorism—are referred to as micropolitical risks.

One of the most basic political risks that you can mitigate is the fluctuations in exchange rates. Exchange rate risk, or currency risk, is the risk of an investment's value changing because of change in the currency exchange rates. For example, a weak dollar is likely to increase both foreign sales and profits. These results are due to the lowering of the selling price of the exported goods, because fewer units of the foreign currency are now required to purchase U.S.-made goods or services. A strong dollar is likely to decrease exports and profits. The appreciation of the U.S. dollar against a foreign currency causes the purchase price of U.S. goods abroad to increase so that it takes more units of the foreign currency to buy a given amount of U.S.-made goods.

Monetary and Fiscal Policy: Managing an Economy's Performance

Monetary policy is the regulation of the money supply and interest rates by a central bank, such as the U.S. Federal Reserve, in order to control inflation and stabilize currency. In the United States the Fed is responsible for managing this process. If the economy is heating up, the Fed can withdraw money from the banking system, raise the reserve requirement, or raise the discount rate to make the economy cool down. This is referred to as a restrictive monetary policy and slows economic growth. If growth is slowing, the Fed can reverse the process—increase the money supply, lower the reserve requirement, and decrease the discount rate. This is referred to as an expansionary monetary policy, with lower interest rates.

Fiscal policy is the decision that the government makes to spend money or increase taxes for the specific purpose of stabilizing the economy. Government increases in spending and lowering of taxes tend to stimulate economic growth, while decreasing government spending and increasing taxes tends to slow economic growth. This makes sense when we think about the individual taxpayer's disposable income. The more money individuals have, the more they will be able to spend on goods and services in the market and therefore stimulate market growth.

The primary sources of government funds to cover the costs of its annual budget are raised through taxation of its citizens, fees collected from business, and borrowing against assets. The U.S. federal budget has gone from a surplus to a deficit in recent years—it is overspending its resources. In order to fund this budget deficit, the federal government will have to borrow billions of dollars in the coming years.

GLOBAL ECONOMIC CHALLENGES
OF THE TWENTY-FIRST CENTURY

As U.S. economies and policies become increasingly interrelated across borders and oceans, we face a more complex economic picture. The opportunities that go along with this more global picture are great, but so too are the challenges. Cellular telephones, computers, disease-resistant crops, satellites, biotechnology, and fiber-optic networks are among the twentieth-century technologies that will shape political, social, and economic realities well into the twenty-first century—realities that include the continuing globalization of business, culture, and health care. So what are the specific challenges that we need to be aware of?

International Terrorism

> Surprise, when it happens to a government, is likely to be a complicated, diffuse, bureaucratic thing. It includes neglect of responsibility but also responsibility so poorly defined or so ambiguously delegated that action gets lost. It includes gaps in intelligence, but also intelligence that, like a string of pearls too precious to wear, is too sensitive to give to those who need it. It includes the alarm that fails to work, but also the alarm that has gone off so often it has been disconnected. It includes the unalert watchman, but also the one who knows he'll be chewed out by his superior if he gets higher authority out of bed. It includes the contingencies that occur to no one, but also those that everyone assumes somebody else is taking care of. It includes straightforward procrastination, but also decisions protracted by internal disagreement. It includes, in addition, the inability of individual human beings to rise to the occasion until they are sure it is the occasion—which is usually too late.

The report, *Countering the Changing Threat of International Terrorism*, written by the National Commission on Terrorism, begins with these words by Thomas C. Schelling. In this succinct and clear description of surprise, the many elements of international terrorism are captured. Terrorism succeeds because of the element of surprise and, unfortunately, surprise is a factor that we cannot always control.

It used to be that international terrorism happened to Americans only when we were not on our home turf. September 11th, however, showed us that we are no longer safe within our own borders. Terrorist attacks are becoming more lethal, too. Most terrorist organizations active in the 1970s and 1980s had clear political objectives. They tried to calibrate their attacks to produce just enough bloodshed to get attention for their cause, but not so much as to alienate public support. Today, as we have seen, the objectives are increasingly religious, economic, or personal (against an ethnic group) in nature.

In his paper "International Terrorism in the 21st Century," Frank Goldstein points out a couple of options to counter the new threats posed to nations due to international terrorism. One option, which received some success after the World Trade Center bombing in 1993, is the economic incentive or bounty. The U.S. government offered a reward of several million dollars for information leading to the person or persons responsible for the bombing. An informant in Pakistan provided the information that led to the arrest of an individual in Islamabad, Pakistan, and he was immediately taken to the United States to await trial.

Although the bounty or reward program seems to have succeeded in 1993, continued terrorist activity demonstrates that these issues of international terrorism are very complicated.

A second option for global nation states to thwart terrorism is "national resolve." It should be acknowledged that a foolproof system against terrorism in democratic societies does not exist. Simple procedures such as better intelligence and improved physical security of critical sites will, in most cases, deter a particular terrorist group.

Economics, technology, and the whims of both criminals and psychotics will produce ongoing and, at times, spectacular events. A result of terrorism in the United States will be more public and political efforts to counter terrorism by the West. Sadly, terrorism in the third world and in developing countries will continue almost unabated.

Shift to a Global Information Economy

The information economy is affecting supply chains, digital technologies, information and communication technologies, technology-enabled marketing; it is pushing businesses to go wireless, changing organizational structures, and increasing the value of intellectual property.

Some think the movement to an information economy is being oversold as the key to economic opportunity. Information technology can help people learn how to absorb knowledge generated elsewhere and combine it with local needs and local knowledge and may help raise real economic returns on investments, but there are still more familiar development challenges (e.g., structural unemployment, social inequality, and an undereducated workforce).

Aging of the World's Population

The world's population is getting older and older as a result of dropping fertility rates and urbanization. Europe provides an excellent example of how the aging population is changing policy and business. Fertility rates have plummeted, especially in southern Europe, to the point that every 10 Italian women are expected to have just 12 children in their lifetimes, and every 10 Spanish women just 11. As a group, the countries of the EU are going to see their populations shrink, unless they allow significant levels of immigration.

The situation right now is not unique to Europe. In fact, well over half of the world's elderly (people aged 65 and older) now live in developing nations (59 percent in 2000), and this is projected to grow to 71 percent by 2030. Many developing countries have had significant downturns in their rates of natural population increase, and as this process accelerates, age structures will change.

Consumers

It is important to consider that businesses ultimately fail or succeed because of consumer preferences and their ability to manage scarce resources. Whether your business provides a product or service to the end user or to an intermediary, your product or service may or may not be chosen depending on consumer preferences. Part of what goes into the consumers' choice is the perception of quality.

U.S. consumers have the perception that certain foreign-made goods are of higher quality than U.S.-made goods. In the past this has been true, for example, of cars and electronic goods made in Japan. French wine and Swiss watches are other examples of goods that some U.S. consumers believe are better than similar domestic products.

Another factor that goes into consumer preferences is as simple as personal buying habits. This includes taking into account where people like to shop, what brands they prefer, and what associations they might have with your product or service.

SUMMARY

Creating a long-term global strategy is a complicated but important task. As is evident throughout this chapter, no country is an economic island, and the economy truly is global. A growing number of businesses have become true multinational firms, with operating facilities around the world. They have figured out how to mitigate their risks both politically and economically, but they have also found how events in one nation can reverberate around the world.

As U.S. businesses contemplate and engage in global expansion, there are endless opportunities, but also potential risks. The U.S. market is also attractive to foreign firms. For an organization to be successful in today's global economy, its owners and stakeholders must look across borders and understand the global community.

REFERENCES

Crooks, Ed. "Europe: EU Feels Pressure to Rethink Policy on Immigration." *Financial Times* (October 9, 2000).

Goldstein, Frank. "International Terrorism in the 21st Century." www.au.zof.mil/au/awc/awcgate/goldstei.doc.

http://usinfo.state.gov/products/pubs/market/mktec1.htm.

National Commission on Terrorism. *Countering the Changing Threat of International Terrorism.* www.fas.org/irp/threat/commission.html. 2000.

Pyzdek, Thomas. *The Failure of Management.* Tucson, AZ: Quality Publishing, 1996.

Reeves, Richard. "Brown's Stealth Socialism Has Backfired: Public Opinion Is Now More Tory Than Ever." *New Statesman* (September 15, 2003).

Roskam, John. "Is Social Capital the New Socialism?" *IPA Review* (September 2003).

"U.S. Economy: Execs Accentuate the Positive." *Modern Bulk Transporter* (January 2004).

World Economic Forum: The Global Information Technology Report. 2003–2004. NY: Oxford University Press, 2004.

www.marketingpower.com.

SECTION III

MARKETS AND STRATEGY

8

Marketing, Strategy, and Competitive Analysis

We've all heard someone in the course of business say that "marketing is fluff and hype." However, the wisest, most savvy, and most successful businesspeople understand that marketing is far from that. Marketing is everything you do on a daily basis to sell a product or provide a service to a customer. Marketing encompasses every way in which a customer perceives a business and everything that generates enough interest from a customer and encourages customers to actually pay for the product or service. As Peter Vessenes suggests, cash may be king, "but marketing is everything."

What does it really mean to market your service or product? Often, people immediately equate marketing with advertising and see only the amount of money that advertising will cost. However, by definition, marketing is actually the process by which we offer goods or services up for sale. Forward-thinking marketing strategists suggest that marketing is not a "cost" or "expense" but rather an investment, because much of the benefit of marketing is longer-term and may take years to fully provide its benefit.

Marketing has also been referred to as a social and managerial process by which individuals and groups obtain what they need and want through creating, offering, and exchanging products of value with others. Additionally, it is all too often equated only with the more focused function of selling. But marketing encompasses a wider range of activities that must be a fully integrated process and, indeed, will form a foundation and catalyst for making sales. Further, the key to successful sales is a consistent proactive marketing strategy.

MARKETING'S KEY COMPONENTS: CREATING VALUE FOR THE CUSTOMER

What, then, is the key to a consistent proactive marketing strategy? First and foremost it is a philosophy that dedicates resources of the firm to ensuring that the wants, needs, and demands of the customer are the firm's focus. This customer-focused mentality is the foundation of the strategy that makes up the entire marketing process.

Second, it is a plan, supported by the firm's philosophy. Once the philosophy is in place, a plan can give direction, guidance, and a structure for proactive strategies that will increase sales and improve business relationships. Often firms find themselves dedicating resources to marketing activities—from trade shows to flyers—and spending money on marketing that is not targeted to the right audience at the right time. This is reactive marketing with a shotgun, rather than a rifle. Conversely, a proactive, focused marketing plan can provide guidance for targeting the right audience at the right place and at the right time, which in turn maximizes the return on investment and increases revenues.

Third, marketing is a process of creating value for the customer. It is a set of activities to educate, communicate with, and motivate the targeted consumer about the firm's services or the company's product and services.

Traditionally, this set of activities, the "marketing mix," is represented by four parts, the well-known "4 P's of Marketing": price, product, placement, and promotion. But to create a marketing strategy and plan that touch on all areas necessary to position a product in the market to maximize sales revenues, there are multiple areas to be tackled.

An effective marketing strategy/plan is an ongoing value-creating process composed of several elements:

- ✔ Marketing segmentation.
- ✔ Marketing strategy.
- ✔ Market research.
- ✔ Pricing.
- ✔ Placement.
- ✔ Value chain.

Market Segmentation

One of the first steps in developing an overall marketing strategy is to perform a market segmentation analysis, as a way to manage the strategy development process and ensure its effectiveness and success. The concept behind market segmentation is intuitive and relatively simple. Market segmentation is simply taking a look at the overall market for your product and service and thinking of it in terms of smaller, more manageable pieces.

Think of market segmentation as what Bert and Ernie from *Sesame Street* sing about when they suggest "One of these things is not like the other . . . one of these things doesn't belong." In a sense, that's what we are doing when we segment a market—we are looking at the whole and trying to determine how we can group the mass market into smaller groups that, while different from each other, within the groups are more alike.

Once we have identified these subgroupings, we can target which of these market segments are likely to be the most productive and be the best fit with our company's strengths and competitive advantages.

A well-used example of market segmentation is the way the players in the hospitality industry look at the market for hotel/motel rooms. Rather than take a "one size fits all" approach to this market, a company like Marriott looks at the overall market and segments it into several smaller, but more focused market segments. For the "travel and leisure" segment of the overall hotel/motel market, Marriott's Fairfield Inn is located near major tourist attractions, is budget priced, and appeals to families. For the middle-level manager who travels a lot and wants some comforts of home while on the road, the Courtyard by Marriott is located near businesses and has a residential "feels like home" atmosphere. For CEOs and top-level executives, Marriott's Ritz-Carlton has all the upscale amenities and top-level customer service that presidents and CEOs of business and industry are used to and expect when they travel. Note in these examples how Marriott has broken this overall mass market into more manageable, more focused segments, and, importantly, how its marketing strategy for each segment is tailored to that segment.

By applying the principles of market segmentation, marketers can make better use of their marketing budgets and more efficiently manage their overall marketing strategy.

Marketing Strategy

To build a strong and durable house, it is necessary to create blueprints. Likewise, to build a strong and profitable business, it is necessary to develop a strategy. Essentially, marketing strategy is a plan that allows a business owner to direct activities that are consistent with the goals of the business owner and organization and spend money wisely in order to create the greatest amount of return on investment.

Market Research and Competitive Intelligence

To thoroughly understand what is happening in the industry in which you operate, it is invaluable to know what the trends in the industry are as well as what the firm's competitors are doing to make money, to improve their businesses, and to improve their own market shares. Market research is necessary to make better firmwide decisions. With marketing being a philosophy where the resources and activities of the firm or company are focused on satisfying the wants and needs of the customer, marketing research is the way a firm with a marketing philosophy determines what those wants and needs may be, and further, how to communicate the associated benefits most effectively and efficiently. Additionally, market research is used to monitor and modify, if needed, the elements of the marketing strategy. Market research includes: defining the problem and research objectives, developing a research plan, presenting the plan, implementing the plan (collecting and analyzing data), and interpreting and reporting the findings. This is the area of marketing where we begin to see science as well as art. This chapter focuses in detail on how to research a market, how to know the competition, and how to leverage that knowledge to improve your business.

Pricing

To sell a product for a particular price, value must be created. Value is the consumer's estimate of the product's overall capacity to satisfy his/her needs. When the value placed on a product or service is high, then satisfaction is achieved. Consumers are savvy and will choose based on the level of satisfaction that corresponds with the price. If a bottle of Coca-Cola were priced at $5 while a liter of Pepsi-Cola was priced at $1, it is likely that the sales of Coke would decrease. If these were the only two options at the supermarket, the likelihood of Pepsi sales increasing is high. Pricing is what your customer is willing to trade in return for a product—that is, the value they place on a product or service. Generally, a "price/quality" relationship exists, where the higher the price, the higher the quality; especially in the case of personal services, consumers will expect a higher level of service if the fee associated with that service is higher relative to other providers of similar services.

Marketers may elect to skim the market with a relatively high price at first, and then, as demand wanes at this relatively high price, gradually lower the price. New, innovative products often use this pricing strategy because their newness and uniqueness may enable a higher price at first. As copycats and competitors enter the market, prices will fall to meet the market price.

Some marketers, though, may use a penetration strategy, where the product or service is offered at a very low price, in order to quickly grab market share and be considered the low price provider. Wal-Mart is an example of a company using a penetration pricing strategy.

Pricing is a powerful tool in developing a marketing strategy with a strong connection to the financial condition of the organization. Pricing too low may result in economic consequences if costs are not covered, and pricing too high may stunt demand and sales of the product or service, also resulting in adverse economic consequences.

Placement

A customer will not likely purchase a service or product unless it can be relatively easily accessed. Placement can be anything from a magazine or candy bar sitting next to the checkout counter at the supermarket—a spontaneous purchase—to gas stations situated on the right-hand corner of the exit from a highway or to the location of a orthodontics office in the same complex as a pediatrician's office. Placement helps make the purchasing process for a customer easier and more convenient. Often the term distribution is used interchangeably for the placement component of a marketing strategy and includes the decisions a company or firm must make to ensure the connection with the customer or client. Placement is how the marketer connects the products or services with the customer—the easier, more convenient, more accessible the product or service may be, the more likely the customer will purchase the product or service.

Value Chain

All of the aforementioned parts of the marketing plan cannot be carried out to the full level of effectiveness without all areas—a value chain—working together. Generally, the value chain includes the following activities:

- ✔ *Inbound logistics*—bringing raw materials into the business.
- ✔ *Operations*—management of processes to create the product or service for the customer.
- ✔ *Outbound logistics*—the means for getting the product or service to the customer (for example, distribution systems and shippers to get products into retail stores).
- ✔ *Marketing and sales*—creating value.
- ✔ *Service*—aligning customer expectations and the performance of the product or service.
- ✔ *Firm infrastructure*—the organization of the firm to maximize service to the customer.

✔ *Human resources management*—creating a structure for the people in the firm, which includes recruitment, training, retention, and compensation of employees.

✔ *Technology*—using technology to maximize service, thereby enhancing customer value.

MARKETING AS AN INVESTMENT

Successful companies that become excellent marketing organizations know themselves, their customers, and what they offer that fills the customers' needs. This requires an investment of time and money to accurately determine whether all three parts of the triangle fit together.

As an example, ABC Company is about eight years old and operates in the online professional services industry. The customer wants and needs this service. Most importantly, the customer is willing to pay for the service and ABC Company is the only company occupying this space at this time. One would imagine that ABC Company is generating a strong and regular revenue stream. Unfortunately, ABC Company's CEO does not believe in investing in consistent marketing strategies and targeted marketing initiatives. Rather, the CEO pays low wages to inexperienced salespeople who have no incentive or support to sell the service. Therefore, due to a lack of investment in marketing, the customer does not even know that ABC Company exists. The fallout of such poor strategic thinking could be that employees often are not paid in a month, morale plummets, and company reputation lags.

BECOMING A MARKETING ORGANIZATION: BE TRUE TO YOURSELF

As set forth in the preceding sections, marketing is the process of building a strategic plan. However, without buy-in from the organization as a whole, becoming a marketing organization is more challenging.

A marketing organization is not a firm that sells marketing services. A marketing organization is a firm—regardless of industry, function, size, or region—in which all levels of the organization adhere to the same ideals and uniform methods for attaining customers. As an example, Southwest Airlines has created a marketing organization. It has three company "policies":

- ✔ Practice the Golden Rule. We have a choice every day and choose to make our employees our first customers and our passengers our second customers.
- ✔ Help each other out.
- ✔ Feel free to be yourself.

Integrate, Integrate, Integrate

Southwest ensures that these messages as well as any marketing message is integrated throughout every part of the organization and in every point of contact with the customer—noting that the customer is both the Southwest employee as well as the purchasing passenger. This ability on Southwest's part to create a marketing organization—or a marketing culture—allowed it to weather economic downturns and adverse industry trends.

Becoming a marketing organization also allows the entire team to understand the value of the firm's products to the customer and behave in a manner in which selling is a way of life. For example, a consulting firm may have strategic consultants working on projects at the client's office. Because of this situation, the consultants are able to observe the client's business processes at every stage, and thus have an inside view of the needs of the client. This can create an "upsell" opportunity. Upselling is the process of adding a product or service to an existing project. For all marketers, gaining more share of an existing customer is a more effective overall marketing strategy than working hard to find more customers. Customer or client loyalty is a much smarter long-term strategy, because satisfied customers become "salespeople" in attracting new customers. Additionally, satisfied customers have trust and confidence in your firm's offerings and are more likely to buy more, buy more often, and, because of the lower marketing costs associated with existing customers, become more profitable. The most expensive customer to acquire is a new customer; the most cost-efficient customer is an existing one.

If the employee doesn't "get it," the customer won't.

There are numerous ways that all businesses can become marketing organizations and create buy-in on all levels.

✔ *Communication.* A firm may ensure that decisions are communicated quickly and honestly on all levels of the company so that employee questions, fears, and rumors do not erupt.

✔ *Training.* Training is important to ensure that every employee knows exactly what the firm does to generate revenue and what impact that individual has on that process. Ongoing training in customer service at all levels of the organization will add greatly to the effectiveness of the company's marketing strategy.

✔ *Tools of the trade.* People take action when empowered with the right tools to do so; therefore, it is important to create the tools to make each employee's job easier—whether it be a technological system or a brochure to distribute to customers or the process to do his/her job with clarity.

STRATEGY

In short, strategy is a bridge that connects a firm's internal environment with its external environment, leveraging its resources to adapt to, and benefit from, changes occurring in its external environment.

Strategy is also a decision-making process that transfers a long-term vision into day-to-day tactics to effect the long-term plan. Although often thought of only as something reflected in a business plan, strategy is rather a continual process of assessment, reassessment, and analysis, which constantly provides direction to the firm. Strategy can be compared to the captain on the bridge of a ship, who is constantly scanning both the horizon and the immediate surroundings and adjusting the course, possibly taking the ship in another direction if a storm appears on the horizon or if an object appears to obstruct the path.

POSITIONING AND STRATEGY

The position the firm fills in the marketplace is an integral part of the strategic process. Positioning can also be thought of as how the firm will stake a claim in a piece of the marketplace in a manner that will differentiate it from competitors. The key to sustainable strategy and positioning is an integrated marketing system. Competitive advantage comes from the ability to identify the firm's position, make strategic plans, and engage an entire integrated marketing system. All activities of the firm should fit together and complement each other to produce a well-oiled machine, which creates differentiation in the customer's mind and competitive advantage.

Strategy involves all areas of the firm from operations to finance to human resources. Choosing the right strategy for the right people for the right goals is challenging yet provides an overarching message for the entire organization. The strategy and message must then be communicated consistently and clearly throughout the firm for its effectiveness to take effect and produce a sustainable organization.

TACTICS

While strategy is the overall direction, the long-term mile markers, and/or the guiding force of how the organization moves forward, tactics are the specific steps that are taken to implement the strategy. Strategy tends toward the longer term; tactics are the shorter-term steps taken to achieve the long-term strategy.

For example, XYZ Company is a health and fitness center. Strategically, the firm leadership has decided to develop a center targeted at the 30 to 65 year-old woman and create a comfortable environment in which she can exercise, lose weight, and learn more healthy life habits. The firm's strategic geographic positioning is to provide centers in suburban areas where the largest number of these women live. The tactics used for carrying out this strategy include developing consistent messages and advertisements reflecting the mission of the firm targeted to this market segment, hiring other women trainers so the women customers will be comfortable, and providing health and fitness educational materials specific to the mature woman customer that will create a relationship between XYZ Company and this market segment.

PEST ANALYSIS

Although easy to remember and easily forgotten by firms in developing a long-term strategy, a "PEST analysis" is an acronym for analyzing the external environment (political, economic, sociological/demographic, and technological) and setting the stage for strategic planning. Also known as "environmental scanning," the PEST analysis reviews the environment of a market—whether emerging or existing—and provides a snapshot of the external situation that may impact an industry or the firms within that industry.

Political Environment

Often considered more relevant when entering a foreign market, the political situation in any new or existing market is invaluable to study and understand. Existing government policies and regulations can deter new entrants into an economy, particularly in underdeveloped or developing areas of the world, or can swiftly affect incumbents in an industry with new regulations and policies that can have both positive and negative results. For example, even though the Graham-Leach-Bliley Act in the 1990s in the United States repealed the New Deal era Glass-Steagall Banking Act and allowed some financial companies to expand their services, it also impacted those firms because they were not permitted to sell both institutional and investment services. Likewise, the Sarbanes-Oxley Act of 2002 prohibited firms such as those in accounting and financial services from providing consulting and auditing services. Additionally, government policies can add extra expense to firms; for example, the HIPAA regulations of the late 1990s required health-care organizations and all related firms to protect patient information, which led to increased costs to these providers.

Economic Environment

The economic health and welfare of a state, nation, or region also impact the firm's decision-making process. If an area is healthy economically and the consumers in a region have the means or potential means for creating purchasing power, then a company may want to consider selling its product or service in that area.

Sociological/Demographic Environment

In this part of an environmental scan, we look at trends and factors of the population of our market—for instance, societal attitudes or population shifts that represent either opportunities or threats to our overall strategy. Included in this portion of the analysis is perhaps the education level of the local market, in terms of creating both a workforce and a customer base for the firm. If the levels are too low, then the cost of creating training programs for potential employees and educational marketing methods for potential customers should be taken into consideration. The aging of the baby boomer demographic has affected the strategies of many organizations; interestingly, AARP has responded recently by becoming "more hip" in its image as a way to woo boomers who, prior to their arrival into AARP age range, have parodied its existence.

Technological

Technology refers not only to technology as it is thought of today with computers and systems to manage business more effectively, but also to the infrastructure necessary to support modern systems and processes. Certainly the diffusion of Web-based technology has affected most organizations, giving even the smallest a global presence and a cost-effective way to reach millions of potential customers. Thus, the strategy of an organization may be affected by technological change, and the velocity of technological change also means this variable must be monitored constantly. Certain areas of the world—even in the United States—cannot support systems without great build-out expense and investment. A firm must look at the condition of the host country or region's communication, transportation, and power systems, as well as the cost of using those systems. If the condition and cost are adequate, then the quality of the end product or service and the reliability of consistently providing the firm's product or service to the end user/customer must be analyzed.

THE MODEL FOR STRATEGIC THINKING: PORTER'S FIVE FORCES

In the 1970s, Harvard economist Michael Porter created the gold standard for how strategy is created and analyzed today. Referred to as Porter's Five Forces, this method analyzes the industry and competitive environment in which a firm operates. When developed correctly, the framework paints a picture of the current environment in which the firm competes, allowing the firm to see the big picture and, in turn, develop long-term strategies for the company that will lead to effective decision making and sustainability. Porter believes that an industry's potential profitability can be expressed as a function of these five forces and that one can therefore determine the potential success of a firm in that industry. Porter's Five Forces provide a model for reviewing the outside environment portion of the strategy bridge and for determining the attractiveness of a particular activity at a particular moment in time. This model can be used on any firm of any size in any location in any industry and can be utilized regularly to keep a constant eye on the market, the direction of the market, and the competitors coming and going within that market.

The essential elements of Porter's analytical framework are:

1. Barriers to entry.
2. Threats of substitute products or services.
3. Bargaining power of suppliers.
4. Bargaining power of consumers/buyers.
5. Rivalry among competitors.

Barriers to Entry

Barriers to entry refer to forces that deter companies from entering a particular market. In general terms, one will hear such references as

"The barriers to entry in the telecommunications market are extremely high" or "The barriers to entry in the ice cream industry appear to be quite low." Barriers to entry are just as important for firms that are incumbent in an industry as well as to the newcomers because of the threat of new entrants.

The barriers generally observed by Porter include economies of scale, product differentiation, capital requirements, cost disadvantage independent of size, access to distribution channels, and government policies (regulation).

Economies of Scale.   These refer to the ability of a firm to mass produce a product and therefore to sell to the customer at a lower price. A competitor that does not have the luxury or means to mass produce would thus not be able to compete on price, but rather be forced to find another way to differentiate itself from the competition to the consumer.

Product Differentiation.   This is the method or tactics used by a firm to give its product a more recognized value than the competitors' products. Brand identity is a powerful tool in creating value and therefore makes it difficult for a new entrant into the market to gain customer loyalty. For example, the leaders in the toothpaste market are Colgate and Crest. Customers tend to be loyal to their toothpaste brands, and it would require heavy expenditures to draw customers away from either of those brands. In addition to brand identity, advertising, first mover advantage (being first in an industry), and differences in products also foster loyalty to products and can easily make entering a market highly expensive.

Capital Requirements.   These refer to the amount of money and investment necessary to enter a market. Not only does this reference the product differentiation and brand loyalty mentioned earlier, but it is also extremely important in an industry in which the infrastructure to produce the product requires large amounts of financial resources. Both telecommunications and aviation are examples of industries that require investment in machinery, technology, and so on.

Cost Disadvantage Independent of Size. Some industries have a high learning curve, whether that is scientific, technological, or experiential. In other cases, companies in a particular industry may have access to raw materials, lower prices, advantage based on history or relationships, favorable locations, or even the benefit of government subsidies. All of these factors can affect the ability for an up-and-comer to set up business, get access to capital, and even be profitable.

Access to Distribution Channels. Incumbents in an industry have relationships that may have been functioning profitably for all parties for years. New entrants to that industry have the challenge of creating new relationships or even new and creative methods of distribution just to get their products to market and in front of the consumer. This may mean using price breaks, innovative marketing, and creative product differentiation. For a service industry, this may refer to selling relationships or even a location of the service or place in society. For example, some law firms build relationships with clients and partners that are a result of years of networking and relationships. Business between the organizations goes back generations and new law firms in the field must be creative in reaching the clients.

Government Policies (Regulations). The government has power over industries in the form of licenses, limits on access to raw materials, taxation, and even environmental regulation and standards.

Threat of Substitute Products or Services

A substitute to a product or service can be any other product or service that serves a similar function. Too often, firms underestimate the competitor by not realizing that the product the competitor sells may be a substitute for its own product or service. Many failed ventures during the dot-com bubble had the misconceived notion that "we have no competition," when, in fact, there are always products or services that compete for a consumer or customer's budget. The key to a substitute is that although it may not be the same product or service and although the competing products or services don't function in the same manner, the competing products meet the same customer need. For example, sugar prices cannot go too high or sugar substitutes such as fructose or corn syrup can be used in various consumable products (beverages, etc.). Other industries also have indirect substitutes such as preventative care and the pharmaceutical industry.

Bargaining Power of Suppliers

By controlling the quality or quantity of a product or service a firm needs to conduct its business, or by affecting the price, a supplier can have power over the firm and impact its ability to enter or function in a new market. The ultimate power of a supplier comes down to the characteristics of the supplier group and the relative importance of sales. According to Porter, a supplier group is powerful—it can affect a firm and possess control over the firm—if and when:

- ✔ There are fewer suppliers than buyers.
- ✔ Its product is unique or differentiated.
- ✔ The buyer group is fairly small.
- ✔ It has created high switching costs. Switching costs are incurred when a customer switches from one supplier/product/service to another. For example, when switching from one deodorant to another, the consumer may not experience a switching cost. However, for a company to switch from one office software provider to another, the costs may involve human resources, time, training, and so on.
- ✔ The supplier can integrate forward or take on the function of its customers; for example, a tire manufacturer may open its own retail stores to sell and install its tires.

Bargaining Power of Consumers/Buyers

Just as the supplier has power in the competition and market wars, the customer has power. Customers can force down prices, demand more service or better quality, and even pit competitors against one another.

As with most situations, when buyers form groups, they become powerful and will remain powerful if and when:

✔ They purchase in volume. A prime example is Wal-Mart or Costco. Not only can the customer purchase in volume, but Wal-Mart can purchase in large volume from the supplier, forcing down prices for the end consumer.

✔ The product is undifferentiated and the alternatives for the buyer increase.

✔ The product that they purchase forms a component of the product they produce.

✔ Switching costs are low.

✔ They can purchase up front.

✔ They can integrate backward.

Rivalry among Competitors

All four of the aforementioned parts—barriers to entry, the threat of substitutes, and the bargaining power of suppliers and buyers—create rivalry among competitors. Analyzing all of these areas provides a platform for studying the competition in the firm's market space.

COMPETITION: DON'T BE JUST LIKE EVERYONE ELSE

Every company and every firm has competition. The competition may be direct or indirect, but there is competition. The health club competes with the television, McDonald's competes with cooking at home, and the design company competes with the do-it-yourselfer. The moment a firm begins to believe that it does not have competition is the exact moment it becomes vulnerable to competition.

Competitive Advantage and the Basis for Competing

Once the firm knows who the competitors are and what they do, it needs to carefully identify and document who it is. This is called creating a competitive advantage. A competitive advantage is creating through differentiation and differentiation is created through branding and imaging.

Any time a customer asks for your product by name, you have achieved differentiation. Although theoretically simple, creating differentiation through brand and image is not as simple as it sounds. It is a process of identifying the firm's strengths, weaknesses, limitations, hurdles, and faulty assumptions, followed by creating a brand that is identified by logos, tag lines, color scheme, and all those additional elements that create a visual or recognizable memory of the firm. The competitive advantage of a product or service also depends heavily on variables such as the level of sophistication of the product, prior experience with that product or service in a certain country or part of a country, and the types of distribution channels available.

Costs and Risks

Creating competitive advantage may require a high level of cost and risk to the firm. Often, a firm will create a branding strategy that "pushes the envelope" and increases risk both in time and in money. However, the brand image that is created is so strong that the customer immediately responds positively. It is imperative that the brand or image created be aligned with the firm's strategic initiatives and goals.

Creating a Perceived Value

There are two packages of cheese, both of which are produced at the same factory. One is sold at the supermarket for $3.50 and carries a brand name. The other package of cheese is a generic brand and sells for $2.50 before the store gives a "VIP card" (frequent shopper) discount. It is the exact same cheese with different labels. However, millions of Americans buy Kraft over the store brand because it is a brand they can trust. This is what is referred to as "perceived value." The customer has no idea that the cheese comes from the same plant, has the same ingredients, and is probably even packaged at the same location.

It is even possible that the same truck delivered both cheeses to the grocery store. The value is not in the cheese, but in the trust that the customer places in a company with which he/she can identify.

The SWOT Analysis: Identifying Firm SWOT

Once the competition and the industry have been assessed, a firm may wish to perform a SWOT analysis. SWOT stands for strengths, weaknesses, opportunities, and threats. The strengths and weaknesses are internal factors, whereas opportunities and threats are external factors. A SWOT analysis can be as high-level or detailed as necessary to understand and bring to light the challenges and next steps for the firm in creating strategic initiatives.

To fully understand the firm's competitors and the competitive environment, it is imperative that the firm compare its SWOT to its competition's SWOT. Most business leaders will want to ensure that a SWOT analysis is performed on the firm at regular intervals and that input on the SWOT is gathered from many areas of the organization, as well as from the customer.

PERFORMING A COMPETITIVE ANALYSIS: KNOWING THE COMPETITION INSIDE AND OUT

Once the firm's internal strengths and weaknesses are realized and the external opportunities and threats are identified, next it is important to turn to a similar process of evaluating the competition. Competitor evaluation not only gives more insight into the strategies and goals of the competition but it also provides a bird's-eye view of the trends and future of the industry in which the firm operates.

Step 1. Identify the Competition

To analyze the competitive landscape, it is necessary to make a list of those competitors that compete directly or indirectly with the firm's product or service by providing the same product or service to the customer. (The need that is fulfilled by a product or service is not necessarily the obvious. For example, in the case of a beauty salon, the customer need is not necessarily a haircut, but rather the need to look good and feel happy and attractive.)

Step 2. Identify the Competitors' Strategies

Analyzing the competitors' strategies provides the firm an indication of current trends in the marketplace. This helps the firm determine how to approach the customer.

Step 3. Determine the Competitors' Objectives and Goals

This step may also be referred to as determining the competition's "internal balance." The key to properly assessing the competitor is to know where its value system lies. Because each competitor is different, it will place various levels of importance on technology, quality, cost, market share, and mission. Understanding the competition's objectives can help the firm identify those things that may differentiate it from the rest of the pack.

Step 4. Identify Competitor SWOT

In this step, it is not only important to assess the competitors' strengths and weaknesses, just as the firm performed on itself, but it is also valuable to recognize those opportunities and threats that may be present for the competition. Identifying the competition's strengths and weaknesses allows the firm to identify and assess future moves and initiatives that could affect both the industry and the firm, while identifying the opportunities and threats will give the firm an idea of the kinds of outside forces that could impact the competitor and therefore attack the firm.

Step 5. Estimate Competitors' Reaction Patterns

Some competitors react quickly to events in the marketplace, whereas other competitors take a different approach and react only to selective events in the marketplace. Others are laid-back and react slowly, while still others don't show a pattern of reaction at all. Looking at these behaviors provides the firm a better understanding of what may occur in an industry if the firm takes certain actions or implements certain initiatives.

Step 6. Select the Competitors to Attack and Avoid

Some competitors are such large financial powerhouses that it may not be financially feasible to attack. Some merely put up the front or the image that they cannot be attacked. It is in this step that it is valuable to the firm to know the competitors for which an attack strategy would be profitable and those for which avoidance would be the best policy. Identifying the weak versus the strong competitors will allow the firm to make efficient decisions.

Step 7. Create a Positioning Map

To create a visual understanding of the entire competitive landscape, it is helpful to create a positioning map to provide a visual representation of the firm's position compared to the competition as depicted in Figure 8.1.

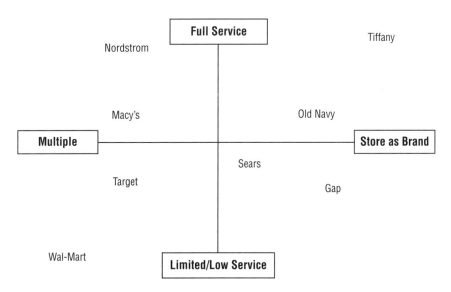

FIGURE 8.1 A Positioning Map

Competition provides the firm the opportunity to look into the future. Once all of the information is gathered, a firm can imagine the competitor's next move and either do the same if the market supports it or take a different route, cutting the competition off at the pass. For example, the home improvement stores Home Depot and Lowe's are often within minutes of each other or even right across the street. Generally, one store decides to move into an area before the other, and the other watches and sets up shop nearby. Once the competitor has found the location, the firm can take action.

Competition creates a sense of urgency and often increases sales for all the competitors who are willing to put up a fight. Once the firm's competition is known and understood, the next opportunity for the firm is to "go deeper" by implementing competitive intelligence.

COMPETITIVE INTELLIGENCE: WHAT CAN YOUR COMPETITION DO FOR YOU?

Competitive intelligence (CI), also referred to as business intelligence, is often seen as the business world's secret agent 007. Although no spy planes or pinpoint cameras are used, competitive intelligence is, according to the Society for Competitive Intelligence Professionals (SCIP), "a systematic and ethical program for gathering, analyzing, and managing external information that can affect [the firm's] plans, decisions, and operations. Specifically, [CI] is the legal collection and analysis of information regarding the capabilities, vulnerabilities, and intentions of business competitors, conducted by using information databases and other 'open sources' and through ethical inquiry." In other words, CI is the company's radar.

Companies use CI for any number of reasons: assessing a competitor's strategies, defining the competitive landscape, discovering and assessing trends in the industry, or identifying new opportunities that may not have surfaced earlier in the competitive analysis process. CI is not market research, as it is more forward looking, nor is it industrial espionage, because it is legal, but rather a systematic and timely process for understanding the current competitive environment. When combined with internal firm analysis, CI can provide a manager with a more complete picture of the decisions that need to be made to retain the firm's competitive advantage.

CI is valuable for many reasons. It can both help decrease the possibility for risk and help the firm avoid unnecessary or additional costs. In terms of savings, it can increase revenues and save time, which translates into cost savings. CI also provides information for innovation, product development, and targeted marketing by validating trends, clarifying events, and providing discovery and insightful information.

Because any effective strategic marketing plan requires that a firm keep close track on a regular basis of the competitors' plans and actions, there are a number of ways that CI can be done. To find out information about the competition, the following are a few obvious or not-so-obvious places where information about the competition can be found:

- ✔ *Annual reports.* Annual reports of publicly held companies are an obvious and easily accessible way to learn how a competitor is revealing itself to its shareholders.

- ✔ *Press releases.* Most firms distribute press releases to generate public relations. Often, the firm will post these on its web site. It is advisable to review the press releases over a few months' time to get a big picture view of where the competitor's strategy is heading.

- ✔ *Trade magazines.* Trade magazines provide an up-to-date and in-depth analysis of the industry and where that industry appears to be headed.

- ✔ *Vendors/partners/customers.* Another source of solid competitor information is the patterns of vendors, partners, and customers.

- ✔ *Salespeople.* Salespeople are often very willing to talk about their companies and provide information that provides insight into the direction the competition is heading.

✔ *Networking.* In the process of creating a network for generating business for the firm, it is possible to hear about the activity of the competition merely through observing the activities or events the senior leadership attends.

✔ *Local news outlets.* Often local, regional, and national news sources track the activities of local private companies.

✔ *10-Ks and 10-Qs.* A public company's SEC filings are especially helpful when considered as an evolving story over a period of years.

✔ *External research or professional organizations.* Often the best place to find information about a company is an event at which representatives of the company have been asked to speak. This may be at any professional organization's monthly meetings or annual conference. In addition, there are plenty of online resources, including organizations such as Hoover's or Dun & Bradstreet, which help if time or money is a limitation.

✔ *Internet.* Search engines can be an invaluable source of information. For example, once the names of the competitors' senior management team are available, it is possible to plug a name into a search engine and reveal a host of information. Search engines may include sources such as www.google.com or www.boardreader.com and even www.cnet.com.

SUMMARY

A firm's strategic goals are based on both internal and external knowledge, insight, and in-depth analysis. Without a strategic plan, resources are spent on events, activities, and functions that may not generate revenue. To make the most of each dollar earned by the firm, all functions must work together to create a well-oiled machine. The marketing plan, which is based on a full understanding of the market, the firm, and the customer needs, dovetails directly with the strategic plan to provide a road map for the firm. This road map is the ultimate tool for guiding leaders toward making decisions that will provide sustainable growth to the company.

REFERENCES

Porter, Michael. "Competition Shapes Strategy." *Harvard Business Review* (March–April 1979).

———."What Is Strategy?" *Harvard Business Review* (November–December 1996).

Secker, Russell. "10 Key Sources of Competitive Data." SCIP.online 1, no. 14 (August 22, 2002). www.scip.org.

Stauffer, David. *The Power of Competitive Intelligence.* Cambridge: Harvard Business School Publishing, 2003.

Vessenes, Peter. "Cash Is King, but Marketing Is Everything." *Journal of Financial Planning* 16, no. 12 (December 1, 2003).

Advertising and Promotion

Every day we are bombarded with different advertising messages, whether it is on the radio while we're driving to work, on television during our favorite programs, or in magazines and newspapers. We're handed flyers while walking down the streets and given tastes of products while walking the aisles of the grocery store. Advertising has entered every area of our lives, and many of us choose to ignore it on many occasions. This might cause you to ask, can advertising and promotional efforts still be effective if we are so saturated with information?

The answer is yes, advertising and promotions can be effective if used properly for targeting the right consumer. One of the main rules in advertising has always been to keep your message simple and consistent, and repeat it often. It has been shown that people remember advertising if they see it with great frequency, which explains why while watching two hours of television you may see the same advertisement two or even three times. That way the message will stand out in your mind.

BRANDING

On the shelves of every grocery store are brand-name products from Oreo cookies to Tide detergent. Strong brands are a great asset to a company and can generate streams of incremental revenue due to the fact that people are willing to pay a premium for brand-name products and over time they reduce marketing costs because a brand's customers present lower or no purchase barriers.

A brand is a name, symbol, term, sign, design, or combination of each of these things, the purpose of which is to identify goods and services of one seller or of a group of sellers and differentiate them from competitors. A brand is also the sum of all characteristics that make a product offering unique. A company can copy a product, but it cannot replicate the brand. In a sense, the brand is the "personality" of the product, what the product means to the customer and the set of emotions evoked when the brand is encountered or used by the customer.

Brand Identity

A brand's identity is the company's vision of the brand and the brand's promise to consumers. It is also the outward visible identity of the corporate brand or family of brands. McDonald's, for example, has the golden arches as part of its brand identity, but it also represents convenient and reliable products. When you order a McDonald's cheeseburger, it should taste the same whether you are ordering it in Los Angeles, Hartford, Shanghai, or Moscow and it should be prepared quickly, because it is "fast food."

Brand Image

The brand image is the consumer's actual view of the brand. Companies will try to bridge the gap between brand identity and brand image. Consistency is the key element when promoting a brand or product, and a clear and consistent promotional campaign will help ensure that the brand's image and the brand identity are very similar.

Brand Loyalty

People who buy only a particular brand of product or service are considered by marketers to be "brand loyal." There are various levels of brand loyalty, from extremely loyal to brand terrorist and everything in between. Think about the products you buy; are you willing to purchase just any brand of detergent or coffee creamer? Some people will use only Clorox bleach or Coffee-mate coffee creamer, while others will be satisfied using private-label bleach or a generic creamer and may not notice a difference beyond price. Others may be loyal some of the time; however, they will take advantage of a sale or promotion for another competitive product. For example, you may buy Coke regularly, but would you buy Pepsi instead if there were a sale? If so, you are not brand loyal to either Coke or Pepsi; you are capable of switching.

People who have bad experiences with brand-name products or services may tell others about their dissatisfaction; these people are deemed "brand terrorists" and may act as an adverse multiplier of reputation. A rule of thumb is that a positive experience will have a one- or two-time positive effect, but a customer with a negative experience will tell 8 to 10 people. If you have a terrible meal at a local restaurant, chances are not only will you not eat at the restaurant again, but also you will tell friends or family about your negative experience. The same can be true with your experience with any kind of product. People who have a bad experience with a brand, product, or service are much more likely to express their reaction to their experience than those who have good experiences.

While there is no way of ensuring that every person is completely satisfied, companies can take measures to try to please their customers through high levels of customer service. They can also take steps to win over customers, or market share, from other products or services in order to equalize the balance between lost customers and new customers.

INTEGRATED MARKETING COMMUNICATIONS

One of the most important aspects of advertising and promoting a product or service is consistency. Companies ensure the consistency of their message by coordinating all of their promotional activities. This coordination of activities into a system or strategic plan is referred to as integrated marketing communications (IMC). IMC creates a unified message and enhances the effectiveness of reaching the target consumer. Firms will create one message that will be used consistently throughout a marketing campaign. It is important that the promotional strategy also be in alignment with the organizational goals.

There are three major aspects of an IMC plan: research, creative aspects, and the implementation. Research and analysis are used to find the best way to design the product or service, the most effective message and media to use, and the best means to distribute the product or service at the optimal price. The creative aspect is the actual advertising, copywriting, and designing of promotional materials. Implementation is the act of putting the plan together, creating a strategy, and seeing it through.

Planning an integrated marketing communications plan also means finding your target market; determining what is unique about the product offering or service you are providing; constructing a positioning strategy for your product or service (building a mental niche in relation to competitor products or services); deciding what the best message would be for your product; and choosing the optimal marketing mix in relation to your allowed marketing budget.

As an example of IMC, suppose Nike comes up with a promotional "Just do it" campaign targeting female athletes for its new line of women's athletic shoes. Marketers will do their research to find what media female athletes use, what time they watch television, what programs they watch, and what types of advertising messages they respond to. Then Nike will create the promotional materials and ads. They learn what's important about the athletic shoes women wear. Nike may have TV and magazine ads featuring women athletes doing extraordinary things. They may also sponsor a women's sporting event such as women's NCAA basketball or hold a contest for a fan to spend a day training with the U.S. women's soccer team. The message would be clear and consistent: Nike cares about female athletes and supports women's athletics.

Ideally, an effective IMC campaign will differentiate the product or service from a competitor's; generate a flow of leads (which are the predecessors to sales); be consistent with and support the overall branding strategy; cause the company to have a more prominent place in the market; communicate the company's experience and knowledge; and help to retain existing customers.

THE PROMOTIONAL MIX

The promotional mix is the use of different advertising and communication channels in a coordinated way to run an effective marketing campaign. These coordinated campaigns are part of an effective integrated marketing communications plan. The four main methods of promotion within the mix are advertising, sales promotion, personal selling, and public relations.

The most important factor in determining the optimal mix is identifying the target market. This can be determined through extensive market research. Once a company knows its target market, it can then research its use of various media outlets in order to come up with the best combination of marketing materials to reach the defined target. For example, if the target market is stay-at-home moms, an organization might find that television advertisements during certain daytime television shows are most effective for reaching them. If the target market is a young professional, the marketer might find that using billboards in a downtown commercial district and morning drive-time radio advertisements are effective for getting the message to this target market.

The size of the promotional budget will greatly influence the chosen mix as well. Television advertising can be very costly and, therefore, may not be a feasible option for a company with a smaller marketing budget, at least not during prime viewing hours on major networks. Often the amount of money a firm spends on promotional activities will be affected by the product life cycle, general economic conditions, and the competition.

The promotional mix may involve a company coordinating its loyalty program with advertising campaigns and a promotional deal. For example, an airline may send out a mailer to its frequent fliers advertising 5,000 free bonus miles for booking a ticket in the next month. In this instance, the airline is coordinating a direct mailing with loyalty program membership and a promotional campaign.

ADVERTISING

Advertising is paid communication brought to audiences through different forms of media such as television, radio, newspapers, magazines, and billboards. A company uses advertising to inform, persuade, or remind its target market of its products or services.

Comparative advertising is used to differentiate a company's products in the marketplace from other similar products. For example, McDonald's and Burger King used to run comparative advertising, comparing their cooking methods for hamburgers. The "Pepsi Challenge" campaign was another form of comparative advertising in which consumers were asked to take blind taste tests to see if they could tell the difference between the products.

Reminder advertising is used once a product has matured in the marketplace—that is, once a product has been around for a while. Credit card companies use a lot of reminder advertising, such as American Express "Don't leave home without it" or Visa "It's everywhere you want to be" campaigns. Coca-Cola uses reminder ads to show us how refreshing the beverage can be on a hot day, and Budweiser wants to remind the consumer to "Make it a Bud night." Some ads use nostalgia to remind us of how much as children we enjoyed a product such as Oreo cookies; and although our taste buds may have matured, we can still enjoy them.

Institutional advertising promotes the company, organization, government agency, or a concept or philosophy, but not a specific product. For example, ads for BASF, one of the world's largest manufacturers of chemicals and chemical-related products, states, "We don't make a lot of the products you buy. We make a lot of the products you buy better." Another example is the U.S. Army recruitment commercials, "Be all you can be."

Industry advertising promotes a whole industry and not just one company or product. The most popular example of this is the "Got milk?" ad campaigns sponsored by the California Milk Processing

Board. Another example is the "Hanker for a hunk of cheese" campaign that was sponsored by the Wisconsin Dairy Board.

Advertising Mediums

There are advantages and disadvantages to each media type, and when selecting the advertising mediums to use, companies must understand who their target audience is and which is the most effective method for reaching them. Marketers must be able to divide their budgets among the various media resources in order to stretch them the farthest to reach the most customers.

Television. Television advertising is the leading medium for reaching U.S. audiences. Although a very expensive form of advertising, television ads reach the largest percentage of the U.S. population at once and can be very appealing due to their visual nature as well as their sound.

TV ads can be classified into national, local, and cable advertisements. The type of network chosen will depend on which audience the marketer is trying to reach. If the advertisement is for a local restaurant, the company may choose to advertise only on local stations or in local ad space on cable channels or national networks. Companies targeting Hispanics may choose to advertise on a Spanish-language cable station such as Telemundo, or advertise during a television show whose viewing audience is predominately Hispanic.

The time an advertisement is shown is also an important decision that companies must make in order to reach the target audience. Budgetary constraints will also be a factor in choosing time slots for advertisements. Super Bowl ads are extremely expensive, but can be cost-effective for reaching an audience of sports fans.

Print Ads. Advertising in newspapers and magazines is another way of reaching customers with a company's message. Print ads are effective because of their visual quality and can be run in many different types of publications. Marketers selling products or services to consumers may choose national publications such as *Time* magazine or local newspapers such as the *Chicago Tribune*. Businesses trying to sell products or services to other businesses will often advertise in trade publications of the industries they are trying to reach. Companies may also target specialized publications; for example, a new computer product may be advertised in *PC World* or another specialty technology publication. Print ads have a longer life than electronic media ads and are good for telling a story about the value of a product or service.

Radio. Although lacking the visual appeal, radio can be an effective medium for reaching target consumers. The average radio listener tunes in for three hours a day, and often on a regular basis. When using radio advertisements in your marketing mix, it is necessary to make sure that the company and product or service is clearly identified. As with television, it is also necessary to find the right station for advertising to the target consumer. If your service is a bar for college students, you may choose to advertise in the evenings on a college station or an alternative rock station; if your target audience is senior citizens, you may advertise on news stations or a talk show.

Internet. The Internet has become an important electronic medium, and its interactive quality is unique. It permits immediacy of purchase and a high level of convenience. It can be personalized and individualized. The Internet and the World Wide Web are becoming essential tools in an integrated marketing plan and effective tools in sustaining customer loyalty and satisfaction.

Direct Mail. Mailing advertisements or promotions directly to people's homes is another commonly used method of reaching consumers. Direct mail campaigns can be expensive, due to printing and postage costs, but these campaigns can be effective if the mailings reach the right consumers. Often companies will purchase lists of consumers or collect data themselves to build a mailing list. The people on these lists will then be sent targeted mailings.

Telemarketing. The utilization of telemarketing has been greatly affected in the United States by the recent implementation of the national "Do Not Call" registry, where millions of Americans signed up to have their telephone numbers removed from telemarketer lists. Internationally, however, regulations regarding telemarketing vary, and it may still be a very effective method of reaching consumers. The downside of telemarketing is that most people do not like the invasiveness of being called at home, though unfortunately many mass marketers find the risk of offending nonreceptive households is offset by the effective results and benefits from these marketing methods.

Outdoor and "Out of Home." The majority of outdoor advertising dollars is spent on billboards. Billboards are a popular way of reaching commuters and consumers in a single geographic location. Other forms of outdoor advertising (known as "out of home") include sports stadium ads, bus shelter posters, or signage on buses and taxis.

Advertising Trends

A very popular way of getting a message across is using celebrity endorsements. Advertising companies are willing to pay top dollar in order to hire celebrities to represent their brands. From *Star Trek* actors advertising cheap travel for Priceline.com to Michael Jordan drinking Gatorade while sweating neon colors, celebrities are part of an advertising message and campaign. Of course, using a celebrity spokesperson can be a risk, for example, using O. J. Simpson as the Hertz Rental Car spokesperson.

When choosing a celebrity to endorse products, it is important to find an appropriate match with the product or service. The relationship should be believable. It is also important that the celebrities endorsing the product be credible; they should either have expertise in the field or be trustworthy characters.

Sponsorships. This is a well-used form of promotion and advertising that allows the company to buy into a sporting event or activity. The amount of investment in a sponsorship can range from an athletic company supporting a college sports team by providing them with brand-name uniforms in order to promote the brand to a company sponsoring a college football bowl game such as the Tostito's Fiesta Bowl.

Infomercials. Another trend in advertising is the infomercial. This is an extended television advertisement and usually runs at off-peak hours or on lower-budget television or cable networks. In-fomercials are usually at least a half hour long. Some of the most popular items that are sold through infomercials are fitness videos, skin care products, and kitchenware. Often they will feature celebrity endorsements and offer products that cannot be purchased in stores. Their low-budget appearance and late-night showing often characterize infomercials. If you turn on the television late at night, a former star is using the Thigh Master or hundreds of uses for a ro-tisserie oven may draw you in. Once the consumer is convinced to purchase the product, he or she will then be able to call and order the product over the telephone, generating a direct response to the infomercial.

SALES PROMOTION

Sales promotion consists of many activities used to sell products. They are activities that give consumers a short-term incentive to make a purchase. Sales promotions are also activities that change the price and value relationship of a product as perceived by the target audience with the possible effect of generating immediate sales. It is possible that a sales promotion can also alter the long-term value of the brand by making what might be a premium prod-uct more affordable.

Sales promotions are generally time-bound programs that re-quire participation on the part of the consumer through either im-mediate purchase or some other action. The fundamental goals of sales promotion are tactical, strategic, and ultimate. The tactical goals are to combat a competitor's increase in market share, to com-bat other competitors' promotional efforts, and to move brands that are either declining, overstocked, damaged, or not selling fast enough. The strategic goals are to motivate consumers to switch from a rival brand, to increase product consumption, to reinforce the marketing communications efforts for the brand, and to moti-vate brand loyalty. The ultimate goal of a sales promotion is to in-crease sales, profits, and market share.

There are different channels for sales promotions, which include consumer promotions and trade promotions.

Consumer Promotions

Consumer promotions are geared toward getting consumers to try a company's products. Some examples of consumer promotion activities include coupons, rebates, sampling, sweepstakes, point-of-purchase displays, and special packs.

Coupons. Whether we're cutting them from newspapers and magazines or getting them in the mail, coupons are a very popular form of sales promotion. They are very effective, especially in economic downturns, for luring people into restaurants or causing them to make repeat purchases of products. E-coupons are another popular form of sales promotion; they are extremely effective for luring in customers and are redeemed by 57 percent of the people who click on them. The most popular uses of e-coupons are for sales of groceries, books, and health and music products. The disadvantage of coupons is that they do not encourage brand loyalty; most consumers who use coupons regularly are willing to switch brands if there is a better discount available.

Rebates. Rebates are partial refunds that are offered by the manufacturers. Often manufacturers will use mail-in rebates as incentives for purchasing. The consumer must purchase the product at full price and then fill out paperwork and mail in the receipt in order to receive some money back. Rebate programs allow marketers to promote a company's product at a reduced postrebate price, offering a substantial savings to its customers, but also requiring that a set of conditions be met to qualify.

Sampling. Companies will often send or hand out samples of products in order to attract customers who may not have purchased their products otherwise. Beverage companies may target college students and hand out soft drinks on campuses, or a food company may set up a stand in a grocery store so that consumers can sample their new chips. You may even receive a trial bottle of shampoo in the mail. Or you may remember receiving the America Online (AOL) CD in the mail, offering you 100 free hours of Internet access. These are all examples of sampling, and the intention of these promotions is to introduce a new product or service to a consumer in order to generate brand loyalty. Sampling can be a costly method of attracting customers, and it often results in wasted distribution; however, it can be a very effective method for getting consumers to switch brands.

Sweepstakes and Contests. Sweepstakes and contests are another strategy of sales promotion. Data will be collected from consumers, and they will be entered to win a prize. Companies can use the information that they collect from entrants in order to develop a mailing list for future promotional campaigns. Organizations must be sure to print all the guidelines for their sweepstakes or contests in order to avoid legal entanglements.

Some of the guidelines companies should follow in order to put on a successful sweepstakes promotion include the following: clarify who is eligible; indicate states where the promotion is not valid; declare the termination date of the promotion; and clarify random drawing procedures. Companies should also detail the prizes, disclose the odds of winning, declare a deadline for entry, and reserve the right to use winners' names and photographs for publicity.

Point-of-Purchase Displays. Point-of-purchase (POP) promotional materials are displays that are set up in stores in order to prominently display products. At a grocery store a POP is usually placed in the front of the store, at the end of an aisle, in the aisle, or on the shelf. POP displays are very successful due to the fact that many people make last-minute purchasing decisions.

Bundling. Sometimes companies bundle products together in order to promote a new product or to encourage consumers to try a complementary product, such as a free small conditioner bundled with a shampoo purchase, or a free disposable razor with a shaving cream purchase. A company may also offer a bonus pack or a special pack with 20 percent more in order to encourage a customer to purchase a product.

Giveaways. Another strategy used by companies is that of special promotional items to be given away. These may be hats or T-shirts advertising the company or brand. For example, many times credit card companies will offer T-shirts if you sign up for a new credit card, or a beer company may be giving away pint glasses to customers who purchase that brand of beer on certain nights. Alcoholic beverage companies often hire young men and women who will go to concerts, bars, and clubs and promote their products by giving away promotional items.

Trade Promotions

Trade promotions are geared toward marketing intermediaries as opposed to consumers. A snack food manufacturer, for example, may offer a discounted price to a retailer who buys a large quantity of a product. These types of promotions are most successful when they offer financial incentives and serve to effectively reduce the cost of the product.

Another form of trade promotion is paying for shelf space. On the shelf at the grocery store, product placement is very important. Items placed at eye level on higher shelves have proven to sell much better than products placed on lower shelves. Knowing this, manufacturers often pay a "slotting fee" in order to have their products prominently displayed on the desired shelf or in a preferred position within a retail store.

PERSONAL SELLING

Personal selling uses a personal sales presentation to influence customers to buy a product. Personal selling tactics are most often used when there are a few geographically concentrated customers; the product is highly technical in nature; the product is very expensive; or when the product moves through direct distribution channels. It is a tactic often used by businesses looking to sell to other businesses, as opposed to businesses selling to consumers.

The sales process involves a personal seller identifying the target customer by determining who is likely to buy his or her product. Once the target customers have been identified, the salesperson will contact them. Upon meeting with a potential customer, the salesperson will make a sales presentation, explaining how the customer needs the product or service that is being sold. The salesperson should be prepared to answer the customer's questions. After the presentation, the goal of the salesperson is to close the sale while the presentation is still fresh in the mind of the customer. Following up with the purchaser after the sale is made is a very effective strategy for developing long-term relationships.

Relationship Strategies

Developing an effective relationship strategy can be the key to forming long-term relationships with customers and in turn creating loyalty. Good customer service and treating customers fairly become the critical first step for ensuring a healthy relationship. Fair treatment includes responding to customer complaints and finding workable solutions to resolving mistakes that have been made. Although the customer may not always be right, the customer should always be treated graciously. Providing customers with truthful information and creating personable contact with them are critical.

A company's internal structure is also very important to its ability to build relationships with customers. The company should be running a cost-effective business, possess interpersonal skills, and have the technical know-how regarding its product offerings. For many professional service providers, their staff may have more interaction with the client than the professional service provider, making it critical that the staff have the same level of concern for customer service and satisfaction as the provider.

Additionally, it's very important that companies recognize who their most valuable customers are. Those are the customers who benefit the company most through their purchases. Companies will want to focus their long-term relationship-building efforts on these types of customers, because it will be more profitable. In a competitive environment complicated by high marketing costs, most marketers are moving toward a relationship-building strategy of "greater share of customers" instead of "greater market share."

Many companies use forms of customer relationship management in order to keep track of their customers' purchases, determine who their most profitable customers are, and target special promotions and product or service offers to their customers using the information they collect. Many banks are starting to offer these services, and you may notice that when you call to get account information the customer service representative will offer you other products. Phone companies have also taken up this practice. It can be a very successful way of introducing new products and services to existing customers, up-selling customers, or influencing them to purchase more products.

Loyalty Programs

Many companies develop loyalty or frequency-marketing programs in order to further engage the consumers with their products and increase customer loyalty. These programs are very effective for targeting the company's most valuable customers. Most airlines develop frequent-flier programs, which allow customers to earn points toward their next flight. Other businesses, such as coffee shops, also offer frequency cards, that entitle the customer to a free beverage, for example, after purchasing a certain number of beverages.

Loyalty programs have been very effective in generating repeat business. They offer an added value to the consumer, whereby the purchaser is not simply enjoying the value of the current purchase, but is being rewarded. It is important, however, that the loyalty program be relative to the product and service offering of the organization and that the award be attainable. Customers may experience frustration if, with an airline ticket as an example, they are unable to redeem their ticket when they want to travel, or if the restrictions on the reward are so high that it is not worth the hassle of redemption.

PUBLIC RELATIONS AND PUBLICITY

An organization's public relations and publicity activities are the means to foster its relationships with its various audiences and to communicate with them. Public relations efforts are undertaken in order to form a favorable view in the public eye. Favorable publicity can enhance an organization's image and increase demand for its products. A positive article or review about a product or service adds credibility, believability, and legitimacy in a much more effective manner than paid-for advertising. Negative publicity, on the other hand, can tarnish an organization's reputation. Most public relations strategies include press releases, special events, and press conferences.

Press releases are articles or brief news releases that are submitted to publications by the firm. They often provide information about company happenings: new hires, new products or services, or changes in management. They can be an effective way of gaining attention and creating or maintaining awareness.

Many organizations sponsor special events such as product launches. A fashion company may sponsor a fashion show to display its new line of clothing. A musician may hold a record release party for his or her new album. The firm will often invite top clientele, industry insiders, and media to these events.

A news conference is an in-person announcement of recent organizational events to the media. It is an effective method of informing the public of recent happenings without causing rumors to be spread, because the information will come straight from the source.

ETHICS AND REGULATORY ISSUES

As in other areas of business addressed in Chapter 4, ethics in promotional activities is very important. Some common ethical violations with promotional campaigns include puffery and deception. Puffery is an exaggerated claim about the superiority of a product. Although puffery is legal, it may cause a company to lose its reputation with the public. As discussed earlier, a brand terrorist can do great amounts of harm to a company's reputation if a product is overhyped and falls short of its inflated expectations.

Deception involves a company deliberately making promises that are not true. A consumer may have legal recourse for deception. An example of a deceptive practice that is illegal is "bait and switch" advertising: A company advertises a low-priced product that is on sale, and when the consumer arrives that product is not available; the company then tries to sell the customer another more expensive product as a substitute.

Another area of ethical debate is marketing to children and teenagers. This is particularly a concern when it comes to tobacco or alcoholic beverages. It is illegal for companies to target those who are legally unable to consume their products.

Other situations of ethical concern when it comes to marketing to children arise when a company such as a beverage company signs a contract with a school to supply solely its brand of beverages on the school campus. This is not an illegal practice, but it is controversial, as some feel that such schools are being controlled by corporations that want to get children to become brand loyal to their products.

SUMMARY

There are many methods used by marketers to attract customers to their brands and products. A successful integrated marketing campaign will deliver a consistent message that is brought to the target audience through different mediums of the marketing mix. Advertising and promotional messages should be consistent and repeated often in order to create a clear image in the mind of consumers. Ideally, these promotional efforts will result in influencing consumers to either try new products, switch from their preferred products, or purchase more products from a company or brand. The end goal of all promotional efforts is to increase the company's product sales and profits through gaining or stealing market share.

REFERENCES

Crockett, Robert O. "Penny Pincher's Paradise." *BusinessWeek* (January 22, 2001).

Kent, Judy. "Relationship Strategies for Acquiring and Retaining Customers." *Credit* (March/April 1991).

Papatla, Purushottam. "Choosing the Right Mix of On-line Affiliates: How Do You Select the Best?" *Journal of Advertising* (Fall 2002).

Chapter

10

Communications and Presentations

Presentations can range from a short talk before a small group of acquaintances or colleagues to a lengthy speech to a group of strangers. No matter the audience or the setting, formal or informal, small or large, the best presentations leave the audience informed and interested. They want to know more about the subject matter and often have insightful comments and questions for the presenter. A bad presentation, in contrast, leaves the audience confused or bored and often makes them wonder why they wasted their time. A poor presentation detracts from the importance of the subject matter and can be detrimental to the reputation of the presenter.

In addition to length and format, presentations can also vary in style. The main purpose of a presentation is to communicate ideas and information. Effective means of communicating ideas and information can also vary and may include persuasion, instruction, inspiration, or entertainment.

Regardless of length, format, or purpose, presentations are an important and useful tool in all aspects of business. Given their importance, it is surprising that few classes are available on how to present more effectively. All too often associates are assigned the task of "giving a presentation" and then left to their own devices. No wonder so many individuals list public speaking as their greatest fear.

This chapter will assist you in becoming a better presenter by providing you with knowledge about the processes of developing an effective presentation style and format. This is accomplished by asking important questions and providing useful tips that will help in examining the different stages of the presentation process.

TO PRESENT OR NOT TO PRESENT

The first and most important question is whether this presentation is a choice or a requirement. If it is a choice you need to ask yourself some important questions before agreeing to present. Preparing for a presentation takes time. A rough estimate for an effective presentation is that it takes 30 to 60 minutes of preparation for each minute of delivery. Do you have enough focused time prior to the presentation to properly prepare? In addition, are you interested, excited, and sufficiently knowledgeable about the subject matter to deliver an effective and enthusiastic presentation? If the answer to either of these questions is a clear "no," you should seriously consider turning down the offer to present.

BEFORE THE PRESENTATION

Some time spent in planning will pay off. Not only will the presentation be better prepared, the planning process will increase your confidence and be reflected in a more convincing presentation performance.

Define the Parameters

Knowing the parameters beforehand will limit uncertainties and surprises and make you better prepared to deliver a targeted, informative, and interesting presentation. The most important parameters are topic and theme, time, program, preservation, audience, place, and questions. Some of these parameters can be determined prior to the presentation. More than likely one or two of the later ones will change slightly by the day of the presentation. It is important shortly before the presentation to redefine the parameters to make sure that none of the changes will dramatically affect your presentation.

Topic and Theme. What will you be talking about? Will you be providing a general overview of this topic or highlights of recent activities? Where do you want to go in your presentation of this material?

Time. How much time do you have to make your presentation? It is a simple question to ask, but all too often a presenter finds himself or herself a number on the agenda or a name on the program. There may be a general sense that the talk will take 10 minutes or an hour, but no specifics are provided.

Program. Will there be other speakers presenting? How will the information in your presentation compare or contrast with the topics covered by other speakers? What is the order of the presentations? Are you expected to provide an exciting introduction to the program or a comprehensive summary?

Preservation. In the age of digital camcorders and cable television, presentations are often recorded or televised for future viewing or public consumption. If you think this could be the case with your presentation, ask. If your presentation is being taped, you should ask for a copy. This will be a valuable resource for reviewing your presentation and your presentation style. It will serve as a useful tool if you are asked to give a similar presentation at a later date.

Audience. To whom will you be presenting? Giving a talk about trees to a group of executives in the lumber industry would be significantly different from giving the same talk to the members of an environmental group. Research your audience beforehand. What is their background and how knowledgeable are they about your subject matter? What are they expecting from the presentation and how can you add value to their experience? Are they expecting to be informed, amused, or challenged? How many individuals are expected to attend your presentation? If you are presenting to a group or an organization, especially one with which you are unfamiliar, take a few moments to find out more about it. Simple and useful information can often be found on the organization's web site or in one of its recent newsletters. What issues are most important to the members? If the group often hosts presenters, look for references to past presenters. What did these presenters talk about, and how were they received?

Place. Where is the presentation going to take place? How are the acoustics of the space? What audio-video resources are available at this location? Will you be able to connect your laptop to the audio-video system at this location or will you need to load your program onto a computer already at the site? Will there be someone there to assist you with audio-video equipment? Will there be a stage, podium, microphone, table, chairs? Will the audience be seated facing you, or will they be seated around dinner tables? (If possible try to avoid big gaps between you and the audience. Make the setting as intimate as possible.) If you are using a screen for your presentation, where will this screen be located? (Try to get the screen set off to the side rather than in the center of the stage or on a back wall. This will allow you to reference it more easily and move around the stage more comfortably.)

Question-and-Answer Component. Will there be questions at the end of the presentation? Will there be a moderator to take questions or will you be expected to handle them yourself? If there are several presenters, will questions be taken at the end of your presentation or after all the presenters have spoken?

Purpose

Knowing your topic and theme is obviously important in delivering an effective presentation. Knowing why you are presenting, however, is equally important. After taking the time to analyze the audience and assess their needs, decide how these needs can best be met. Four common purposes for a presentation include persuasion, instruction, inspiration, and entertainment. Persuasion is a method for bringing an audience around to your point of view. Instruction is used to share basic information about your topic. Inspiration is effective when used during a change of process, procedure, or direction. Entertainment lightens the mood. Often these purposes are used to varying degrees in a presentation. The important point is that in preparing for your presentation you take a moment to think about what purpose is the most important and effective for your presentation and your audience. To help determine the purpose of your presentation, ask yourself what you want people in the audience to do as a result of having heard your presentation. What concepts do you want your audience to leave with?

Preparing Your Presentation

As mentioned earlier, for an effective presentation you can expect to spend 30 to 60 minutes of preparation time for each minute of delivery. This means that to deliver a one-hour presentation, one can expect 30 to 60 hours of preparation. This is realistic given the research, preparation, and practice that must go into developing effective presentation materials.

In the current business environment it is often difficult to find time to focus on any one particular project. Interruptions are common, and it always takes a little extra time to mentally reengage and focus on what you were previously doing. If you want to give an engrossing presentation you need to dedicate your full attention to your presentation. Schedule an appointment with yourself well ahead of your presentation date to make sure that time will be available. Forward your calls, turn off your cell phone and pager, resist the urge to check your e-mail, and put a Do Not Disturb sign on your door. Sometimes the best approach is to find a location to work on your presentation outside of your normal office environment.

Materials. After you have taken time to define the parameters and ask some important questions about the topic and purpose, it is time to begin assembling materials for your presentation. This process involves several steps including collection, organization, writing an outline and rough draft, editing and then reviewing the draft.

1. *Collection.* Pull together information that you think best suits your topic while addressing the purpose of your presentation. What information do you have on hand? Is there any information that is out of date or needs to be supplemented with

additional materials? Is there anyone who may be able to provide you with further useful information?

2. *Organization.* Go through the materials you have collected and sort them into groups based on themes and topics.

3. *Outline and rough draft.* Develop a rough outline of your presentation. What topics and themes are appropriate for the beginning, middle, and end of your presentation? Expand on your outline to develop a rough draft of your presentation. Remember, this is a rough draft. Try to determine what are going to be the key points of your presentation. Write several sentences addressing each of the themes and topics contained in your outline. Try to identify at least five key points. More than seven key points is an indication that you may be trying to convey too much information in your presentation. Does starting with these key points, in light of your overall theme and purpose, succinctly tell your audience what you are going to say? Taken together do they successfully summarize your presentation?

4. *Editing.* For many novice presenters, this part of the presentation process receives the least attention. Given time and energy constraints, one may decide to wing it with a rough draft in hand. For most, however, taking the time to edit the rough draft will be well worth the time and effort. It makes the difference between a fair presentation and an excellent one. Editing the rough draft is best begun by letting a bit of time to pass between the writing and the editing. This allows for a fresh approach. In the editing process think about how the presentation can move from the written to the spoken word. This can be done by simplifying and solidifying the text. Cut unnecessary ideas and words, remove or clarify any jargon, and shorten sentences. In addition, support your ideas with anecdotes and examples. At the end of this process you should have a written copy of what you'd like to say in your presentation and how you'd like to say it.

5. *Review.* Take the time to thoroughly review your edited draft. Read though it out loud several times. If possible do this in front of friends or colleagues. Ask them for criticism and feed-

back on delivery, content, and style. Is the length appropriate for the time allotted? Are the ideas conveyed clearly? Are the overall theme and purpose maintained?

Preparing for Delivery

Once the material has been pulled into a spoken format that stays true to the theme and purpose of the presentation, it is time to refine the delivery process. This can be done through the identification of key words and phrases, the selection of appropriate presentation aids, rehearsal, and preparing for questions.

Keys to an Effective Delivery. One of the most important keys to a successful presentation is eye contact. With a written draft in hand, some presenters will keep their eyes glued to the printed page and neglect to make eye contact with their audience. Unless you are delivering a very formal address or speaking to the press, sticking to the exact words of the draft can be unnecessary and stifling. For a more spontaneous and original approach, which involves more eye contact with the audience, it is useful to identify key words and phrases in the draft. These prompts will be the basis of your draft or your visual aids. Stepping away from the script, rehearse your presentation using these prompts. What do these key words and phrases convey? How do they fit into the presentation as a whole? Transfer these prompts to index cards and practice giving your presentation using these cards. Work toward linking these prompts together in your mind and using fewer and fewer of the cards. Continue practicing this process.

Presentation Aids. Even though the rough draft developed from the materials you collected is the main structure of your presentation, there are a variety of aids that can be used to support your topic, theme, and purpose. These include computer-generated graphics, multimedia, and overhead transparencies. There is nothing more disconcerting, however, than a presentation with poor presentation aids. Instead of supporting your presentation, they detract from it by drawing the audience's attention away from what you are saying. A Microsoft PowerPoint slide with a solid paragraph of text will accomplish one of two things: It will either put the audience immediately to sleep or pull all eyes to the screen for the next five minutes as people carefully try to comprehend the meaning of the words before them. Use presentation aids to support the presentation and encourage conversation between the audience and the presenter. Make sure to have a printed copy of each of your visual presentation aids in case there are problems with technology and you need to refer to an important number or point. Regardless of which aids you use in your presentation, it is important that all aids meet the following criteria:

- ✔ Fit with the script you have developed from your rough draft. They should either summarize or add value to what you are saying at a particular point in your presentation.

- ✔ Flow with the script. Do the aids fit smoothly together with the topic, theme, and purpose as they develop in your script?

- ✔ Are they appropriate for the size and type of audience and the venue where the presentation is taking place? Does an informal audience of five need a multimedia presentation?

- ✔ Look clear, readable, and consistent from all places in the room where the presentation is to take place.

- ✔ Display content simply and effectively. Cluttered and complex slides take attention away from your presentation.

- ✔ Use appropriate graphics such as drawings, charts, and graphics to support a particular point or issue.

Remember that the main structure of the presentation is the script, not the presentation aids. The simpler, clearer, and more precise you can make your presentation aids, the more effective they will be in supporting your topic, theme, and purpose. If you have questions about the quality and clarity of any presentations aids, rehearse your presentation for a trusted colleague, friend, or family member and ask for constructive feedback and criticism.

What's the Point of PowerPoint? Advances in technology have increased the percentage of information we receive visually. This has been especially true since Microsoft brought PowerPoint into our lives and dramatically changed the nature of presentations. Microsoft released PowerPoint in 1987 and since then over 400 million copies have been installed on computers worldwide. Estimates are that it is used in approximately 30 million presentations each day. Some people are now surprised if they attend a presentation and PowerPoint is not part of the program. Many of us, however, look forward to a PowerPoint presentation with all the excitement of a root canal. A dark room, a blue background with white lettering, and we struggle to stay awake and wonder what all that information was about that was flashed up on the screen only minutes ago. PowerPoint is not a required element of a presentation, but it can be a useful tool. Remember, it's not the slides themselves that are the problem so much as it is the content of the slides and how well the presenter uses them.

One of the biggest problems with PowerPoint is that although some organizations encourage its use there is rarely any emphasis on teaching people how to use it effectively. In addition, some companies and organizations require the use of a particular template or insist that the organization's logo be present on each slide. This results in poorly designed and ineffective presentation aids that detract from a presenter's ability to establish a personal relationship with the audience. Some of these problems can be dealt with, while others must be worked around.

One way to counter these problems is to focus on PowerPoint basics rather than on text animation, clip art, video clips, and colorful backgrounds. The more complex a presentation, the more likely it will upstage the presenter. To keep slides visually simple, use a limit of six words to one line and five lines to a slide. Also use no more than three colors per slide.

PowerPoint should be used to provide a map of what you are talking about and to help provide context for the rest of your presentation. Don't use PowerPoint as a surrogate for your speech. PowerPoint is not a teleprompter. In fact, putting less material on a slide can provide a unique opportunity for discussion, but make sure that you know the material you are presenting so as to fill in the details. When working with the program make sure that you know the technology well: What cable goes where? How do you advance a slide? These questions should be answered before you enter the room. Use the "Notes" view of PowerPoint to write out what you'd like to say in your presentation. This will serve as a valuable check in making sure that what is shown on the slide directly relates to what you are saying. In addition, it preserves a more detailed copy of your presentation to share with others or to review at a later date. Don't spend too much time on PowerPoint, though, especially if you are not an expert with the program; time can be better spent working with the core materials of your presentation and rehearsing your delivery. Minimize the number of slides you use in a presentation. The fewer slides the better. If there is additional material that needs to be shared, use handouts. Learn to use the "B" key, which will black out the screen, giving your audience a chance to shift their focus away from the screen and back to the most important part of the presentation: you.

If you are comfortable with PowerPoint and feel that your presentation of the basics is sufficiently covered, take a step or two away from the bullet point format presented in the PowerPoint templates. Alternatives do exist, and these can add meaning and depth to your presentation. Some examples of these are the use of PowerPoint's text boxes, diagramming tools, and AutoShapes. If you want to use more graphics in your presentation, PowerPoint makes it easy to add images—a chart, table, or diagram. Think about symbols and analogies that can be used to emphasize your point.

Rehearsal. Similar to the process of editing the rough draft mentioned before, rehearsal is another part of the presentation process that is often skipped over. With a script, a few prompts, and some clever presentation aids, some presenters are ready to go. Once again, however, taking the time to rehearse the presentation will prove worthwhile in the long run. It will smooth over rough patches, reveal areas that may need further attention, and make you more comfortable about delivering the presentation. Rehearsing in front of others can be particularly beneficial and can bring up certain things that may have been overlooked earlier, such as a lack of eye contact, forgetting to smile, putting your hands in your pockets, or turning your back to the audience. If you want to make sure you are mindful of these issues during your presentation, write them down on an index card and place the card in front of you during your presentation.

During the rehearsal process take a moment to reflect on the style and content of your delivery. Does your presentation stay focused and avoid wandering off on tangents? Does it deliver a clear message to your audience? Don't be afraid to fine-tune your presentation in order to address some of these issues. This will help maintain the focus and attention of your audience.

Preparing for Questions. Try to anticipate some of the questions your audience might ask. How can these questions be answered referencing your presentation or your visual aids? Are there any questions that might require a bit more research on your part?

The Eleventh Hour

After defining the parameters, developing a script, and preparing the delivery, the time will finally come to give the presentation. There are several important things to think of in the hours before this moment arrives. To cover any last-minute problems, you should redefine the parameters, check yourself, double-check your materials, and arrive early.

Revisit the Presentation Parameters. As mentioned earlier, some of the parameters can be determined prior to the presentation; others will change slightly by the day of the presentation. It is important to take another look at the parameters to make sure that none of the changes will dramatically affect your presentation. Review the parameters and address any concerns or problems. Have there been any changes in the program or agenda? Has your presentation been moved in the program? Will someone be introducing you? Who is that person, and does he or she need anything from you prior to your introduction? Will someone be asking audience members to turn off their cell phones and pagers? You should request this if possible.

Another parameter that often changes the day of the presentation is the size of the audience, which will have a lot to do with how you choose to address the formality and style of your presentation. For small groups of 5 to 10, the presentation will often be informal. You can remain seated and work to develop a more personal relationship with your audience members. For an audience containing between 10 and 30 individuals, it is still possible to develop relationships, but the style will probably be more formal. With an audience of this size, visual presentation aids become useful. When the audience size is closer to 100, good presentation aids will become even more useful. An audience of this size will increase formality further and make it more difficult to develop personal relationships. When the audience size surpasses 100, your presentation will be more of a performance. It is best to use a microphone and try to exaggerate facial gestures and arm movements.

Changes and difficulties at the location of your presentation can be a real headache. Give yourself at least a couple of hours before the presentation to double-check the audio-video resources available at the location. Are they working? Are you still able to connect your laptop computer to the audio-video system? Do you need to load your presentation program onto an on-site computer? Do all of your computer-based audiovisuals run smoothly with the projector? Will you be using a remote to advance your slides? Who will help you with the audio-video equipment if there are any problems? In addition, find out exactly where you will be presenting in the room. Where should you be prior to your presentation? Will a glass of water be available? Where are the restrooms?

Speaker's Podium and Its Use.　A podium has always been a central fixture of lecture halls and auditoriums. For the most part, if there is a podium in the room a presenter will often be drawn to it like a magnet. This is not always for the best. Although a podium can provide a sense of authority and a convenient place to rest one's water glass, it can also serve as a barrier and hinder one's efforts to connect with an audience. If a podium is present and there is a convener for the meeting, ask where presenters are expected to deliver their presentations. If the choice is up to you, think about the size and nature of your audience. With a smaller, less formal group, step away from the podium so that you can develop personal and individual relationships with your audience members. With a larger, more formal audience, a podium can serve as a means to minimize stage fright and help the audience focus on the presenter.

Speaking Attire.　What are you going to wear for your presentation? With all the thought you have put into preparing what you will say and how you will say it, it is possible that this item has been sidelined until the last minute. The most important thing to keep in mind is that your choice of attire should not detract from the message you are delivering. Dressing conservatively and neatly will convey the professionalism of your presentation. In the minutes before your presentation make sure to double-check your appearance. And did you remember to turn off your cell phone and pager? In general when planning on what to wear for your presentation, consider these questions and the following list of do's and don'ts from the Executive Communications Group at http://ecglink.com.

Clothing "Do's"

- ✔ Always look professional.
- ✔ Dress for the audience, the circumstance, the corporate culture, and yourself.
- ✔ Wear clothes that fit.
- ✔ Make sure your clothes are pressed.
- ✔ Keep jackets buttoned (formal).
- ✔ Err on the side of conservative.
- ✔ Keep your hair neat and trimmed.
- ✔ No hair in eyes.
- ✔ For women: simple manicure, conservative makeup.
- ✔ Mild (or no) fragrances.
- ✔ Ties should be conservative and reach the middle of your belt buckle.
- ✔ Lace-up shoes (usually black) with a suit.
- ✔ A traditional starched business shirt, preferably white cotton with a suit.
- ✔ Shirts with a simple collar and cuffs.
- ✔ A formal but simple watch.
- ✔ Hair, usually parted to one side, not reaching the top of your shirt collar.
- ✔ Over-the-calf socks for men; hosiery should be skin color or darker for women.

Clothing "Don'ts"

✔ Wear clothes that talk louder than you do.

✔ Undo multiple buttons on your shirt or blouse.

✔ Wear clothing that no longer fits.

✔ Wear wrinkled clothing.

✔ Use fabrics that have a noticeable sheen.

✔ Let hair fall in your face or obscure your eyebrows.

✔ Have a hair style that requires continual adjustment.

✔ Use a fragrance that smells from a distance.

✔ Wear an ID badge when you're presenting.

✔ Wear busy patterns.

✔ Wear garish ties.

✔ Sport untrimmed facial hair (in some organizations, any facial hair can be career-inhibiting).

✔ Wear shiny tie pins or clips or big belt buckles.

✔ Wear visible jewelry (other than a watch and/or a single simple ring).

✔ Wear distracting lapel pins for men, or dangles, bangles, or anything noisy for women.

✔ Leave top shirt button open with a tie.

✔ Wear short-sleeved dress shirts.

✔ Wear short socks.

✔ Wear loafers with a suit for men, or open-toe or ultrahigh-heel shoes for women.

Other Appearance Considerations. Your audience should be able to see your eyes clearly and easily. If you wear glasses, consider an antiglare coating for the lenses, which makes it easier to see your eyes. Avoid any tint (unless medically necessary) and avoid heavy frames that can obscure your eyes. Any perfume, cologne, or perfumed grooming product should not be noticeable at normal business proximity. This means that you can exit the elevator and no one entering should be able to guess that you were there. Also, if you will be in a health care setting, you should not wear anything scented because colognes can aggravate certain medical conditions and allergies.

Importance of Backup Plans and Preplanning

Do not make the mistake of leaving an important presentation aid behind at your home or office. Put the materials you will need for your presentation in a separate and secure location. Check them carefully the day before and the morning of your presentation to make sure that nothing is missing or broken. Bring a backup copy of your visual aids in a folder or on a CD in case something happens to the originals. Are there any handouts you want to provide to your audience during or after your presentation? If so, make sure that you have more than enough copies available well in advance of the presentation day. Do you have that index card of what to be mindful of when presenting (such as looking your audience in the eye)?

In order to do a last-minute check of the parameters, arrive early. Knowing that the audio-video equipment and your laptop are working will put your mind at rest and add to your confidence about your presentation. Take a minute to look over your notes and run through your key words and phrases. In addition, and if it is appropriate given the size and formality of your audience, playing host before your presentation can be a good way to begin developing a relationship with your audience. Greet audience members individually as they arrive, and ask people if they are comfortable in their seats and can see the screen. Developing a personal relationship with your audience in this way will also help alleviate some of your stage fright.

DELIVERING THE PRESENTATION

The time has finally come to take the stage. There are a couple of important steps that can be taken to engage your audience and make your presentation informative and interesting. To overcome stage fright, remember that for most situations the audience wants the speaker to succeed. The audience is there because they want to hear what you have to say. Once you have been introduced to the audience, take a moment to establish your presence. This is not very difficult, but it does involve patience and a bit of confidence. It is done by taking a deep breath, looking your audience in the eye, relaxing your frame, and, most importantly, smiling.

The Introduction

Even if someone has already taken the time to introduce you, it is helpful to take a moment to introduce yourself. This will quickly clarify a couple of important points. It lets your audience know who you are, what you have come to speak to them about, and what credentials you possess to speak on this subject. This also shapes the audience's expectations of your presentation.

The best presentations are engaging as well as informative. In order to engage the audience, you need to begin developing a relationship. Get your audience's attention by showing them that you understand their concerns and issues, that you are aware of their expectations, and that you respect their opinions. You can do this by asking an engaging question, doing something unexpected, or showing them a unique visual aid. This not only serves to break the ice but also shifts some of the attention from you back to the audience. One of the most effective tools for developing a relationship with your audience is to tell a story. This is not always easy, but an engaging story that is relevant to your presentation will get your audience's attention quickly and effectively.

Sometimes, especially during a long presentation, the audience's attention might begin to drift. Don't hesitate to take a break during your presentation at an appropriate point. A five-minute break can do wonders for reviving your audience. You might even plan for a break during the initial stages of planning your presentation.

It is important to remember that when you are developing a relationship you need to be yourself. Use your emotion as well as the raw information contained in your presentation to convey your message. Having a sense of conviction about what you are saying will serve not only to strengthen your relationship with the audience, but also to alleviate some of the initial stage fright you might feel.

Sometimes, through no fault of your own, you will find yourself in front of an unresponsive audience. It could be due to the poor quality of previous presenters or the fact that attendance was mandatory.

Perhaps it's just that it's 7 A.M. on a Monday morning after a three-day weekend. Regardless of the cause, no matter what you try, the audience refuses to display any emotion about your presentation. In this case it's best to face facts and move on. Focus on your material and speak passionately and convincingly. Remember that just because the audience as a whole was cold and unresponsive, this is not necessarily true about the individuals that make up the audience. Given another time or space and some one-on-one contact, you may find that members of the audience were receptive to the topic, theme, and purpose of your presentation.

Body and Voice

Having conviction in what you are saying will be conveyed not only in the words you use, but also in the way you stand and the way you speak. In establishing your presence you took a deep breath, relaxed a bit, and smiled. This process is meant to prepare your body and voice for the task ahead. During the presentation your stance should be erect and focused. Your feet should be shoulder-width apart and your weight should be balanced. Remember to keep your hands out of your pockets and look your audience in the eye. If you have your index card in front of you, you won't make the mistake of forgetting this during your presentation. Avoid turning your back to your audience, don't lean casually against a podium or table, and don't fidget with clothing or jewelry. Your casual stance can come across as disinterested, unprepared, and disrespectful. This is not the impression you want to leave your audience with after the presentation is finished.

If you are having trouble looking your audience in the eye, look just over the head of the person sitting in the last row. In this way it will seem to people in the audience that you are looking directly at them. Another option is to look at the center of people's faces rather than at their eyes. You can also select a few people around the room you feel comfortable making eye contact with and focus on them. Choose the option that best suits your comfort level.

In addition to a straight and focused posture, your body language should also be positive and as natural as possible. When you are trying to share important information with family members or friends, how do you approach them? Do you move around and use hand gestures and facial expressions? Do you sometimes smile and laugh? Use this same approach with your audience. It will convey to them that you are confident, sincere, and respectful.

If you are uncertain about your posture and body language during your presentation, make a video recording of yourself during your rehearsals. Watch the video and keep an eye out for poor posture or body language and any tendencies that might detract from the focus of your presentation.

To be truly effective, however, an erect and confident posture combined with a positive and natural manner must be accompanied by an effective use of voice. One of the biggest problems that people experience when giving a presentation is that they begin speaking very quickly. The material rushes by in a blur and the audience is left squinting at the visual aids trying to figure out exactly what was said. Speaking quickly also has a tendency to raise the pitch of your voice and wear you out quickly. There are a few steps that can be taken to guard against the tendency to speak too quickly. First, take a deep breath and relax. Breathing normally will help pace your speech. Second, listen to yourself. Do you seem to be rushing your sentences? Do you feel short of breath? Is the tone of your voice rising? If so, slow down, work on lowering your voice, and take a breath. Third, if, despite forewarning and practice, you still find yourself speaking too quickly, get a trusted colleague, friend, or family member to sit in the front row during your presentation. Visually check in with that person every couple of minutes and have him give you a subtle hand gesture if you need to slow down.

Another problem people often experience when giving a presentation is hesitating and saying "um" or "er" when they have lost their train of thought. A better approach is to pause, take a breath, and refocus. Be conscious of whether or not you have these tendencies. If you are unsure, make a recording of yourself giving your presentation. While listening to the recording, follow along in your rough script. How often do you hear yourself say "um" or "er"? Are there certain places in your presentation where you have more trouble than others? Be aware of these problems and work to correct them.

An additional and important element to consider in regard to the use of your body and voice during your presentation is variation. This is part of the process of conveying emotion to your audience. While rehearsing your presentation, think about ways to change your body language or voice to convey the importance of particular material. Change the speed and tone of your voice and use inflections and emphasis. One of the most effective ways of making a point during a presentation is the use of silence. After making a particularly important point or summarizing several previous points, pause for a moment and allow the audience to absorb and reflect on what you have said. Vary gestures and other body language to convey similar messages.

Humor

The use of humor in your presentation is a great way to further build on your relationship with the audience and lighten and vary the mood. Make sure you are confident in your use of humor and use it to support points in your presentation. Confident, relevant, and natural are the qualities you want to project to your audience. Avoid using humor to belittle or make fun of people in the audience. It will detract from the theme, topic, and purpose of your presentation. As the presenter, you are the only legitimate target for humor in the room.

Expect the Unexpected

As Dwight D. Eisenhower once said, "In preparing for battle I have always found that plans are useless, but planning is indispensable." Despite the importance and necessity of all the planning and practicing you have done in order to deliver a successful presentation, learn to expect the unexpected. This requires flexibility both in the way you relate to your audience as well as in the way you deliver your presentation. When mistakes happen, and they will, don't try to ignore them; this just makes them more obvious. Acknowledge them, deal with them, and move on. This can be done by deflecting them or countering them with the use of light humor. Don't, however, be overly sensitive to mistakes. In many cases the mistake may be small enough that the audience may not have even noticed it.

A level of flexibility should also be present in the delivery of your presentation. A presenter who is too polished, overly confident, or too prepared can alienate an audience. Be sensitive to how the audience is relating to you and be flexible enough in your presentation to lighten the mood or change the style of your delivery. Leaving room for improvisation will add an element of freshness, realism, and sincerity to your presentation.

Flexibility will also be important if there are any problems with your presentation aids. Instead of dwelling on any problems, try to address them and, if you cannot solve them quickly, make a humorous aside and talk directly to your audience. Remember that the presentation is not about the visual aids; it is about you. You have prepared and you are ready.

CONCLUDING THE PRESENTATION

In developing the outline for your presentation, you organized the material you collected into themes and topics with an eye on what would be appropriate for the beginning, middle, and end of your presentation. Over the course of your delivery you have carefully developed these themes and topics in light of the purpose of the presentation. At the end of your delivery make sure that you bring your presentation to a close with a concise and effective conclusion. The conclusion should be succinct so that it leaves your audience with a clear message about your main topics and themes. Don't repeat the main text; summarize it. In addition, end on a positive note with energy and confidence. This will leave your audience interested in learning more about your topics and themes.

QUESTION-AND-ANSWER PERIOD

Dealing with questions can be as intimidating as delivering the presentation itself, and some presenters might prefer to skip the process entirely. To properly conclude your presentation and respect the relationship you have developed with your audience, you need to allow for questions. When answering questions, acknowledge the speaker and repeat the question so that the entire audience can hear it. Avoid getting into a debate or argument, and if you do not know the answer to the question, admit it. Ask for the contact information of the person asking the question and offer to get back to them with a response later.

POSTPRESENTATION CONSIDERATIONS

After a presentation, the script and visual aids often end up in a folder casually tossed and forgotten on your desk. It is time to get on with other things, and if you need to deliver the presentation again, you can always dig up the folder and use the same materials. This approach is a mistake and wastes a valuable opportunity to take advantage of your initial assessment of the presentation. Even letting a couple of days pass before reviewing your presentation will cause you to forget valuable points.

If you were fortunate enough to get a video recording of your presentation, use it as a tool to examine your presentation for content and style. If possible watch the video twice, focusing on a different aspect each time. It would be difficult to cover both aspects at the same time.

SUMMARY

Presentations and communications are critical success factors in today's competitive organizational environment. Managers find they are spending more and more time preparing for presentations, and in communicating their ideas with colleagues, customers, investors, and other stakeholders. It is essential that managers consider these presentation opportunities as important to advancing the organization's purpose and in achieving its goals and objectives. Properly prepared, managers can use presentations as an effective tool for success and opportunity.

REFERENCES

Adubato, Steve. "Put Power of Low-Tech in Presentations," *Star-Ledger* (May 25, 2003).

Bobo, John. "How to Repair and Resuscitate an Audience Abused by Boredom," *Presentations* 18, Issue 1 (January 2004): 58.

Bunzel, Tom. "Successful Speakers Know How Presenting and Preparation Go Hand-in-Hand," *Presentations* 17, Issue 10 (October 2003): 58.

Couzins, Martin. "How to Make Effective Presentations," *Personnel Today* (July 22, 2003): 25.

Daley, Kevin. "Meeting the Challenges of Group Presenting," *Presentations* 17, Issue 11 (November 2003): 66.

Executive Communications Group, "Best Business Attire," *PS: For Business Communicators*, http://ecglink.com/newsletter/dress spk_men.shtml.

Finkelstein, Ellen. "A PowerPoint World without Bullets Is Possible, and Beautiful As Well," *Presentations* 18, Issue 1 (January 2004): 20.

Hill, Julie. "The Attention Deficit," *Presentations* 17, Issue 10 (October 2003): 26.

Messmer, Max. "Public Speaking Success Strategies," *National Public Accountant* (November 2003): 26.

Murphy, Herta. *Effective Business Communications*. New York: McGraw-Hill, 1991: 392–395.

Ross, Emily. "The Podium Set," *Business Review Weekly* (Australia) (December 11, 2003).

Stafky, Aaryn. "Taking the Fear out of Public Speaking," *Rural Telecommunications,* (July–August 2003): 46, 49.

Wahl, Andrew. "PowerPoint of No Return," *Canadian Business* 76, Issue 22 (November 23, 2003): 131.

SECTION IV

SYSTEMS AND PROCESSES

Chapter 11

Project Management

In this chapter we explore a concept and a practice that has grown in importance as organizations have become more complex and are continuously evolving and implementing new ideas, products, and services or seek to improve existing ones. An organization will create a project as a way to focus resources on an opportunity or issue and to serve as a way to effectively organize its efforts to achieve a specific goal or objective. In a small firm, practice, or business, a project may be the installation of a new accounting software system or the introduction of a new product or service. In large, complex organizations, several projects may be in play at the same time, with some midlevel managers whose only responsibility is the management of a stream of these short-term assignments. In the dynamic nature of today's organizational environment, project management is an important concept and tool to understand and effectively implement.

According to the Project Management Institute (PMI), 74 percent of all projects fail. The projects can fail from a processes standpoint (initiation, planning, executing, controlling, or closing), or they can fail from a weakness in project dynamics (scope, time cost management, quality management, human resources management, communications, or risk). Project management covers a wide range of topics and issues and is defined as the application of knowledge, skills, tools, and techniques to a broad range of activities to reach a predetermined goal or objective. (See Figure 11.1.)

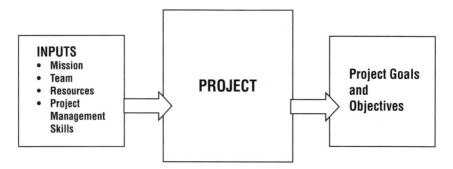

FIGURE 11.1 Simple Project Management Process

ROLE OF PROJECT MANAGER

It may also be concluded that a considerable number of projects fail from not having a skilled and experienced project manager to manage the process. This hole is quickly being filled, however, as companies recognize that successfully managed projects increase productivity, yield a greater return on investment, increase profits, and improve customer service.

But project management isn't new. Project management coordination and planning skills have been used for centuries—even as far back as the Roman Empire. Project management has also almost always dealt with the same elemental challenges: incomplete project specifications and scope definition, insufficient labor, unforeseen challenges, or unsure funding. The role and job title of the person responsible for managing these elements, however, the project manager, was not recognized until the twentieth century.

Another reason for the importance of the role of a project manager is the increasing rate of change in the workplace. Project management skills transcend corporations and industries; with change happening at such rapid rates, whether in technology, business, or construction, project managers are increasingly in demand.

It is important, however, for all project participants to understand the process of project management. As project-based change increases, every project participant from part-time team member to executive sponsor will be more effective in their role if they understand the process of project management.

PROJECT SCOPE AND WORK BREAKDOWN STRUCTURE

Let's begin with a discussion of the vocabulary and processes that encompass project management. The project scope involves subdividing the major project deliverables into smaller, more manageable components. Often this includes the work breakdown structure (WBS). The project scope is a deliverable-oriented grouping of project elements that define the total scope of the project. The WBS is almost like a giant task list of what needs to get done to successfully complete the project. It is often used to help confirm a common understanding of what the project scope is. It has the ability to transform one large, unique, and sometimes mystifying job into many small, more manageable tasks.

The WBS helps to define deliverables and figure out the tasks that need to get done. The WBS is also a useful tool to help monitor the progress, verify the schedule estimates, and build project teams necessary to complete the project. It lists the tasks that need to get done in a prioritized, hierarchical structure in relation to what needs to get done in the overall project. Each task should be specific enough to be able to put a person's name next to it who will be able to execute the given activity.

Some of the items on the list will be open-ended tasks. Open-ended tasks include activities that we are familiar with doing, but don't have a specific deliverable or hard product being produced. Examples of open-ended activities that might appear in a WBS are things such as "research," "perform analysis," or "interview." Another type of task might be on the list to perform but need more clarification. "Database" might be listed, but what does that really mean? Does it mean sort the database? Clean the database? Load the database? Test the database? You can see that just putting the word "database" on the list could refer to numerous activities; therefore, a greater level of detail about the task needs to be achieved.

The WBS should include a plan for the project and output quality.

Be sure to take the time necessary to get the quality high enough to meet expectations. It is cheaper to design and produce a product correctly the first time than it is to go in after development is in process and fix it. Steve McConnell, in his book *Rapid Development,* pointed out that if a defect caused by incorrect requirements is fixed in the construction or maintenance phase, it can cost 50 to 200 times as much to fix as it would have in the requirements phase. Each hour spent on quality assurance activities such as design review saves 3 to 10 hours on downstream costs.

Product scope and project scope have different qualities. The product scope can remain constant throughout the process of the project, while the project scope can change and evolve and expand. The project may also focus on the creation and delivery of a service. If there is no detailed product description, then creating one should be the sole deliverable for a project. Defining what the project constraints are (costs, schedule, resources, material, etc.) won't have any meaning unless the product specification is complete. This makes sense because if the project team doesn't have a clear idea of the product specification, they don't know what they're building or what they're working toward.

Given that a product scope is understood, then, it is important to define what the deliverables are. What is being produced? Is it a product? A service? A new design? Fixing an old problem? It is critical that the team know what they are working toward and it helps to create boundaries and focus the team on the outcome.

Deliverables can be either end deliverables or intermediate deliverables. The end deliverable is what the final outcome of the project is expected to be. The intermediate deliverables are the small pieces of the puzzle that help the team get there. An intermediate deliverable, for example, could be the creation and description of a target market, when the end deliverable is the mass media advertising campaign for a product or service.

Setting project objectives is critical. They serve as quantifiable criteria that must be met in order for the project to be deemed successful. Project objectives should be specific and measurable so that they can provide the basis for agreement on the project. Measurability provides supporting detail that may be necessary to make a strong case for a particular outcome.

PROJECT SCOPE MANAGEMENT PLAN

When the product scope is understood, a project scope management plan needs to be created. This plan describes how the project scope will be managed and, therefore, any changes in scope will be integrated into the project. It also serves as an assessment of the anticipated stability of the project scope. In other words, it documents the characteristics of the product or service that the project was undertaken to create. As shown in Figure 11.2, the project scope management plan begins at initiation of the project and moves through scope planning, scope definition, scope verification, and scope change control (should this be needed).

The initiation phase includes beginning to develop the scope statement. The scope statement serves to put some boundaries on the project and keeps the scope from increasing as you delve into the meat of the project, which is a common phenomenon. The scope statement should describe the major activities of the project so clearly that it can be used to assess if extra work is necessary as the project process gets going. More simply, it serves to detail exactly what has been agreed to from the beginning. It is understood that changes in the project scope require changes in the cost, schedule, and resource projections as these assumptions are made during the project planning and scope writing. Additionally, the scope statement can be used to help define where the project's placement is in a larger picture. This is the ideal place to clarify the relationship of this project to other projects in the total product development effort.

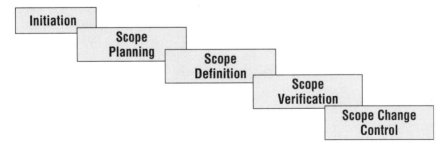

FIGURE 11.2 Project Stages

Also considered in the initiation phase is the overall strategic plan of the organization. All projects should be supportive of the performing organization's goals, and having a strategic plan helps to make this possible. The project selection criteria are also very important to clarify in this phase. This is a good time to look at historical information and look to the results of previous project selection and performance.

The elements included in the initiation phase may include creating a project charter. The project charter is the product description and business needs the project addresses. Identifying and assigning the project manager should also be one of the results of the initial phase. It is important as well during this phase to identify constraints that will limit the project team's options and also identify the assumptions. The assumptions can include factors that will be considered true, real, or certain during the planning process and that will be more rigorously examined in the risk analysis phase of project planning.

The scope planning phase includes the scope statement (scope justification, project product description, project deliverables, project objectives, and supporting detail).

When the major project deliverables are subdivided into small, more manageable components, the phase is called scope definition. The scope definition phase is also where you'll see the creation of the WBS.

The scope verification portion of the system is what may be used to determine if the job is complete. The process can actually proceed as soon as a deliverable is complete and can be measured, examined, and tested. Once verification is attained, you can move on to the next component of the project.

After formal acceptance of the scope (scope verification), scope change control takes place. It is likely that changes will occur after a project is under way. This phase influences factors that create scope changes to ensure that the changes being made are beneficial.

A change control system will include:

✔ Recognizing that a change is needed.

✔ Reviewing all requested changes.

✔ Ensuring that any change is beneficial.

✔ Evaluating the benefits of the requested change.

✔ Identifying alternatives that would achieve the same result.

✔ Identifying all impacted tasks.

✔ Analyzing these impacts and how they affect project performance in terms of time, money, and scope.

✔ Approving or rejecting the request.

✔ Communicating the approved changes to all stakeholders.

✔ Changing the baselines for performance monitoring.

✔ Updating the project scope definition.

✔ Implementing the change.

✔ Documenting the change.

It is critical that all change gets documented by the client prior to the change taking place. The agreement should detail not only what changes need to take place, but also how each change will occur and what the impact of the change will be on the overall scope.

Jeb Riordan created a useful flowchart to describe the typical change control process. It is easier to picture how the decision flows through question points on a diagram, and it makes the change control process seem a lot more intuitive.

Once a need for a change has been identified, the request for change needs to be reviewed. If it is deemed a bad idea to make the change suggested at that time, the issue is registered but there is no change order created or acted upon. If it is deemed a good idea to make the change at the time, it must be determined if the impending change will impact the project plan. If it will not impact the project plan, you can go ahead and make the change. If it will impact the plan, the impact must be assessed and clearly identified, a change order must be prepared outlining the anticipated changes, and then that change order must be approved before the change can be made.

PROJECT SCHEDULE

In order to adjust for things such as scope changes, we need to be sure that there is a solid project schedule in place. The project scheduling process needs to include the activity definition, activity sequencing, activity duration estimating, schedule development, and the schedule control.

Examples of the primary tools used for project scheduling are Gantt charts, or Critical Path Method (CPM), PERT (Program Evaluation and Review Technique). Critical Path Method and PERT are powerful tools that help you to schedule and manage complex projects. They were developed in the 1950s to control large defense projects, and have been used routinely since then.

Gantt charts are simply a visual look at the major activities involved in a project, arranged so that the viewer will see the time-based relationships of the component parts of the project. Figure 11.3 is a Gantt chart showing the activities involved in the purchase and implementation of a new accounting software system.

CPM helps you to plan out all tasks that must be completed as part of a project, and it acts as a basis both for preparation of a schedule and for resource planning. When you are managing a project, this tool can help you monitor the achievement of your project goals to date. It also helps you to see where you can take action to put a project back on track if it has fallen behind or deviated from its course.

	March	April	May	June Weeks 1–2	June Weeks 3–4	July	August	September	October	–	January	June	December	Person/Team Responsible
Assessment of the needs and tasks the new software would perform	X													Joan lead/ accounting team and managers
Research the programs available in the market	X													Accounting team
Request proposals from software vendors		X												Joan
Evaluate proposals			X											Joan/ accounting team
Reassess needs given capacity of software packages			X											Joan lead/ accounting team and managers
Make selection			X											Joan lead/ accounting team and managers
Install software				X										Sam/IT team
Train staff on use of software					X									Sam/IT team

FIGURE 11.3 Sample Gantt Chart

CPM is useful because it:

✔ Identifies tasks that must be completed on time for the whole project to be completed on time.

✔ Identifies which tasks can be delayed if necessary if resources need to be allocated somewhere else to catch up on missed tasks.

✔ Helps to identify the minimum length of time needed to complete the project.

PERT is a variation on CPM that takes a slightly more skeptical view of time estimates made for each project stage. To use it, you estimate the shortest possible time each activity will take, the most likely length of time, and the longest time that might be taken if the activity takes longer than expected.

Project scheduling essentially takes the definition of what the project is and breaks it down into smaller, more manageable tasks. It also identifies the relationships of each of the tasks to the other tasks. It illuminates in complete detail the actions that need to take place in order for the project to get accomplished. It then ensures the necessary order by using information about the activity duration as well as any external constraints that might exist. Finally, the project schedule ensures that the deadlines are met given the identified constraints such as labor, materials, and other resources.

PROJECT BUDGET

The next step is figuring out the project budget. Project budget estimates can be derived by using a variety of techniques ranging from pure estimation based on experience and knowledge to complicated financial models. An accurate, detailed cost estimate is necessary as soon as the project concept gets approval. The cost estimate created will become the standard for keeping the project costs in line and can be used by the client, the management team, the project manager, and the project management team.

A detailed and accurate budget also helps forecast the project funding needed and during which phase it will be needed. As the project progresses, the cost information will also be used to help control the project, monitor the progress, identify potential problems, and help to find solutions.

The calculation of the budget isn't what's difficult. We all know that it's just a matter of adding up the numbers that we have associated with the costs of performing different tasks. The trick is getting those numbers to be as accurate as possible before the expenses have been incurred. The source of data for the budget, then, is where most of the time will be spent when it comes to the budgeting process.

The first thing to think about is the internal labor costs. One of the biggest oversights that occur during the budgeting process is leaving out the cost of internal staff. This can be derived by using the detailed planning model to figure how much of each person's time is going to be needed to get the job done. Then you can use the burdened labor rate. Although the hourly rate of each salaried employee may vary, you can look to your finance department to create a standard burdened labor rate. This rate is calculated by taking the average cost of an employee to the firm. It includes the costs for wages, benefits, and overhead. Most company finance departments keep this established rate on record so it is not necessary to calculate and recalculate it from the project manager's point of view.

Getting an accurate cost for internal equipment used can be more complicated. If you will be purchasing and using equipment for a single project, then it is fairly straightforward to add up the cost of each piece and add it to the budget. If, however, you will be using equipment that gets used on multiple projects, you should use a unit cost approach to estimate how much of the equipment will be used for a specific project. One way to do this is to spread the cost over the time period of the expected use. Do you expect to use the equipment on 5 projects? 10? 50? Based on these assumptions you can create a unit cost, or hourly rate, for using the equipment, which can be applied to a project estimate.

External labor cost and equipment costs are usually simpler to figure out. This is because contractors have already calculated their costs for products or services ahead of time. Sometimes these rates can be negotiated. Under a cost-plus contract, the labor and equipment rates are written into the contract and the vendor bills the project for the amount of labor, equipment, and materials supplied to the project. Once this has been figured out, you just add it to the overall cost estimate for your budget.

The final piece to consider is the cost of materials. Material costs will vary widely depending on the nature of the project that you are working on. The range can expand from materials needed to construct a building to the materials needed to develop software. The percentage of the total costs attributed to materials varies just as widely. The first place to look for the expected costs of materials is in the product specification or service plan.

Once the project's schedule and costs have been determined, you may generate a cash flow projection. Again, it is important to realize that estimating the costs that go into the budget is the responsibility of all of the project stakeholders. A cooperative approach yields more accurate results and it helps to reduce the uncertainty of the project.

RISK MANAGEMENT

Next, it is time to manage the project's risk. Not many project managers realize that managing risk is their primary responsibility, but they tend to do it without even thinking about it. Risk management is the total process to identify, control, and minimize the impact of uncertain events. The objective of the risk management program is to systematically reduce risk to increase the likelihood of having the project objectives met. In effect, as project managers know, all project management is risk management. As mentioned earlier, outside obstacles are assessed and accounted for when planning the project.

The project definition takes into account a lot of risk management activities. The project definition establishes what the goals and constraints for the project will be. In this process it is critical to identify what the risks for your project are. You must identify the sources of risk in your project. You must then develop a response to each risk by examining the potential damage and the degree of likelihood of that risk taking place. Finally, you should implement the strategies that you develop as a response and monitor the effects of whether these changes will impact the project. If there are changes that need to take place, be

sure that all stakeholders are again apprised of the situation and noti-
fied of what changes will take place.

At the end of this whole process, you end up with a solid project
plan. You have identified the key or required staff; the key risks including their constraints and assumptions (and have planned responses for
each); the scope and schedule management plans; the project charter;
a description of the project management approach or strategy; a scope
statement that includes project deliverables and the project objectives;
WBS to the level at which control will be exercised; cost estimates,
scheduled start dates, and responsibility assignments that stem from
WBS; performance measurement baselines for schedule and cost; and
finally, major milestones and target dates for each.

PROJECT ESTIMATION

Although estimation, by definition, is making an attempt at forecasting
the future and trying to predict the time and money necessary to produce the stated result, it is important for your stakeholders that you
get good at accurately estimating when a project will be done and what
will be needed to ensure its completion. This means getting the right
people on board to help make the estimate, making estimates based on
personal or institutional experience, and taking the time and making
the effort required to make good estimates.

One technique used for estimating is called phased estimating.
This means that cost and scheduling commitments need to be given
for only one phase of the project at a time. Not surprisingly, this is a favorite estimating technique among project managers because it doesn't
require the whole project time line and costs to be determined all at
once, which is considered unrealistic for some; they prefer to base the
future phases of the project on how the first one or two phases go. The
uncertainty that every project faces at the beginning diminishes as
the project progresses. This approach takes place by first making an
order-of-magnitude estimate for the full development life cycle, with
a detailed estimate for the first phase of the project.

The conclusion of the first phase also means the first meeting of
a phase gate. Phase gates specifically refer to decision points for evaluating whether the project development should continue. Reaching

the first phase gate also means the beginning of the second cycle or phase of the estimate. Once sign-off has been granted for the first phase, another order-of-magnitude estimate is made, along with a detailed estimate of the second phase. And the cycle continues like this. Through this process, the order-of-magnitude estimate gets more and more accurate and each phase requires assessment and evaluation in order to continue.

Another technique used in project estimation is called apportioning, or top-down, estimating. With this method, a total project estimate is given and then a percentage of the total project is assigned to each of the phases and tasks of the project. The WBS can provide a good solid breakdown for using this estimation technique.

In order for this method to be as accurate as possible, however, it is critical that, first, the overall project estimate is correct; otherwise the project estimates for the smaller pieces won't be accurate. Second, apportioning is based on a formula derived from historical data/experience of other similar projects. Because of this, it is critical that the previous projects be very similar to the project at hand. This technique is rarely as accurate as a bottom-up approach, but can be very valuable when assessing whether to select a project to pursue.

Parametric estimates are made when a basic unit of work is created to be used as a multiplier to size the project as a whole. The estimates are useful for figuring the entire project scope or cost on a smaller scale and applying it to the whole. It is created by using historical data of how long something took or what resources were used, and it requires that the estimator develop a parametric formula. Parametric formulas take into account certain variables that might occur during the working process. Will the process be faster or slower at some times than others due to holidays, seasonal influences, or other projects that need to be worked on? Will there be a shortage or surplus of materials for any reason? Parametric estimates are more accurate when done at lower levels, but they can still be useful when used to measure order-of-magnitude estimates. It is most useful when used during the construction phase of the product life cycle because it allows you to really detail the product specification, and this feeds into a more accurate estimate.

The most accurate type of estimation is bottom-up estimating. Bottom-up estimating, however, also requires the most amount of work because it makes an estimation of all of the detailed tasks individually and then adds them all up for the project as a whole. Although the most accurate form of estimating, this level of detail usually isn't available at the very beginning of the project, so it's best used for building the detailed phase estimates.

PROJECT TEAM

During the estimation phase, it is critical that you know the skill sets of the team with whom you will be working. You must know the expertise of others, even if you don't know them personally, and be able to ask for help. It is also important to look at what technology will be required to complete the project. Does it rely on new technology? Will you need members of your team to have a new skill set to accommodate for the technology? What is the reliability of the technology you will be using?

The team of people you will be working with on your project management team is probably the most critical ingredient of the whole process. It is the responsibility of the project manager to motivate and guide the team to complete the project at hand. This may oblige the leader to administer a variety of management techniques to develop a cohesive group. Change in the process must also be aptly managed. Managing the execution of the project requires being constantly aware of the project deliverables, project objectives, project schedule, project costs, and the quality. Monitoring all of this will allow the project manager to quickly assess when the work of the team is deviating from the original plan and allow the manager to bring the team back on track.

Project managers have a large task. They must be able to define and manage quality throughout the project. They must be able to accurately determine the human resource requirements and be able to manage them. They must know how to develop and manage project planning and costs using the techniques discussed in this example. They must be effective communicators with all stakeholders—senior management, team members, clients, outsourced resources, and so on—and they need to be familiar with the supply and contract management techniques.

The most successful leaders, however, create outstanding teams.

A successful team has numerous links between team members and frequent and comfortable communication among them. It is important not to overly rely on one person too much with critical information, and put the project at risk by consolidation of data or information. Just as it is important not to rely too heavily on one individual, it is critical that there isn't someone in the middle who slows down communication or decision making. It is best to allow forums to be created to draw in resources as needed for decision-making purposes. Finally, you should always make an effort to look outside your own beliefs to try to ascertain another perspective on what's going on. True project leadership means looking outside of what your interests and outlook are and trying to approach the project from an unbiased perspective. It might sound simple, but it's more difficult than you might think.

In an effort to communicate effectively, the project team should make responsibility or task assignments and deadlines very clear from the beginning. They need to emphasize, again, the importance of communicating with all of the stakeholders: the managers and clients throughout the execution of the project. Expectations should be stated and effectively managed throughout the process so that surprises or disappointments are kept to an absolute minimum. It is also important that at completion the project is properly closed out.

REPORTING

Close-out reporting is possibly the most neglected activity in project management. When the project is complete, it is tempting to have the final product speak for itself. What has been found, however, is that closing-out activities can bring a high return to the project managers. The closing out of a project can bring closure to the project in the eyes of the stakeholders and can also provide an excellent learning opportunity. It provides an opportune time to take a poll of the project participants and find out how they perceived the process. What can you change/improve next time as the project manager? Did you learn anything about how the estimation process was done? What did the participants perceive to have gone well?

One way to keep all of these learning points from surfacing all at once at the end of the project is to measure the progress of the project. This is also referred to as project control. Part of successfully controlling a project is to have project performance measures. These measures indicate when tasks have been accomplished. It helps you to measure whether you've completed what you thought you would by the dates previously established.

You can also take a measurement referred to as earned value reporting, or sometimes earned value analysis, which is a method for measuring project performance. The method takes into account the planned and actual costs for all completed tasks and compares them. It combines cost and schedule status to provide a complete current picture of the project. It indicates how much of the budget should have been spent in view of the amount of work done so far, and the baseline cost for the task, assignment, or resource. There are various ways of calculating the earned value reporting that take into account variables such as the budgeting cost of work performed, the actual cost of work performed, the cost variance percentage, and the estimate of completion.

SUMMARY

Project management in its simplest form of understanding is all about planning. Proper planning can be somewhat complicated, and to do it well requires delving into what needs to be done from the very beginning.

Although the practice of project management has been around for centuries, scholars and project management professionals are still studying how to make project management better. The value of face-to-face interaction does not deteriorate, even with the deployment of virtual project management teams. Projects require leaders who are trained in both business and technology and have teams with qualified project management professionals when possible. There are various preferences and cultural values that weigh different communication techniques and interpersonal skills differently. Perceptions of communication techniques will have an impact on the end user and the end result of the project, so it is important to clarify preferences at the beginning.

REFERENCES

Armstrong, Dan. "Six Degrees of Project Management." *Baseline* (February, 2004).

Godbout, Jaques. "Project Management Mainstays." *CMA Management* (December/January 2004).

McConnell, Steve. *Rapid Development*. Seattle: Microsoft Press, 1996.

Ramirez, Holley, and Michelle Meyer. "Project Management: Is It Right for You?" *Certification* (March 2004).

Riordan, Jeb. "Scope Management." *Project* (December, 2001).

Salidis, Frank. "Taming the Wild Project." *Mobile Radio Technology Sourcebook* (December 2004). www.iwce-mrt.com.

Tesch, Debbie, Timothy Kloppenbourg, and John Stemmer. "Project Management Learning: What Literature Has to Say." *Project Management Journal* (December 2003).

"Unwritten Rules of Project Management." *Times* (Malaysia) (February 19, 2004).

Verzuh, Eric. *The Fast Forward MBA in Project Management*. New York: John Wiley & Sons, 1999.

Chapter

Management Information Systems

How have management information systems (MIS) and information technology (IT) had such a profound impact on business in the past 10 years? Maybe the better question to ask is has information technology changed business or has business actually created information technology in the past 10 years? Surprisingly, if we take a look at business in the 1990s, it's actually less about technology and more about competition: A continued focus on increased productivity and efficiency has intensified competition and driven business toward technology. However, as Diana Farrell relates in the *Harvard Business Review*, "With the technology sector in shreds, more than a few believe that IT changed scarcely anything [in business] at all."

Today's business owner or professional can tell that technology does in fact play a key role in the day-to-day operations. In fact, some businesses no longer even have a tangible presence but rather exist only in cyber-land. The transformation from bricks-and-mortar businesses into e-businesses has leveled off but the role of technology and management information systems in business is undeniable. In this chapter we focus on giving an overview of the essentials for today's cyber-environment and technology-driven organizations and give a particular focus to MIS.

MANAGEMENT INFORMATION SYSTEMS

Management information systems can be described as tools that help managers organize and make decisions from their data. More simply, effective MIS aids communication. Unsurprisingly, it's still true that people generally accomplish more together than they do apart, and the old concept of collaboration and communication is still at the core of business. Management information systems strive to efficiently collect, format, and communicate information to a wide variety of people. A number of software packages and applications designed to help you collaborate more and communicate better will be described later on in the chapter. First, it is important to have a solid understanding of computing hardware, since these are the tools of processing and communication used in management information systems.

Key Components of Computing Hardware Tools

Computer hardware is a term to identify the tools that we typically see when looking at someone's desk: the computer itself, the monitor, the input devices such as the keyboard, disk drive, CD-ROM and DVD-ROM, the mouse, and so on. There are also the components inside the computer that store and process the data that is entered into the systems.

There are all kinds of computers that range from mainframe computers to handhelds. Mainframe computers are large computers that are mainly used by companies to manage bulk data processing—they are very powerful and very expensive. Handhelds, or personal digital assistants (PDAs), are small, increasingly inexpensive, portable devices that allow the regular consumer to connect to calendars, e-mail accounts, phone books, telephones, games, cameras, and much more.

Software

The real power and use of what the computer can do, however, is largely a function of the software that is installed into these various systems. The most fundamental of the software functions is the operating system OS that runs the computer. Examples of the OS include Windows XP, Windows 2000, Linux, Mac OC, and Unix.

These provide different processes through which we operate and work on our computer systems.

The software directs the computer to perform very specific tasks such as creating a financial spreadsheet/statement/model, preparing a slide presentation, or writing a document on a word processing program. Specific applications software include programs such as Microsoft's Word (word processing), PowerPoint (presentations), and Excel (financial spreadsheets).

Managing the hardware and software that are used in any business is a difficult task because it requires understanding the functions of each and understanding their purposes.

ROLE OF THE CHIEF INFORMATION OFFICER

For the small business owner or professional, you are probably reading this chapter to learn about the role and purpose of management information systems and, in effect, to become the "CIO" for your business. The chief information officer, or CIO, is the person in the company responsible for managing all the information collected from the various hardware and software applications and making sure that the information and communication flow is sufficient to meet the needs of the company objectives.

The CIO Insight Research Company has identified the different roles of the chief information officer. CIOs are responsible for evaluating the fit between the company's strategy and the technology used to implement its strategy. They are responsible for interviewing and hiring, vetting IT risks and opportunities, monitoring large investments, auditing IT infrastructure for reliability and risk, and counseling IT staff on selected strategic issues. This is no small job.

In an article in the *Harvard Business Review*, Diana Farrell suggests the CIO should be able to answer each of the following 10 questions:

1. Is the company leveraging IT in our most important business initiatives?

2. Is our management and shareholder information of the highest accuracy and integrity?

3. Are we leveraging technology to ensure business continuity?

4. Are we getting the best return on our technology expenditures?

5. Are our businesspeople capable of using and managing information and technology effectively?

6. Are we leveraging IT for business innovation and learning?

7. Are we capitalizing on the business potential of the Internet?

8. Are we optimizing the supply and delivery of IT services?

9. Do we have the right IT partners?

10. What do we expect from the CIO and IT organization?

It is likely that at least one of these questions has crossed your mind during the course of running your business or practicing your profession. The information in this chapter will help you to better answer the questions and become a more effective CIO for your business.

FUNCTIONS OF MIS: TOOLS TO SHARE DATA IN A UNIFORM CONTEXT

Microsoft Word is one of the most basic software tools and is commonly used. It is a word processing application that allows users to input, store, retrieve, edit, print, and share various types of documents. These documents can also be easily attached to e-mail messages and sent to various locations where collaborators can work on the same document. Microsoft Word also has an editorial tool that allows users working collaboratively to track and illustrate changes to a document without altering the integrity of the document.

For example, this chapter has been written using Microsoft Word. An author first writes the content; other contributors and editors change, format, and edit the content, and then the content from this specific chapter can be integrated into the larger work. In this sense, Word is an effective tool in a management information system because it is facilitating the way a business operates. Think of the time and effort saved because with this word processing technology a document can be shared, stored, transmitted, worked on, and printed.

As even the most basic word processing capabilities grow, it is increasingly possible to keep fewer paper files—a movement toward the "paperless office." Although we've seen a large trend in this direction, many business owners and professionals are still uncomfortable getting rid of paper copies altogether.

One of the software applications commonly used for desktop publishing is Adobe. You may be familiar with Adobe Acrobat, which is one of the applications of this software that allows people to upload documents on the Web and have others download the same document; but unlike a Word document, the formatting and content cannot be changed, altered, or extracted. Adobe allows the user to input the content and design and format it in a more intricate manner than a word processing application allows, for example, into printed material. Often a desktop publishing application will be used for functions such as producing brochures, newsletters, calendars, and reports.

Other very useful applications for the small business are spreadsheet programs such as Microsoft Excel. This software is a very dynamic and powerful tool that can create reports and worksheets that the user can manipulate by using simple formulas such as addition and division, use complex models that link sheets to each other, and have them interface with real-time data, depending on the needs of the business. The program can also compute statistics, run financial models, create a variety of charts, and monitor performance. Although many people are intimidated by numbers, spreadsheets can simplify and sort data in a user-friendly manner. Spreadsheet programs can also create graphics or charts generated from data that you input. The graphics can then be inserted into word-processing documents or presentations.

The impact of electronic mail, or e-mail, has revolutionized personal and professional communication. E-mail provides a rapid communication tool that can share information, provide updates, and transport data almost instantly in most cases. E-mail has been adopted to communicate both inside and outside an organization; it can carry such important documents as contracts and agreements through the use of file attachments or simply provide basic messages such as reconfirming a meeting. Not surprisingly, software has been created to help users manage the information that comes through their e-mail accounts. One such tool is Microsoft Outlook, which allows users to receive, send, and manage not only their e-mail accounts, but also their calendars, contacts, tasks, and notes. Software applications such as Outlook have proven to reduce paperwork and decrease time wasted in playing telephone tag, with a corresponding impact on increasing productivity.

One of the easiest ways that a small company can make a big impact is by looking professional in all its communication with stakeholders. An opportunity to set your company apart from the competition is by having outstanding presentations that aren't merely based on agendas and notes but, technology permitting, have a polished look projected onto a screen to accompany your ideas. As discussed in Chapter 10, presentation software such as PowerPoint allows you to create entire presentations, replete with graphics, audio and video clips, impressive effects, and even prerehearsed timing tools. It ultimately allows you to combine text with multimedia and design that are consistent with the professional image that you would like to project.

If PowerPoint can't handle all of the multimedia computing that you would like to use, there are technologies that can integrate media—voice, video, graphics, and animation—and convert them into computer-based applications that can be shared and duplicated with others. One of the expanding uses for multimedia computing is employee presentations, client presentations, use in conferences, and use in the classrooms of some of the more advanced educational institutions. Presentation software has the power to focus an audience, project an image, and aid communication with unparalleled success when used effectively.

Another important software application combines information sharing through a common database with communication via e-mail so that employees or associates can collaborate on projects. This groupware application allows employees to work together on a single document simultaneously while seeing what their collaborators are changing in real time.

As is the case with all of these applications, groupware allows a company to increase the scale and efficiencies of its business. Software allows users to use, copy, edit, share, and track data at record speed and then allows the diffusion and reach of their work to increase exponentially. Metcalf's Law states that, in fact, the use of applications such as those just described increases exponentially by the number of users that adopt it. For example, e-mail would be fairly useless if just one person had an e-mail account. E-mail has increased value the more people adopt it and use it to communicate and share information. It is important to think about how your business's stakeholders are communicating; which applications are they using to understand the information you need to share? In evaluating technologies and applications, you should always choose those that the majority of your stakeholders use, if they offer the desired functions, to ensure comprehension and effectiveness of company outputs.

INFORMATION SYSTEMS FOR DECISION MAKING

MIS is used for communicating, but the ultimate goal is to use these tools to help make better decisions. In this way, the software used for managerial decision making should be based on characteristics of the individual, the task being performed, and how information is presented.

Jane Carey and Charles Kacmar demonstrate the variety of factors that go into deciding which technology is best suited for a particular decision-making situation. These tools and processes have a variety of functions and purposes, ranging from managing customers through customer relationship management software, to knowledge management functions (sharing and disseminating the "institutional memory" of the organization), to shipping and tracking the company's products or services.

Decision support systems (DSS), for example, are information systems that quickly provide relevant data to help people make decisions to choose a particular course of action. For example, a DSS tool may be able to simulate a situation and predict various outcomes based on known variables. What will the revenue of an airline be given the possible number of flights completed (taking into consideration weather delays and other unforeseen obstacles), how many passengers will be on each flight, what number of seats they are sold, at which price, and so on. A DSS can take into account all of these variables and come up with various revenue projections based on the possible outcomes. These tools might be complicated to figure out at first, but prove to be invaluable in the long run for the amount of time and monetary resources saved.

Executive information systems (EIS) allow managers to access the company's primary databases utilized specifically by top managers. These systems can be highly customized and typically cater to a specific industry. For example, one such system describes itself as:

> The first comprehensive decision-support system designed for property/casualty companies. You can project financial results, discover and mitigate unacceptable risks, optimize reinsurance structures, test alternative investment strategies, allocate capital and reveal the sources of value within your company. Don't spend your time building models, spend it refining strategies. Financial decision-making requires reliable and thorough projections of the macro-economy and financial markets. [Our tool] is the most comprehensive economic scenario generator, incorporating individual security classes, inflation indices and macro state variables. It models historical relationships across markets, for realistic simulations that allow for stress-testing that simpler models can't achieve.
>
> —DFA Capital Management, Inc. (www.dfa.com)

CHALLENGE OF PROTECTING AGAINST COMPUTER CRIME

As explored earlier in the chapter, e-mail is an extremely valuable tool that has found a secure place in today's business environment, but it should also be noted that e-mail does have significant limitations with regard to privacy, piracy, and filtering. Not only is there a risk to your company through electronic mail, but computer crime, cyberterrorism, and viruses all pose a threat to your business operating systems.

Intellectual property is the most valuable part of any business and as an intangible asset it is also extremely difficult to protect. Just as computers and software programs offer efficient ways of communicating, they also provide gateways to unintended/illegal information sharing that is difficult to monitor.

The Computer Security Institute conducted a survey in 2003 that had disturbing results. The survey showed that 15 percent of businesses didn't know whether their systems were attacked the previous year. And of those who reported that they had had attacks on their systems, more than half of them never reported it to anyone. Just as crime on the street has law enforcement officers monitoring and trying to control it, so does computer crime.

Although the data may seem hard to believe, consider that employees or outsiders can change or invent data in computing programs to produce inaccurate or misleading information or illegal transactions or can insert and spread viruses. There are also people who access computer systems for their own illicit benefit or knowledge or just to see if they can get in, which is referred to as hacking. Almost as if it were a very challenging game, computer hacking has been responsible over the past several years for some of the most serious crimes in business. One hacking technique referred to as the Trojan horse allows hackers to take over a computer without the user knowing and capture the password of an investor's online account, for example. These are the security issues that clients and companies have to face as online investing, banking, and account management become more the norm.

Identity theft, international money laundering, theft of business trade secrets, auction fraud, web site spoofing, and cyber-extortion are all schemes that were carried out in 2002 and involved at least 125,000 victims and more than $100 million. And these crimes didn't make the Computer Security Institute's Computer Crime and Security Survey.

Computer viruses are programs that secretly attach themselves to other computer programs or files and change, export, or destroy data. Because viruses are frequently spread through e-mail, it is important to know who the sender is before opening the message or an attachment. It is best to use antivirus software to see if the document has a virus or whether the message should simply be deleted.

Not only is the Federal Trade Commission (FTC) concerned about viruses, but Microsoft, together with the FBI, Secret Service, and Interpol, announced the introduction of an antivirus reward program in November 2003. Microsoft is involved with funding the program to help law enforcement agencies identify and bring to justice those who illegally release damaging worms, viruses, and other types of malicious code on the Internet.

Other computer crimes consist of actual theft of computing equipment (laptops and PDAs are particularly vulnerable due to their small size), using computer technology to counterfeit currency or other official documents (passports, visas, ID cards, etc.), and using computer technology to illegally download or "pirate" music and movies that are copyrighted. With so much potential for computer crime, what can small business owners do to protect themselves?

The U.S. Department of Homeland Security suggests taking the following steps if you are worried that your systems have been attacked:

- ✔ Respond quickly.
- ✔ Don't stop system processes or tamper with files if you are unsure of what actions to take.
- ✔ Follow organizational policies/procedures.
- ✔ Use the telephone to communicate.
- ✔ Contact the incident response team of your credit union.
- ✔ Consider activating caller identification on all incoming lines.
- ✔ Establish contact points with general counsel, emergency response staff, and law enforcement.
- ✔ Make copies of files intruders may have copied or left.
- ✔ Identify a primary point of contact to handle potential evidence.
- ✔ Don't contact the suspected perpetrator.

In addition, it is important to prevent access to your system and viewing of your data by unauthorized users. Passwords, firewalls, and encryption software are useful in this regard.

Finally, it critical to back up your data and computing systems in case your system is attacked and you need to retrieve data that has been altered or destroyed in the process. There are many systems and ways for backing up data and it doesn't matter which you choose, but rather that you consistently and accurately back up your data for your records.

INTERNET, INTRANET, AND EXTRANET

As businesses and professional practices implement the use of technology and management information systems, it becomes important to link these tools together and provide a means for the machines, the information they produce, and those who use and benefit from the system to communicate with each other. Thus, computers in an organization and computers in different organizations form networks to facilitate the exchange.

You may have heard someone refer to an "extranet" before and thought the individual actually meant "Internet" because we all know that that's what most people use to find and share information; but there are three major types of networks that allow people to access and share information.

The Internet is what a company uses to connect to the World Wide Web and communicate with clients and the broader outside world. This communication happens through e-mail, web sites, and researching, or accessing, public information.

The company intranet, on the other hand, doesn't connect the company to the outside world, but rather to an internal network. This wide area network (WAN) connects all of the company's computers to allow them to access the same hard drive and therefore be able to share files and information from a central, internal location.

An extranet occurs when the business or practice is networked to a variety of stakeholders such as suppliers, dealers, manufacturers, or distributors. This is a network that is shared among a select set of businesses that work together closely and need to share information quickly to efficiently plan and execute their business.

These larger networks define where information is shared and who can access it; the importance of other computer networks is that they define how the information is shared.

COMPUTER NETWORKS AND THEIR IMPORTANCE

Computing systems consist of hardware and software and also networks. A local area network (LAN) has the capacity to connect computers to the network from one physical site in the company's offices and within different buildings. At the designated site, people can share both the hardware and software of the system set up in that location.

LANs are changing, though, as they move toward a wireless application (WLAN) that provides the benefits of networking equipment without the use of cables and being hardwired. Before you decide which is best for your business, you should consider the number of wireless access points, the type of information/data that will be transmitted, the speed with which you will need the data transmitted, the bandwidth that applications require, mobility coverage for roaming, and whether the system you purchase will be easily upgradable as the technology advances.

You should also consider that the WLAN's speed as it appears when you buy it might not necessarily be the product's real-world speed, because the WLAN is a shared medium and divides available throughput rather than providing dedicated speeds to the connected devices such as a dial-up connection. This limitation makes it a little more challenging to figure out how much speed you will need in the end. Therefore, it is critical to try to purchase a model that is upgradable.

Because wireless networks utilize technology that is a form of broadcasting data through the air, instead of a tailored system of wires, they present a concern over the security of such systems. When choosing a wireless system, internal security measures must be included to make sure the wireless data cannot be "hijacked" or hacked into by a cyberthief or pirate.

Throughput is a major consideration for your wireless deployment. Consider what types of traffic—e-mail, Web traffic, speed-hungry enterprise resource planning (ERP) or computer-aided design (CAD) applications—will ride across your WLAN most often. Network speeds diminish significantly as users wander farther from their access points, so install enough access points to support not only all your users but the speeds at which they need to connect.

One certainty, however, is that with the advent of wireless, the requirement of sitting in one place connected to a wall to access the Internet is becoming obsolete. A virtual office might be everyone's reality in the not too distant future.

Another type of network that is used is the broadband wide area networks. These are more powerful networks that have the ability to connect computers in different places by microwave, satellite, or telephone and can link together a large geographical area. These types of networks are growing, especially in the restaurant business. Restaurants are deploying these networks to have a virtual private network for managing supply chain integration with Web-based food-ordering and back-office functions. Some restaurants even use them for "front-of-the-house" applications such as credit card authorization. Restaurants that are using this high level of technology include Au Bon Pain, Chevy's, McDonald's, and Arby's. These restaurants have also shown a preference for satellite technology for transmitting their data, and this seems to have been a growing trend in 2003 according to Spacenet, a WAN service provider. It is not surprising as satellites' speed and reliability continue to improve.

But the limits of WANs have yet to be reached. Optimization offerings are hitting the market promising to accelerate applications with high-end units. They are more scalable and more compressible, boosting the performance of even the e-commerce sites that carry the heaviest traffic volumes. This higher-powered technology comes at a price, though. These systems represent significant costs depending on the scale of compression, acceleration, and speed you need for your business.

CATEGORIES OF MANAGEMENT INFORMATION SYSTEMS

There are three primary MIS categories: transaction processing systems, management support systems, and office automation systems.

These basic terms are descriptive. Transaction processing systems handle daily business operations; they collect and organize operational data from the activities of the company. Management support systems are used to help analyze the data that is collected and organized; they help the manager make decisions by forecasting, generating reports, and performing other types of analysis. Office automation systems facilitate communication between people who use the same operating systems through word processing, e-mail, fax machines, and other types of technologies.

HOW COMPANIES MANAGE INFORMATION TECHNOLOGY TO THEIR ADVANTAGE

Before any purchases are made it is imperative to look at what applications or combination of applications will be best suited to your company or small business. The technology packages should be planned out to ensure that the right technology is being used.

The first step in that process is evaluating what your goals and objectives are for the purpose of the technology. It's a good idea to have a collaboration of the needs of the executives, the IT managers, and other managerial staff who will have specific needs or ideas about the technologies being used; this can help shift the traditional bottom-line-driven point of view to a top-down, strategic perspective and increase the staff's perceived value in the technology.

It is then useful to map the information flow to analyze how information is transferred from one point to another within an organization. While this concept itself is simple, it is important to understand that mapping the information flow can also support a ranking system to identify the most valuable potential client for information resource center (IRC) services, create a picture of the competitive landscape, and help define the necessary actions for short- and long-term budgeting.

There are three primary benefits to mapping information flows. The first enables an understanding of how information is used and by whom. You should ask yourself the basic question of what information you already have within your organization and then figure out where it is located and how you can access it. The second pinpoints the ultimate client or key stakeholder for various types of information services, as well as where information touches as it passes through the organization. The third primary benefit helps to focus information services on the highest potential opportunities. In other words, it helps you clearly identify which information has the highest value and how you can do a better job at capturing it. This realization can make the value of the information center even more obvious.

There are numerous consultants who specialize in helping small businesses map their information flows; here are the generally accepted five steps to the information mapping system that a consultant will use.

1. Describe the current situation. What is the company organization chart? Who are the clients? Who aren't the clients but still use the system? Once the general idea is generated, it is of critical importance to drill down even deeper and ask yourself how well you really know what the client's needs are. Which departments do they interact with? What is the sphere of influence over the account?

2. Describe the potential clients in other business units within the company and discuss their specific information needs. This helps to give a better understanding of which information needs are, and are not, being met currently.

3. Mapping the potential clients is the next step. This allows a visualization of the potential areas for overlap, potential for consolidation of resources, and new solutions for optimal information flow.

4. As effective decision making becomes more difficult with complex, competitive, and dynamic working environments, it is critical to rank the solutions for prioritization. This process helps you decide which solution will meet the majority of the company needs while using the budgeted resources. The ranking process can be conducted by assessing the risk activity within the organization. Even by just assigning each activity with low-, medium-, or high-risk levels, you can create a priority scheme for the organization, which allows the best solution to be found for the least amount of time and effort.

5. The final step in the process is then creating the information map. Mapping the final solutions to show each department and the suggestions for their information needs creates an un-

derstanding of each subset of the organization, highlights the ultimate client, and results in information solution recommendations for each.

At the core behind mapping information flows is knowledge management. Many companies have found that as the organization grows, information that is critical to the company's success ends up getting lost, or no one is quite sure who should know it or where to access it. As a result, mapping information flows is getting increased attention, but so too is basic knowledge management.

A case study to show how critical knowledge management is for success is found in the Brixco story. Ashley Braganza of the Cranfield School of Management noted that Brixco, a 4,000-employee utility company, found it needed to make radical changes to its working practices, but was hindered by outdated IT systems and poorly managed knowledge, especially customer knowledge across its four main functional communities—customer operations, finance, sales, and marketing. Brixco decided to turn its IT solution project around by creating, in effect, a "community of communities of practice" that spanned its four main functional communities. Rather than putting employee requirements at the center of the system, Brixco asked the board to prioritize the key objectives linked to the business strategy for the company. When this was accomplished, a small group of people formed a team to identify stakeholders in the process and then backed into what knowledge the employees needed to deliver to these stakeholders. This meant that the company was consistent in the messages being sent out to clients and that the necessary information was more easily managed. The findings from this company suggest that people/employees are able to articulate the linkages between knowledge and their day jobs, and through the links to stakeholders' expectations they can tie their knowledge back to the organization's business strategy.

Knowledge management is about sharing organizational collective knowledge, improving productivity, and fostering innovation within the organization. It ends up making information more easily accessible to all who need it and increases the efficiency and productivity of the company.

LEADING TRENDS IN INFORMATION TECHNOLOGY

Experts are forecasting a trend toward increased spending on technology after a cyclical drop soon after Y2K concerns passed. With antiquated legacy systems getting more and more expensive to fix, old computers breaking down, and the benefits of mobile computing continually being realized, new technology is expected to enter the business world with renewed speed. As is often the case with the gradual diffusion of technological innovation into the marketplace, telecom and storage services are simultaneously decreasing in cost.

According to Michael J. Miller, editor-in-chief of *PC* magazine, the biggest growth opportunity for management information systems technology is in Web services. He predicts that emerging Web service standards will promote integration and let companies tie together existing applications within an organization, connect to outside applications, and create applications that are entirely new. Due to the increasing number of applications in the corporate world, Miller also does not see that just one player (such as Microsoft or Sun Microsystems) will dominate the market.

Mimicking the security issues discussed earlier, Miller sees that security is the biggest obstacle for continued growth in the sector and that both consumers and businesses will need to address issues of security better.

Another trend in MIS is what is referred to as business process management (BPM). As has been illustrated in this chapter, there are myriad applications and packages that can be used for the IT enthusiast. A new trend that is emerging in the area, however, is business process management. BPM is recognized as one of the fastest growing technologies in the software world with a market value of over $400 million in 2003 (according to an analyst in the Delphi Group). The innovation of the technology finds its roots in automating the processes that involve people. It includes capabilities derived from process modeling, process monitoring, application integration, and rapid application development tools.

Additionally, there is a trend toward integrating different technologies. As mentioned earlier, PDAs can now include telephones and cameras, but there has also been the creation of "palmtops" and Web phones. These innovations in technology are going outside the communication realm and now migrating toward regular household appliances such as washers, refrigerators, and even microwaves.

One of the greatest trends in the world of information systems, however, is a shortage of the people who can help integrate, install, and run these information systems. Companies are finding it increasingly difficult to stay current with the latest technologies and are facing a shortage of IT personnel. This can be seen as an excellent opportunity for the technologically inclined, but can be a competitive hindrance to a company that simply can't access the resources needed to keep up in its industry, and to its clients as well. In the future, the trend toward IT outsourcing will continue and most likely make the reliance on consultants even greater.

REFERENCES

Birchard, Bill. "CIOs Are Being Tapped to Sit on Corporate Boards, but Those Who Don't Broaden Their Executive Presence and Business Smarts Need Not Aspire." *CIO Insight* (June 2003).

Boone, Louise, and David Kurts. *Contemporary Business* 11th ed. South-Western, 2002.

Braganza, Ashley. "A Better Way to Link Sharing to Your Strategy." *KM Review* 6, no. 6 (September/October 2003).

Carey, Jane, and Charles Kacman. *Journal of Managerial Issues* (Winter 2003): 430.

Computer & Internet Lawyer 21, no. 1 (January 2004).

Computer Security Institute, Eighth Annual Computer Crime and Security Survey, 2003. www.gocsi.com/press/20030528.jhtml.

Farrell, Diana. "The Real New Economy." *Harvard Business Review OnPoint* (October, 2003).

Gitman, Lawrence, and Carl McDaniel. *The Future of Business*, 4th ed. Thomson South-Western, 2003.

Goldsborough, Reid. "Arming Yourself in the Virus War." *Tactics* (December 2003).

Hibberd, Betty Jo, and Allison Evatt. "Mapping Information Flows: A Practical Guide." *Management Information Journal* (January/February 2004).

Liddle, Alan. "Kiosk, WAN Use at Restaurants Spreads Far and Wide." *Nations Restaurant News* (October 27, 2003).

Lindeman, Jesse. "Surveying the Wireless LANscape." *Network Computing* (January 22, 2004).

Madura, Jeff. *Introduction to Business*. South-Western, 2003.

Middlemiss, Jim, and George Hume. "Feds Crack Down on Cyberfraud." *Wall Street & Technology* (December 1, 2003).

Mink, Mary. "Awareness Can Reduce Computer Crime." *Credit Union Executive Newsletter* (January 26, 2004).

Musich, Paula. "Pushing the Limits of WANs." *eweek* (January 19, 2004).

13

Chapter

E-Commerce and Uses of the World Wide Web

T he Internet is the starting point for an exploration of e-commerce, and the World Wide Web is a worldwide collection of computer networks, cooperating with each other to exchange data using a common software standard. Though considered by many as a new technology, the Internet has been around for several decades. Originally known as ARPAnet, the Internet was created in 1969 by the U.S. Department of Defense as a nationwide computer network that would continue to operate even if the majority of it were destroyed in a nuclear war or natural disaster. It was not until 1992 that commercial entities started offering Internet access to the general public, and the business world has not been the same since.

THE EFFECT OF THE INTERNET ON BUSINESSES

Over the past decade, widespread Internet and e-mail access have radically changed the way companies do business and communicate with their employees, vendors, and customers. Consumers and businesses purchase products and services such as $2,000 laptops and airline tickets by paying with credit cards via the Internet without ever speaking to a customer representative or salesperson. Many companies allow customers to track the status of their orders online to see when their products shipped and when they are scheduled to arrive, again without ever speaking to a customer representative. When companies such as Amazon and Priceline emerged, their business models revolved around conducting 100 percent of their business online, eliminating the need for costly bricks-and-mortar outlets. More and more consumers are paying their bills online as they become comfortable with online security, thus eliminating the need to pay postage and write checks for each bill using the traditional snail-mail method. Today thousands of adults are getting their undergraduate and master's degrees online without ever attending an actual class or meeting their peers or professors, who teach the classes online. There are few businesses or organizations isolated from this transformational wave of technology and innovation.

INTERNET FACTS

According to www.internetworldstats.com, the total number of Internet users worldwide as of February 2004 is 719.3 million. This is approximately 11.1 percent of the total world population of 6.45 billion. IDC Research predicts that this number will exceed one billion users by the end of 2005. The United States is still the country with the highest number of Internet users at 186.5 million, 63.3 percent of the total population of the country, which stands at 295.5 million. Asia ranks highest as the continent with the most number of Internet users with a total of 229.82 million. North America is second at 203.38 million versus 203.28 million for Europe. Additionally, the countries with the highest percentage of the population using the Internet include Sweden (76.9 percent), Netherlands (66.0 percent), and Australia (64.2 percent).

DESCRIPTION OF TYPICAL INTERNET USERS

According to the UCLA World Internet Project's findings based on research collected from 2002 to 2003, in general, around the world men are more likely (in some countries, such as Italy and Spain, *much* more likely) to use the Internet than women. However, in countries such as the United States, Sweden, and Taiwan, the ratio of men to women who use the Internet is nearly 1:1.

It is interesting to note that according to the study, the average Internet user watches less television than non-Internet user counterparts. For example, in the United States, Internet users watch 5.2 hours less television per week. Internet users are also more likely to spend time reading books and engaging in social activities. They also tend to be more educated and have higher total household incomes.

DEFINITION OF WEB-BASED SYSTEMS AND E-COMMERCE

A Web-based system is a business process that is supported and accessed online. For example, e-commerce, a Web-based system involving purchasing products online, may include features such as charge card approval systems and customer order tracking systems, which provide companies with the opportunity to sell their products and services online more efficiently. Many internal employee Web-based systems such as payroll, vendor selection and ordering, time sheet, and expense report submissions are also examples of Web-based systems.

As an example of how Web-based systems are changing the way organizations harness the power of the Web, let's look at the payroll function. Companies have to provide their employees with benefit information, taxes paid, vacation/sick days remaining, and so on each time they get paid. To complicate matters even further, of the people on payroll, some are contractors and part-time workers, while others are considered regular employees. If the company's payroll system is Internet-based, data can be entered by disparate reporting units, in a wide array of geographic locations, away from the headquarters' accounting and payroll office, if needed. The online system is able to keep better track of the number of vacation days, amount of 401(k) contributions, and health insurance deductions on each employee's pay stub.

The process of accounting for employees' time can also be automated, eliminating the need for manually totaling payroll hours and time cards, reducing the number of errors, and providing immediate real-time data for managers, allowing them to make more department-specific, accurate, time-sensitive decisions. A Web-based payroll system is beneficial not only to human resources staff, but also to employees. They no longer have to make copies of their time sheets when they turn in the originals because past time-sheet records are available on the Internet for viewing and printing, and they no longer have to worry about calculational errors while adding numbers because the time sheets are automatically calculated online. The system also enables employees to fill out their time sheets while they are away from the office, which is especially convenient for those who spend a significant amount of time in the field.

Clients also appreciate suppliers and service providers who use Web-based systems. Not only does providing clients with access to information on your web site save them time, it saves you time as well. Allowing clients to access old reports and data from previous and current projects by using a password online saves you from having to take time out of your busy day to print out the report and ship it to the client. The client is able to log in online and make copies of the report himself, and the benefit to him is that he can access the information immediately. He does not have to wait for you to return from out of town to print his file and then wait another day or two to receive it in the mail. Clients can also access project and budget updates, participate in virtual conferences and meetings, and retrieve invoices online. While clients find the online process to be convenient and quick, your company saves time and money and also benefits from the "stickiness" factor. Once a client gets used to accessing information using your system, she will be less likely to switch her business to one of your competitors. As discussed in Chapter 8, this notion of switching costs is a key driver of customer loyalty and competitive advantage. Once clients understand and build trust in your system, they will be less likely to risk working with a company that does not offer this service to its clients or spend the time to learn how to use another company's system.

An example of a company that takes advantage of the stickiness factor is Bank of America. The company used to charge customers for online banking, but now it offers the service for free. The bank realized that once customers spend time inputting all the information required to use online banking and learning their system, they will be less likely to move their account to another financial institution.

Another Internet-based system that many companies have implemented is electronic bidding for products and services, meaning that proposal bids are sent electronically instead of via regular mail or paper-based systems. Benefits to companies of the electronic bidding system include the arrival of bids in a consistent, legible format free of calculation errors, and a reduction in the amount of man-hours and other resources needed to print, distribute, and edit bids. The suppliers who are bidding also benefit from the process because they have access to project bidding information 24 hours a day, and they can send in their bids even when they are away from their offices. Additionally, the number of errors made on the forms is reduced because the system detects them and will not accept them unless they are completed in their entirety and are free of errors. Other advantages of electronic bidding are the elimination of travel expenses and confirmation of delivery of bid on the supplier side.

Although they may cost several thousand dollars to set up and their maintenance and support functions may have to be outsourced, in general Web-based systems are more cost-efficient since they save on printing, human labor, mailing, and invoice costs.

As customers grow more comfortable with security issues regarding purchasing products online, Jupiter Research predicts e-commerce—purchasing products or services online—will continue to grow over the next five years, specifically among small businesses that have established a reputation among consumers for being entities that are legitimate and trustworthy. In addition, Jupiter Research predicts e-commerce will grow from $65 billion in 2004 to $116 billion by 2008, and the percentage of U.S. consumers who purchase products online will increase from 30 percent in 2004 to 50 percent by 2008.

ADVANTAGES AND DISADVANTAGES OF E-COMMERCE

While e-commerce is expected to continue growing over the next several years and trending toward wide adoption to sell products and services online, there are many challenges that should be considered before implementing an online selling system for your company.

One major concern among consumers is that of security and privacy of personal information. Consumers want to be assured that the personal information they provide on a company's site will not be sold to other companies for marketing purposes. Others are wary about technology that tracks personal information such as web sites visited and items purchased by customers. A major barrier for consumers who still do not purchase products online is the fear that a web site is not secure and that their credit card number or other personal information will be accessed by hackers.

Another reason many consumers choose not to purchase online is because of viruses. While in the past viruses were often spread by opening an infected e-mail, these days simply surfing the Internet is enough to be vulnerable to getting a virus. System downtime is another problem associated with e-commerce sites. Whether the downtime is a result of system maintenance, server issues, hackers, or poor system administration, it can have a negative impact on sales. If customers are unable to purchase from your site due to technical problems, they may become dissatisfied and visit the web site of your competitor instead.

Although there are several challenges associated with e-commerce, there are also many advantages to selling products online for companies and customers. One advantage for companies is cost savings through lower inventory management, customer service, administration, and communication costs, order tracking, and integration with the company's accounting system. Web orders can be sent directly to the warehouse, which allows customer service representatives to focus on larger customer orders, while smaller orders can be handled more efficiently online. Detailed purchase history reports on each customer allow companies to design customized online purchase deals for customers who have not purchased from their sites in several months or reminder notices to order specific products for customers who purchase specific products on a regular basis. Current online inventory reports can aid in projecting inventory depletion and assist with product restocking information.

Manufacturers of products have the advantage of being able to sell directly to customers by bypassing the intermediary if they sell online and are able to pass along some of the savings to their customers. Another advantage to companies is that sending e-mails to customers is an effective low-cost way of sending customized messages about upcoming products, special online purchase offers, or shipping and order confirmations. Additionally, specific customer information can be stored for repeat customers, making it easier to analyze customer groups. Benefits to consumers include 24-hour shopping, convenience, lower prices, special online promotions, comparative shopping, and proactive feedback from the company regarding stock-outs or delays in shipping.

E-COMMERCE TRENDS

Mitchell Levy of CEOnetworking has compiled a list of top technology-related trends for 2004. Of the top 10 trends on his list, two are related to e-commerce: the increase of spam and viruses and the continued growth of e-commerce.

According to *The Washington Post*, spam or unsolicited commercial e-mail accounts for about 50 percent of all e-mails. With the help of special software, spammers can generate various combinations of letters and numbers and place the name of a common Internet service provider (ISP) such as AOL after each @ to create a list of millions of e-mail addresses, many of which are actual e-mail accounts. Although as of 2003, 26 states had antispam laws, many people still continue to send out spam since they are unlikely to get caught, and it is an inexpensive way to reach customers. The fact remains that although only a handful of people out of a thousand people who receive a spam message open it and eventually make a purchase, spammers find it worth their time to spam because the amount of sales generated is higher than the cost to distribute spam. This creates a problem for legitimate companies that are sending out e-mails to current or past customers who may delete them thinking they are spam. Even though many believe there should be a ban on spam similar to the ban on unsolicited faxes that came into effect in 1991, others argue that banning spam violates spammers' rights to free speech.

As more and more small businesses go online, e-commerce will continue to grow in the coming years. According to e-Marketer, 80 percent of small business were online as of 2003.

> E-commerce will continue to grow based on wider acceptance, reliability and security and that growth will accelerate on a multiplier to economic recovery. That is to say that e-commerce as a route to market will gain disproportionately from economic recovery.
>
> —Jeff Drust, vice president, e-business, Autodesk, Inc.

> Online sales will continue to rise. Convenience and familiarity are at work here. Those who have not bought will and those who have will buy more.
>
> —Jim Sterne, president, Target Marketing

STEPS IN DEVELOPING AN E-COMMERCE STRATEGY

Depending on whether your company is currently selling online, the following section may either help you set up a web site or make your web site more successful. The first thing you should do before you begin the setup is determine what you expect to achieve by creating a web site. Without determining the scope of the project, it is impossible to be fully prepared for all the steps involved in the process. Be sure to consider the following:

- ✔ What are your goals and objectives for creating this web site?
- ✔ Which products or services will be provided?
- ✔ Who will the target market be?
- ✔ Should you hire an outside firm to help develop and maintain the web site or should you handle it internally?
- ✔ If the system will be handled internally, can you afford to hire a system administrator, Web copywriters, Web designers, project director, and/or software engineer?
- ✔ How will selling online affect your current relationships with your vendors, salespeople, and employees?

✔ Will a Web presence contribute to "channel conflict" or the concerns by intermediaries that they may be bypassed by customers, who will be reaching you directly?

✔ Where will the funding for the web site come from?

✔ How much do you expect the total project will cost?

✔ Can your current purchasing, accounting, and supplier systems be integrated into the web site's system?

✔ Do you have the infrastructure and customer response capabilities to support volume from the Web?

Setting Up a Web Site

Once you have determined the scope of your web site project, the next step is to begin setting it up. First you have to create a domain name that is unique, yet descriptive. To make sure that you choose a unique company name, you may want to consider working with a lawyer or name consultant to avoid the hassle of having to change the name of your company later after finding out the name you picked already belongs to another company. After you have picked out a unique domain name, the next step is to contact a Web hosting service to secure and register your new domain name. A Web hosting service hosts your web site on its server. It also offers many features that you may select from such as offering a shopping cart on your site. Although it is possible to host your web site on your own server, this method is not recommended because of the high costs involved in doing so. The more people who visit your site, the more storage space you will need and the more money you have to pay; make sure the plan you pick allows for growth.

Although you may hire an outside firm to develop and maintain your web site, if you plan to make minor changes such as changing prices on the site you may want to consider having the necessary tools in your office to handle these minor changes yourself. For example, you need to consider how your site interacts with major Web browsers your customers are likely to use, such as Netscape Communicator and Microsoft Internet Explorer browsers. Since your customers will use either one of these browsers to access your web site, you need to test any changes you make in both formats to make sure the changes will not cause problems for customers using either browser. You should also consider purchasing a file transfer protocol (FTP) program to upload any new files to your web site and a text editing software program such as Notepad that comes with Windows. Other tools you may want to purchase include HTML editors and tutorials, a digital camera, and graphics equipment.

Web Site Content

There are many things to keep in mind when developing the content for your web site. In general, web sites should be easy to use, clear, and concise, and should contain accurate and updated information. While you want to make sure your web site is interesting enough to entice visitors to continue browsing and clicking, you do not want to use graphics that take so long to appear that visitors become frustrated and leave your site. Be sure to offer visitors the option of viewing your page in another format if it takes too long to download, and keep your pages short so they download faster and eliminate the need to use the scroll bar. It is important to remember that your web site should be consistent with your company's established brand, logo, mission, culture, and philosophy to avoid confusing customers, employees, and suppliers. Make sure your web site is user-friendly and easy to navigate. Also include a site map, and "contact us," and FAQ (frequently asked questions) pages.

Alicia Sequerah, CEO of Womenetwork.com, also suggests using effective marketing copy on your web site, as the site is a part of an integrated marketing strategy. Sequerah suggests that companies should use more "you" phrases rather than "we" phrases to show customers how they will benefit from purchasing your products. For example, try using "You get . . ." rather than "We offer . . ." solutions to problems your target market is experiencing.

Test Your Web Site before Going Live

Once the web site is set up, all pages and features should be tested. Try to send an e-mail from the "contact us" section; try to purchase something from your shopping cart using a credit card; make sure that a confirmation e-mail is sent to your e-mail address and another e-mail is promptly sent to your supplier; see how long it takes your home page to appear completely; try to send in a bid. Just make sure you test all parts of the web site. Upon successful completion of internal testing, the next step is to conduct focus groups or one-on-one interviews with current customers, vendors, clients, and prospective customers to find out what they like and dislike about your site, as well as to ask for suggestions on how to improve it. Once the system goes live, if it does not work properly you risk frustrating or alienating customers, employees, and suppliers; so it is best to test it thoroughly and get feedback before going live even though you may have to spend more money than you initially thought.

Web Site Maintenance and Refreshment

Just because your web site is up and running does not mean that your work is done. Your web site needs constant refreshment, refinement, and incremental, continuous improvement. Product prices, availability and descriptions, phone numbers, employee contact information, news and press releases, and all other sections of your web site must be updated on a regular basis. Additionally, to increase the number of times customers visit your web site, you should give them a reason to revisit your site. Give them the option to bookmark your web site, automatically add them to your newsletter, customer discount, and order reminder lists (also extend them the option to decline this offer), offer links on your web site to complementary web sites your target market would find interesting, offer sweepstakes or contests online, and make changes to the web site based on customer feedback. Every visitor to your web site is a potential customer. Implement ways to capture, and keep in touch with, visitors to your web site!

Promoting Your Web Site by Attracting a Target Market

Your company may have a great web site, but you should not subscribe to the *Field of Dreams* approach to web site development ("If you build it, they will come"). You need to make some adjustments so you can reach your target audience, and conversely, so your customers will find you. According to Dr. Ralph Wilson, an e-commerce consultant, there are many things a company can do to try to reach its target audience. One thing he suggests companies do is track the number of visitors who visit their web sites. Your hosting service should be able to provide these figures to you each month. Some specific things you can track include:

✔ *Agent log*—record of links used by those who visited your site.

✔ *Browser*—Which browser do your visitors use?

✔ *Entry page*—Which page of your site do visitors see first?

✔ *File*—number of times a particular file is accessed.

✔ *History*—analysis of specific features over several months' time.

✔ *Impressions*—number of times a logo is viewed.

✔ *Path*—page sequence followed by visitor.

✔ *Repeat visitors*—number of repeat visits from same address.

✔ *Sales*—by frequency, volume, and sales amount.

✔ *Sessions*—number of times site has been accessed by the same user in a specific amount of time.

✔ *Time*—amount of time visitors spend on each page.

Something else Dr. Wilson recommends is submitting your URL to search engines such as Yahoo! by clicking on the "Add your URL" link on their web sites, and submit your site to directories such as About.com. You will be prompted to write a short description of your web site, so think about what words people would plug into search engines to search for your products and services before submitting the description of your web site.

Additionally, you should try to find web sites that complement your products and services and place reciprocal links or banner ads on them. Writing articles for another web site's newsletter is another effective way to spread the word around about your web site. Try developing your own newsletter, and e-mail it to those who visit your web site once a quarter. This helps keep your company on their minds. Providing readers with the option of e-mailing your newsletter to a friend is another great way to make people aware of your web site. Lastly, don't forget to add your web site address on all your company's brochures, stationery, and so on.

Efficiencies of E-Commerce

Once you take the time to set up e-commerce on your web site, you can leverage the benefits. When a customer places an order, an e-mail is sent to his e-mail account, thanking him for placing his order with your company. Another e-mail is sent to your company's warehouse, a supplier's warehouse located nearby, or a manufacturer—whichever is responsible for shipping the products. Products can be shipped directly to the customer without having to be sent to your company, which not only shaves a few days off the total shipping time, but it also eliminates additional shipping, inventory tracking, and storage costs. When the order has shipped out, an e-mail is sent to the customer's account alerting him of an estimated shipping arrival date and a link to the shipping company's online package tracking system. Because the customer paid for the products and services with a credit card, there are no invoices or late payment hassles to deal with, which eliminates the need for more staff. The automated system can also e-mail reminders to customers about purchases, special online offers, and upcoming new products and services.

You should consider outsourcing the product fulfillment and inventory management processes so that you can focus more on your company's competencies. These companies handle everything, including setting up the software; running daily, weekly, and monthly warehouse inventory reports; packing and verifying your orders; and shipping them out.

Monitor and Track Visitors and Sales

A major advantage to having a web site is being able to track visitors' behavior. All customer and visitor data should be tracked and analyzed on a regular basis. Once the data is properly analyzed, customers can be grouped and targeted with customized offers, which can enhance sales. It is important to monitor the success of your web site so that you can make changes to enhance efficiency and sales even further.

HARNESSING THE POWER OF A WEB INSIDE—CREATING A SUCCESSFUL INTRANET

While the Internet is an international network of computers linked together, an intranet is an internal network that can be accessed only internally and usually is accessed through a password by authorized users such as employees, existing clients, or customers. Allowing clients to access project and budget data, invoices, and old reports through a password is an example of an intranet.

The key advantage to implementing an intranet is improved communications; an intranet facilitates employees sharing knowledge with each other, collaboration on work-related documents, learning the latest company news, and socializing outside of work and forming stronger bonds. Additionally, intranets can save companies money on printing, paper, and distribution costs. They can also increase productivity and efficiency.

For example, if employee directories, benefits information (401(k), health insurance, etc.), holidays, upcoming events, company organizational charts, and policies are posted on the intranet, employees spend less time searching for paperwork or calling employees in other departments for answers to their questions. Employees can also receive information regarding news and announcements simultaneously and in a timely manner rather than having to wait for the information to be announced in the next staff/team meeting or distributed in their internal mailboxes. This sharing of information makes employees feel like they are an important part of the organization. As a result of improved communications and efficiency, employees are more likely to be satisfied with their jobs and become more loyal to the company, thereby increasing employee retention and improving customer service.

To ensure that an intranet is successful, the information on it must be consistent with the company's brand, business objectives, and mission. Additionally, enough staff and resources should be allocated to promote and implement the intranet as well as adequate staff to maintain and refresh it.

When thinking of a domain name for your intranet, think of a name that is consistent with your brand. For example, Southwest Airlines' intranet is called Freedom Net, based on its external brand "A

Symbol of Freedom," which is easier to remember, more energizing, and powerful than www.southwest.com/employees/intranet.

The best way to find out what information should be included in your intranet is to conduct interviews or focus groups with employees from various departments.

Incorporating intranet objectives in regular strategic planning helps to ensure that the intranet is aligned with your company's goals and objectives each year. Ideally, you should consider a team approach, incorporating input from a diverse set of users' needs and perspectives to review and refresh the intranet. The intranet strategist would monitor performance against objectives, track the budget and resources allocated to the project, and ensure that standard procedures are implemented in the layout of pages. The intranet operations person would be responsible for the day-to-day operations of the site, which includes interacting with other departments such as human resources and marketing to obtain updated materials. The intranet developer's main job is to determine ways in which to improve and enhance the intranet. However, depending on how large your company is, you may assign only one person to be responsible for all three major tasks or find this function to be well served by outsourcing to a consultant.

Along with analyzing suggestions that employees send via the on-line suggestion box, employees should be surveyed on a regular basis about the intranet's content and design, and results should be available on the intranet for all employees to see. If changes are made as a result of feedback from employees, be sure to mention this on the intranet to prove to your employees that you value their feedback and make them feel like they are actively involved in the process.

Simply alerting your employees via e-mail that your company has implemented an intranet may not be enough to entice them to use it. You need to get them energized and excited about the intranet. Perhaps you could provide lunch for your staff one day and explain how to use it and what the benefits are to them and to the company. You can also create a formal implementation plan and publicize it internally by using testimonials and specific stories from employees who have tested it, with confirmation about how easy it is to use and what the specific benefits to them are. In addition, you could also mail out an announcement letter or even hold an intranet launch party.

The success of your intranet depends not only on adequate staff, funding, and site content, but also on senior management buy-in. If senior management fails to actively support the intranet, it will be a challenge to convince others to use the system. If company leaders expect their employees to use the intranet, they must lead by example and use it themselves.

SUMMARY

Harnessing the power of the Web and technology is a vital part of an organization's success and future. To remain competitive in today's business environment, companies must retain their employees, improve communications with clients and employees, improve productivity, increase efficiency, and reduce costs. Implementing an intranet and integrating the Web into a strategic plan can help achieve these goals. While web sites can be used as marketing and sales tools, they can also be used to improve internal organizational efficiency by streamlining the order, tracking, and vendor bidding processes. In today's complex, competitive world, technology can be a powerful element in attaining competitive advantage, lowering costs, increasing customer satisfaction, and achieving long-term success.

REFERENCES

Catauella, Joe, Ben Sawyer, and Dave Geely. *Creating Stories on the Web.* Berkeley, CA: Peachpit Press, 1998.

Gilbert, Matthew A. *Intranets: Catalysts for Improved Organizational Communication.* White paper, 2003. www.clearpixel.com.

Hensell, Lesley. "How Small Businesses Can Afford E-Commerce." *E-Commerce Times* (November 7, 2003).

Jamison, Brian, Josh Gold, and Warren Jamison. *Electronic Selling: 23 Steps to E-Selling Profits.* New York: McGraw-Hill, 1997.

Krim, Jonathan. "Spam's Cost to Business Escalates, Bulk E-Mail Threatens Communication Arteries." *Washington Post* (March 13, 2003): A01.

Lebo, Harlan and Stuart Wolpert. "First Release of Findings from the UCLA World Internet Project Shows Significant 'Digital Gender

Gap' in Many Countries." UCLA Anderson School of Management (January 14, 2004). www.anderson.ucla.edu/admin_dept /media_rel/releases/2004/04worldinternet.html.

Levy, Mitchell. CEOnetworking's Top Ten 2004 Business Trends. www.ceonetworking.com/businesstrends/2004top10withquotes.p df.

Nielsen, Jakob. "Intranet Usability: The Trillion Dollar Question." *Useit.com Alertbox* (November 11, 2002).

Sequerah, Alicia. "Your Checklist for a Profit-Generating Marketing Web Site." www.womenetwork.com.

Swinnerton, Kelly. "Quick Marketing Checklist—14 Ways to Promote Your Site." www.itwales.com/cgi/showsite/showpage.cgi?999558.

"Top 10 Items to Post on Your Intranet." www.intranets.com.

U.S. Department of Transportation. "Internet Bidding for Highway Construction Projects." (November 15, 2002). www.fhwa.dot .gov/programadmin/contracts/interbid.htm.

White, Martin. "Creating an Effective Intranet." *Intranet Focus Ltd* (January 2003). www.intranetfocus.com.

Wilson, Ralph. "The Web Marketing Checklist: 29 Ways to Promote Your Web Site." *Web Marketing Today*, no. 125 (June 4, 2003).

Quality Management Systems

For more than two decades "quality" and "quality management systems" have been leading buzzwords in the business world. Numerous consultants have built their careers around these topics, and quality issues in business have been responsible for the development of new organizations and even industries, for instance, the American Society for Quality and Six Sigma consulting.

The notion of quality in business focuses on the savings and additional revenue that organizations can realize if they eliminate errors throughout their operations and produce products and services at the optimal level of quality desired by their customers. Errors can take almost any form—for example, producing the wrong number of parts, sending bank statements to customers who have already closed their accounts or sending an incorrect bill to a client. All of these errors are very common, and the costs incurred seem minimal. But over time when mistakes are repeated the costs add up to a significant amount, so eliminating errors can result in significant increases to the bottom line of a business.

WHAT IS QUALITY?

According to the American Society for Quality, "quality" can be defined in the following ways:

- ✔ Based on customer's perceptions of a product/service's design and how well the design matches the original specifications.
- ✔ The ability of a product/service to satisfy stated or implied needs.
- ✔ Achieved by conforming to established requirements within an organization.

What Is a Quality Management System?

A quality management system is a management technique used to communicate to employees what is required to produce the desired quality of products and services and to influence employee actions to complete tasks according to the quality specifications.

What Purpose Does a Quality Management System Serve?

- ✔ Establishes a vision for the employees.
- ✔ Sets standards for employees.
- ✔ Builds motivation within the company.
- ✔ Sets goals for employees.
- ✔ Helps fight the resistance to change within organizations.
- ✔ Helps direct the corporate culture.

Why Is Quality Important?

Business success may simply be the extent to which your organization can produce a higher-quality product or service than your competitors are able to do at a competitive price. When quality is the key to a company's success, quality management systems allow organizations to keep up with and meet current quality levels, meet the consumer's requirement for quality, retain employees through competitive compensation programs, and keep up with the latest technology.

HISTORY OF THE QUALITY MOVEMENT

As early as the 1950s, Japanese companies began to see the benefits of emphasizing quality throughout their organizations and enlisted the help of an American, W. Edwards Deming, who is credited with giving Japanese companies a massive head start in the quality movement. His methods include statistical process control (SPC) and problem-solving techniques that were very effective in gaining the necessary momentum to change the mentality of organizations needing to produce high-quality products and services. Deming developed his 14 points (Appendix 14.1) to communicate to managers how to increase quality within an organization.

Deming believed that 85 percent of all quality problems were the fault of management. In order to improve, management had to take the lead and put in place the necessary resources and systems. For example, consistent quality in incoming materials could not be expected when buyers were not given the necessary tools to understand quality requirements of those products and services. Buyers needed to fully understand how to assess the quality of all incoming products and services, understand the quality requirements, as well as be able to communicate these requirements to vendors. In a well-managed quality system, buyers should also be allowed to work closely with vendors and help them meet or exceed the required quality requirements.

According to Deming, there were two different concepts of process improvement that quality systems needed to address: (1) common (systematic) causes of error, and (2) special causes of error. Systematic causes are shared by numerous personnel, machines, or products; and special causes are associated with individual employees or equipment. Systematic causes of error include poor product/service design, materials not suited for their use, improper bills of lading, and poor physical conditions. Special causes of error include lack of training or skill, a poor lot of incoming materials, or equipment out of order.

Another influential individual in the development of quality control was Joseph M. Juran, who, like Deming, made a name for himself working in Japanese organizations focusing on improving quality. Juran also established the Juran Institute in 1979; its goals and objectives were centered on helping organizations improve the quality of their products and services.

Juran defined quality as "fitness for use," meaning that the users of products or services should be able to rely on that product or service 100 percent of the time without any worry of defects. If this was true, the product could be classified as fit for use.

Quality of design could be described as what distinguishes a Yugo from a Mercedes-Benz and involves the design concept and specifications. The quality of a product or service is only as good as its design and intention. Thus, it is important to include quality issues in the design process, as well as to have in mind during the design phase the difficulties one might have in replicating the product or service with the intended quality level.

Quality of conformance is reflected in the ability to replicate each aspect of a product or service with the same quality level as that intended in the design. This responsibility is held by individuals to develop the processes for replication, the workforce and their training, supervision, and adherence to test programs.

Availability refers to freedom from disruptive problems throughout the process and is measured by the frequency or probability of defects—for example, if a process does not have a steady flow of electricity and this causes defective parts, or when an employee must complete two jobs at once and is therefore forced to make concessions on the quality of both products or services.

Safety is described by Juran as calculating the risk of injury due to product hazards. For example, even if the product or service meets or exceeds all quality standards and expectations, but there is a possibility that if it is not used properly it could injure someone, the product will not be considered high-quality.

Field use refers to the ability of the product to reach the end user with the desired level of quality. This involves packaging, transportation, storage and field service competence, and promptness.

Juran also developed a comprehensive approach to quality that spanned a product or service's entire life cycle, from design to customer relations and all the steps in between. Juran preached that an organization should dissect all processes and procedures from a quality perspective and analyze for a "fitness for use." Once this is completed the organization can begin to make changes based on the "fitness for use" model.

The Quality Revolution Comes to the United States

The push for increased quality began in American manufacturing companies in the 1980s, following in the footsteps of Japanese manufacturers. Japanese companies found themselves with a distinct competitive advantage over American companies with their ability to produce much higher quality products with fewer defects.

The Ford Motor Company was the first to invite Deming to help the company transform itself into a quality-oriented organization. As a result, Ford was able to achieve higher quality standards than any other American automotive manufacturer and substantial sales growth in the late 1980s even when the rest of the U.S. automotive market was declining. Ford attributes the ability of its Taurus to overtake the Honda Accord in annual sales to the high quality standards set by the company.

The U.S. Congress, seeing the need for American companies to strive for increased quality, established the Malcolm Baldrige National Quality Award, modeled after Japan's Deming Prize. This spawned a substantial increase in the resources American businesses allocated for quality improvement, and within 10 years an American organization, Florida Power and Light, was able to capture Japan's Deming Prize for quality.

Since the early 1980s and on into the twenty-first century, quality issues have surfaced in every industry and almost every organization in the United States. The quality movement started in manufacturing and then moved to service industries. Initially service organizations did not feel quality systems would transfer very easily from manufacturing, but today service companies are reaping substantial rewards from implementing quality programs.

Throughout the history of the quality movement there have been several approaches to quality and even the development of several organizations dedicated solely to setting standards for quality.

Standardized Systems

ISO 9000 is a series of quality management systems (QMS) standards created by the International Organization for Standardization, a federation of 132 national standards bodies. The ISO 9000 QMS standards are not specific to products or services, but apply to the processes that create them. The standards are generic in nature so that they can be used by manufacturing and service industries anywhere in the world.

An organization that would like to have ISO certification needs to meet all the criteria stated in the ISO standards and pass a detailed audit performed by an ISO auditor. In some industries ISO certification has become necessary; for example, some large manufacturers require all suppliers to be ISO certified. While ISO certification is highly respected, if it is not a trend in your specific industry, the additional cost of certification is a deterrent to most managers. It is very possible to reach the desired quality level within an organization with a well-planned quality system and without going through all the additional steps for ISO certification.

QS-9000, released in 1994, is the ISO 9000 derivative for suppliers to the automotive Big Three: DaimlerChrysler, Ford, and General Motors. This quality management system standard contains all of ISO 9001:1994, along with automotive sector-specific, Big Three, and other original equipment manufacturer (OEM) customer-specific requirements.

Total Quality Management (TQM)

TQM is a management approach in which quality is emphasized in every aspect of the business and organization. Its goals are aimed at long-term development of quality products and services. TQM breaks down every process or activity and emphasizes that each contributes or detracts from the quality and productivity of the organization as a whole.

Management's role in TQM is to develop a quality strategy that is flexible enough to be adapted to every department, aligned with the organizational business objectives, and based on customer and stakeholder needs. Once the strategy is defined, it must be the motivating force to be deployed and communicated for it to be effective at all levels of the organization.

Some degree of employee empowerment is also encompassed in the TQM strategy and usually involves both departmental and cross-functional teams to develop strategies to solve quality problems and make suggestions for improvement.

Continuous Quality Improvement (CQI)

Continuous quality improvement came into existence in manufacturing as a different approach to quality and quality systems. It does not focus as much on creating a corporate quality culture, but more on the process of quality improvement by the deployment of teams or groups who are rewarded when goals and quality levels are reached. CQI allows individuals involved in the day-to-day operations to change and improve processes and work flows as they see fit.

CQI implementation attempts to develop a quality system that is never satisfied; it strives for constant innovation to improve work processes and systems by reducing time-consuming, low value-added activities. The time and resource savings can now be devoted to planning and coordination.

CQI has been adapted in several different industries. For example, in health care and other service sectors, it has taken on the acronym FOCUS-PDCA work:

> **Find** a process to improve.
>
> **Organize** to improve a process.
>
> **Clarify** what is known.
>
> **Understand** variation.
>
> **Select** a process improvement.

Then move through the process improvement plan:

> **Plan**—create a time line, including all resources, activities, dates, and personnel training.
>
> **Do**—implement the plan and collect data.

Check—analyze the results of the plan.

Act—act on what was learned and determine the next steps.

The FOCUS-PDCA acronym is an easy system for management to communicate to teams, and it helps them stay organized and on track with the end result in mind. The system has proven to be very successful for the CQI team approach.

Six Sigma

Six sigma was developed at Motorola in the 1980s as a method to measure and improve high-volume production processes. Its overall goal was to measure and eliminate waste by attempting to achieve near perfect results. The term *six sigma* refers to a statistical measure with no more than 3.4 defects per million. Numerous companies, including General Electric, Ford, and DaimlerChrysler, have credited six sigma with saving them billions of dollars.

Six sigma is a statistically oriented approach to process improvement that uses a variety of tools, including statistical process control (SPC), total quality management (TQM), and design of experiments (DOE). It can be coordinated with other major initiatives and systems, such as new product development, materials requirement planning (MRP), and just-in-time (JIT) inventory control.

Six sigma initially was thought of as a system that could be used only in manufacturing operations, but more recently it has proven to be successful in nonmanufacturing processes as well, such as accounts payable, billing, marketing, and information systems.

At first glance six sigma might seem too structured to be effective in analyzing processes that are not standard and repetitive as in manufacturing situations, but the theory of six sigma is flexible enough to suit any process. Nevertheless, many of the lessons learned on production lines are very relevant to other processes as well.

The following is a brief description of the steps involved in the six sigma process:

1. Break down business process flow into individual steps.
2. Define what defects there are.

3. Measure the number of defects.
4. Probe for the root cause.
5. Implement changes to improve.
6. Remeasure.
7. Take a long-term view of goals.

ELEMENTS OF A QUALITY SYSTEM

There are several elements to a quality system, and each organization is going to have a unique system. The most important elements of a quality system include participative management, quality system design, customers, purchasing, education and training, statistics, auditing, and technology.

Participative Management

The entire quality process, once started, will be an ongoing dynamic part of the organization, just like any other department such as marketing or accounting. It will also need the continuous focus of management. The implementation and management of a successful quality system involves many different aspects that must be addressed on a continuous basis.

Vision and Values. The starting point for the management and leadership process is the formation of a well-defined vision and value statement. This statement will be used to establish the importance of the quality system and build motivation for the changes that need to take place, whether the organization plans to exceed customer expectations, commit to a defined level of customer satisfaction, or commit to zero defects. The exact form of the vision and values is not as important as the fact that it is articulated and known by everyone involved. This vision and value statement is going to be a driving force to help mold the culture that is needed throughout the organization in the drive for quality. It is not the words of the value statement that produce quality products and services; it is the people and processes that determine if there is going to be a change in quality. The vision and value will be very important statements to set agendas for all other processes used to manage the quality system.

Developing the Plan. The plan for the quality system is going to be different for every organization, but there are similar characteristics:

- ✔ There should be clear and measurable goals.
- ✔ There are financial resources available for quality.
- ✔ The quality plan is consistent with the organization's vision and values.

The plan for the quality system might also include pilot projects that would entail setting up small quality projects within the organization. This will allow management to understand how well the quality system is accepted, learn from mistakes, and have greater confidence in launching an organization-wide quality system. The plan should provide some flexibility for employee empowerment, because, as has been demonstrated, the most successful quality systems allow employees at all levels to provide input.

Communication. Change, especially a movement toward higher quality, is challenging to communicate effectively, yet the communication process is essential for the company's leaders to move the organization forward. Communication is the vital link between management, employees, consumers, and stakeholders. These communication lines also bring about a sense of camaraderie between all individuals involved and help sustain the drive for the successful completion of long-term quality goals.

Communication systems also must allow for employees to give feedback and provide possible solutions to issues the company must face. Management needs to allow for this in both formal and informal ways, such as employee feedback slips and feedback round-table meetings.

The responsibility for fostering a culture that values communication lies with senior management. They alone have to ensure that goals and objectives are communicated to all. They are also responsible for setting up the system for feedback from the employees.

Rewards and Acknowledgment. Rewards, compensation, and acknowledgment for achievements in quality are very effective ways to motivate employees. They tell employees at the end of the day exactly what management is trying to accomplish. Rewards, compensation, and acknowledgment may also be seen as a form of communication—they are tangible methods that senior management uses to let employees know that quality is important. This could come in the form of individual rewards or team rewards. Rewards, compensation, and acknowledgment take many forms, and it is up to management to ensure that this type of program is in line with the goals and objectives of the quality system and the goals and objectives of the organization. Organizations have found that the best and most cost-effective reward, compensation, and acknowledgment programs are geared to meeting specific criteria. These programs motivate managers who in turn motivate their employees to strive toward predefined goals.

Quality System Design

A quality system is composed of the standards and procedures that are developed to ensure that the level of quality desired is repeated in every unit of a product or service. This portion of the quality system is very concrete and can be measured and managed. Before you start, your organization should establish a core team to carry the performance system design process forward.

The eight steps of the design process are:

1. *Understand and map all business structures and processes.* This forces employees involved in designing a performance measurement system to think through and understand the entire organization, its competitive position, the environment in which it operates, and its business processes. This will also allow for complete understanding of customer touch points and how the different operations in the organization affect the customer's perception of quality. See Figure 14.1 for an example of a process map.

2. *Develop business performance priorities.* The performance measurement system should support the stakeholders' requirements

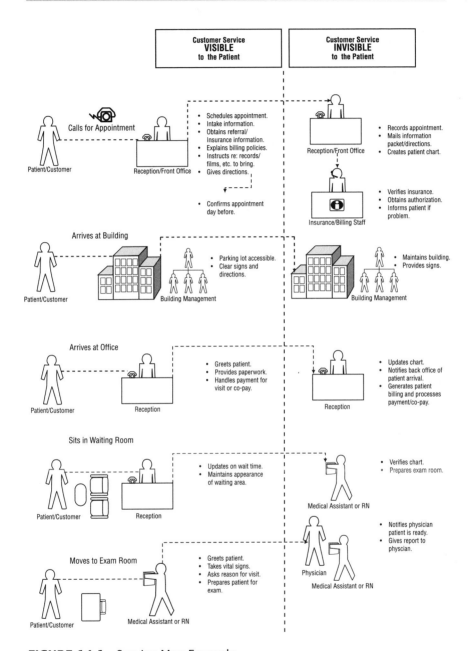

FIGURE 14.1 Service Map Example

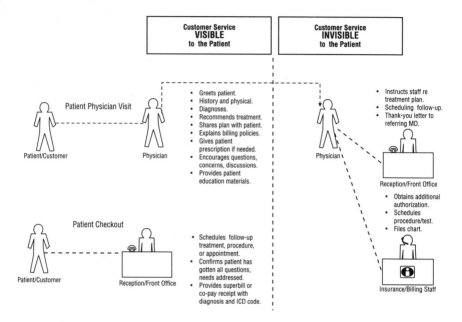

FIGURE 14.1 *(Continued)*

from the organization's strategy through to its business processes. This order of priorities must be in place well before the process enters the actual design phase.

3. *Understand the current performance measurement system.* Every organization has some kind of measurement system in place. For this reason, there are basically two ways to approach the design and implementation of a new performance measurement system. Either you can scrap the old system and introduce a new one as a replacement, or you can redevelop the existing system. Both approaches can work, but the former approach is more likely to lead to trouble. People will cling to the old measurement system and either use both systems simultaneously or use the old one and simply go through the motions of the new one. You can eliminate this outcome by taking the second approach.

4. *Develop performance indicators.* The most important element of a performance measurement system is the set of performance indicators you will use to measure your organization's perfor-

mance and business processes. This is the point in the design process where the top-down approach meets the bottom-up design approach and where the broad masses of the organization become involved. The purpose of this step is to develop the performance measurement system with an appropriate number of relevant and accurate performance indicators.

5. *Decide how to collect the required data.* Developing perfect performance indicators that will tell you everything you ever wanted to know about what goes on in your organization is one thing, but being able to collect the data required to calculate these performance indicators is a completely different matter. This issue must initially be addressed during the development of the performance indicators so that you avoid selecting those that can never actually be measured. There will be trade-offs of cost and time versus the benefits of collecting data, but a likely middle ground between perfect data/high cost and no data/no cost will be found.

6. *Design reporting and performance data representation formats.* In this step, you decide how the performance data will be presented to the users; how the users should apply the performance data for management, monitoring, and improvement; and who will have access to performance data. After you finish, you should have a performance measurement system that has a solid place in your organization's overall measurement-based management system.

7. *Test and adjust the performance measurement system.* Your first attempt at the performance measurement system will probably not be perfect—there are bound to be performance indicators that do not work as intended, conflicting indicators, undesirable behavior, and problems with data availability. This is to be expected. In this step you should extensively test the system and adjust the elements that do not work as planned.

8. *Implement the performance measurement system.* Now it's time to put your system to use. This is when the system is officially in place and everyone can start using it. This step involves issues such as managing user access, training, and demonstrating the system.

This is not an absolute process that needs to be followed to the letter in order for it to work. In some cases, one or more steps may be unnecessary; in others, additional steps may be needed. It's up to you to make the necessary adjustments to the process to maximize the probability of the system's success.

Designing Part Two of the Quality System

This portion of the quality system is conceptual. It is more about management's role in increasing motivation and the determination to make the first part run smoothly. It is rooted in the communication between management and employees, which was discussed earlier. In most cases, the employees who are performing the activities and process know how to improve the quality. This part of the system should allow employees to make recommendations and motivate them to want to improve quality.

Customers

The inclusion of customers in a quality program can take many different avenues, including the cost of losing a customer, the customer's perception of quality, and the satisfaction level of the customers. The customer portion of a quality program is going to be unique for every industry and organization, but it must capture how quality plays into the customer's value system and how quality drives the purchase decision.

In service industries, in particular, quality is measured in customer retention rates and the cost of losing a customer. If typical accounting measures could capture the exact cost of losing a customer it would be easy for managers to allocate the exact amount of resources needed to retain customers. According to the *Harvard Business Review*, companies can increase profits by almost 100 percent by retaining 5 percent more of their customers. Customers over time will generate more profits the longer they stay with the same company.

Perceived quality by customers leads to referrals; in service industries, referrals can equate to more than 60 percent of new business. If a company can increase the number of referrals through increased quality, it is going to have a substantial effect on the bottom line of the business.

Purchasing

Purchasing is an area in an organization where substantial gains in quality can be realized through the implementation of just a few policies and procedures designed around quality. Today's suppliers need to be partners in the quality effort. A company's products or services are only as good as the combination of all the inputs.

The first step in molding the purchasing system to collaborate with the entire quality system is to take all the standards developed for all incoming materials that can be qualified as an input to routine process or activity. If the quality system's performance standards and procedures are completed as described in the design phase these standards should already be established.

The second step is educating the purchasing personnel on how the standards are important to the process flows of the organization. If standards are not upheld, the quality of the product or service will be jeopardized. The employees should also be educated on how to measure and communicate the required standards. This may involve materials or statistical process control education, and it could even be as simple as cross-training the purchasing personnel so that they know exactly how the inputs fit into the organization. Once the purchasing area knows how the products are used and what problems can arise, they will have a better chance of procuring inputs that meet all the specifications.

Once steps one and two are complete it will be the purchasing department's responsibility to communicate the requirements to suppliers and hold them accountable for the quality. This sometimes may not be a simple task and could involve finding new suppliers or working with current suppliers to develop higher quality standards.

Education and Training

The education of employees for the purpose of reaching higher quality standards has many different facets. For example, the quality education of management is going to be different than the quality education of the general workforce, because they play different roles in the process.

Because most quality problems start at the top, so too should education. The education of management on quality issues should start with a general discussion of quality systems and the roles management plays in quality programs. With respect to general knowledge, management must understand the history of the quality movement, who the major players were, and how quality programs have affected the business world. More specifically, managers must know how quality programs have affected their specific industry in the past, and they should have an idea of what role quality programs play in the future of their industry. Management must also keep abreast of new developments in quality. The discussion of the roles that management must play in a quality system is the most important aspect of their education. Management must understand how employees view their actions or inactions, how their individual actions and jobs impact quality, and the overall importance of dedication to quality by management. Managers must understand that without strong leadership and reinforcing dedication to quality, a quality program will not be meaningful.

The education of employees for a quality program will include a discussion of how these programs will affect their jobs on a daily basis. It should also include a brief overview of quality as well as the tools employees will use in order to ensure outputs and how their roles add to the overall quality goals of the organization.

Data Development and Statistics

Statistical analysis is a very important aspect of quality systems. It could be considered a cornerstone of the quality improvement process and is very closely tied to auditing a quality system, which is discussed later in the chapter. Statistical process control (SPC) was what Duran taught as a decision maker in quality systems. Statistical analysis is the measurement portion of quality systems and allows it to be managed. A very common saying in management, which relates well to quality, is "you cannot manage what you cannot measure," and statistical analysis will give you the measurements necessary to make management decisions.

Statistics was a key tool that Deming used to distinguish between systemic and special causes, and the key to quality management in general was statistical process control. SPC was developed by Walter Shewart while working at Bell Labs in the 1930s, and Deming took Shewart's concept and applied it to quality management. Deming believed that SPC was necessary because variation is a fact of life in any process. Deming believed that it was very unlikely that two products/services when produced by the same procedure and operator would be identical.

Control Charts and Their Role in Quality Systems. Control charts are the most widely used tool in quality systems. Control charts communicate a lot of information effectively. Figure 14.2 shows a process in which all the outcomes are within the specified limits. The upper control limit (UCL) is .18 and the lower control limit (LCL) is .02, and all the points fall between these two limits. This means the process is in control and operating correctly. If some of the points were to fall outside of the UCL or LCL, it would signal that the process is not in control and action needs to be taken to correct the problem.

We discussed earlier the two different types of errors, (1) systematic and (2) special causes. Systematic errors will show up on a control chart as one or two points outside of the control limits with the rest of

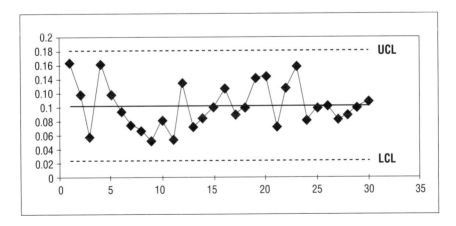

FIGURE 14.2   Control Chart

the points within the limits. Special causes will show up on a control chart with numerous points outside of the control limits.

The exact use of statistical measures is going to be different for each organization. Some statistical analysis will be very easy to set up and use. For example, the length or weight of a particular part can be measured and analysis can show if the parts are within the required specifications. In service industries the statistical analysis will be more abstract, but is just as valuable. For example, one could survey customers regularly and ask them on a scale of 1 to 10, "How would you rate the service?"

Here are some common traits of statistical measures used in quality systems:

- ✔ Are driven by the customer.
- ✔ Reflect vision and values.
- ✔ Benchmarked to the competition.
- ✔ Are achievable.

Auditing

Auditing a quality management system is just as important as any other aspect of the system. The audit process allows everyone involved to see if the quality management system is working correctly and if the goals and objectives are being reached. Auditing also plays major roles in motivating employees and allows for rewards and acknowledgment measures to be assessed as well as possible compensation.

Auditing of quality management systems can take many forms, and each organization will have a unique auditing process that fits its system. Service industries will have a very different auditing system than a manufacturing organization, but the end result of the systems is going to be the same. Here are some examples of auditing systems used in service organizations.

Mystery Shoppers. Shoppers are sent to businesses to interact with employees and assess the overall service quality and report back to management. This is usually done on a regular basis, and reports are produced for the employees.

Customer Surveys. Customer surveys are now well used as a means to find out how your business is viewed by consumers. These surveys can range from mail-in forms to short forms the consumers complete at the time of purchase or even having a saleperson or clerk asking the customer to rate the product or service at the close of the purchase. Getting direct input from your customers is invaluable and should be done in some form in every organization.

New Customer Measures. Measurement over time of the number of new customers can be a very effective tool to assess quality levels. Customers who are very happy with your service are going to tell others—60 percent of new customers in service organizations come from referrals. New customers can be an important litmus test of quality.

Quality in Services. Quality in service industries has more recently come into the mainstream, and the benefits reaped by service organizations initiating solid quality management programs have been substantial. The basis for quality management systems in service organizations is to proactively measure and manage the quality level of the services; some of the metrics applied as the basis of service quality are:

✔ The "iceberg principle," in other words, the average service company never hears from more than 90 percent of customers who are not happy with the level of service they received. For every legitimate complaint received there will be more than 20 customers who feel they have had problems, and at least 25 percent of those problems could be considered serious enough to warrant investigation.

✔ Of the customers that make a complaint, more than half will do business again if the complaint is addressed and resolved. If the complaint is resolved quickly, and the customer feels the organization cares about its customers, the number will jump up to almost 100 percent.

✔ If a complaint is not resolved, the average customer will tell more than eight other individuals about the negative experience. If the complaint is resolved, the customer will tell at least five others about the positive experience.

✔ On average it costs six times more to gain a new customer than to keep an existing one.

As you can see, quality in service industries can have substantial influence on the bottom line. A well-designed and managed quality system can be the key to providing the quality of service desired.

SUMMARY

The quality movement and quality systems have had many different names or terms of reference in the past few decades, and might look like a short-lived business management trend at first glance. With ever-increasing competition and consumer expectations, professionals and business managers cannot ignore quality issues and expect to maintain or improve their competitive position. Quality systems, time and again, have been responsible for substantial increases in the bottom line of businesses in every industry and have given organizations the boost they need to meet overall goals and objectives. Organizations that do not accept that quality improvement is going to be ingrained into every part of their business are not going to be around to see what the future brings.

RESOURCES FOR QUALITY

Agency for Healthcare Research and Quality

www.ahrq.gov

A U.S. government agency established to improve the quality of health care.

American Customer Satisfaction Index

www.theacsi.org

An organization dedicated to tracking customer satisfaction and providing benchmarks and insights into customer satisfaction.

American Society for Quality

www.asq.org

A nonprofit organization dedicated to the development of quality. The organization offers a wide range of resources for quality professionals.

Baldrige National Quality Program

www.quality.nist.gov

Center for Quality of Management

www.cqm.org/index.html

International Organization for Standardization

www.iso.org/iso/en/ISOOnline.frontpage

Quality Leaders Network

www.qualityleaders.net/qnet/default.htm

APPENDIX

Deming's 14 Points

1. Create constancy of purpose toward improvement of product and service, with the aim to become competitive and to stay in business and to provide jobs.

2. Adopt the new philosophy. We are in a new economic age. Western management must awaken to the challenge, must learn their responsibilities, and take on leadership for change.

3. Cease dependence on inspection to achieve quality. Eliminate the need for inspection on a mass basis by building quality into the product in the first place.

4. End the practice of awarding business on the basis of price tag. Instead, minimize total cost. Move toward a single supplier for any one item, on a long-term relationship of loyalty and trust.

5. Improve constantly and forever the system of production and service, to improve quality and productivity, and thus constantly decrease costs.

6. Institute training on the job.

7. Institute leadership. The aim of supervision should be to help people and machines and gadgets do a better job. Supervision of management is in need of overhaul as well as supervision of production workers.

8. Drive out fear, so that everyone may work effectively for the company.

9. Break down barriers between departments. People in research, design, sales, and production must work as a team, to foresee problems of production and in use that may be encountered with the product or service.

10. Eliminate slogans, exhortations, and targets for the workforce when asking for zero defects and new levels of productivity. Such exhortations only create adversarial relationships, as the bulk of the causes of low quality and low productivity belong to the system and thus lie beyond the power of the workforce.

11. (a.) Eliminate work standards (quotas) on the factory floor. Substitute leadership. (b.) Eliminate management by objective. Eliminate management by numbers, numerical goals. Substitute leadership.

12. (a.) Remove barriers that rob the hourly worker of his right to pride of workmanship. The responsibility of supervisors must be changed from sheer numbers to quality. (b.) Remove barriers that rob people in management and in engineering of their right to pride of workmanship. This means, inter alia, abolishment of the annual merit rating and of management by objective.

13. Institute a vigorous program of education and self-improvement.

14. Put everybody in the company to work to accomplish the transformation. The transformation is everybody's job.

REFERENCES

American Society for Quality. www.asq.org, accessed February 15, 2004.

Biolos, Jim. *Six Sigma Meets the Service Economy*. Boston: Harvard Business School Press, 2002.

Garvin, David, and Artemis March. *A Note on Quality: The Views of Deming, Juran, and Crosby*. Boston: Harvard Business School Press, 1981.

Reichheld, Fredrick F., and W. Earl Sasser Jr., "Zero Deflections: Quality Comes to Services," *Harvard Business Review* (September–October 1990).

Wolkins, D. Otis. *Total Quality: A Framework for Leadership*. Management Leadership Series. New York: Productivity Press, 1995.

Index